Praise for

THE PRIMARY SOLUTION

"America's political problem is not a lack of talent; it is a corrupted system that incentivizes extremism while punishing the compromise essential to democracy. Nick Troiano's sobering but brilliant analysis of our political primaries nails the problem and offers realistic solutions."

—Stanley McChrystal, General, U.S. Army (Retired);
Chairman & CEO, McChrystal Group

"Unique insight and thoughtful analysis into our elections."

—U.S. Senator Bill Cassidy (R-Louisiana)

"The one book every American should read first this year. Nick Troiano makes a compelling argument that reforming primaries is the most viable of the many possible solutions to our dysfunctional political system. Buy this book, read it, and then immediately give it to a friend!"

—U.S. Senator John Hickenlooper (D-Colorado)

"If you feel frustrated by gridlock, exhausted by extremism, or just want the yelling match to end—read this book, now! Excellent, readable, and important, it's a guide to why politics went so wrong, and how to put it right."

—Dr. Rachel Kleinfeld, Senior Fellow,
Carnegie Endowment for International Peace

"Smart, convincing, and practical."

—Andrew Yang, Founder, Forward Party

"Nick Troiano is an activist and patriot, and *The Primary Solution* makes one of the best structural arguments I've read. . . . Reformers interested in fighting extremism have a great new road map with this book."

—Reid Hoffman, Cofounder, LinkedIn and Inflection AI

"With the precision of an exceptional political player, Troiano offers meaningful, measurable solutions that will have a positive impact on every voter in every community."

—Dr. Frank Luntz, Pollster;
Washington Post Crystal Ball Award winner

"Thoughtfully researched, elegantly argued, and delightfully written."

—Lee Drutman, Senior Fellow, New America

"A tour de force that synthesizes political strategy, scholarly research, and philanthropic vision to chart a course for policy change to reduce extremism."

—Christian Grose, Professor of Political Science,
University of Southern California

THE
PRIMARY
SOLUTION

RESCUING OUR DEMOCRACY
FROM THE FRINGES

NICK TROIANO

SIMON & SCHUSTER

NEW YORK   LONDON   TORONTO   SYDNEY   NEW DELHI

1230 Avenue of the Americas
New York, NY 10020

First Simon & Schuster hardcover edition March 2024

SIMON & SCHUSTER and colophon are registered trademarks of Simon & Schuster, LLC

Simon & Schuster: Celebrating 100 Years of Publishing in 2024

For information about special discounts for bulk purchases,
please contact Simon & Schuster Special Sales
at 1-866-506-1949 or business@simonandschuster.com.

The Simon & Schuster Speakers Bureau can bring authors to your live event.
For more information or to book an event,
contact the Simon & Schuster Speakers Bureau
at 1-866-248-3049 or visit our website at www.simonspeakers.com.

Interior design by Ruth Lee-Mui
Images courtesy of Unite America Institute.

Manufactured in the United States of America

3   5   7   9   10   8   6   4   2

Library of Congress Cataloging-in-Publication Data has been applied for.

ISBN 978-1-6680-2825-4
ISBN 978-1-6680-2827-8 (ebook)

To Doug Bailey
& Jake Brewer

Whose mentorship and dedication to
our democracy inspired my life's work

I am not an advocate for frequent changes in laws and Constitutions, but laws and institutions must go hand in hand with the progress of the human mind. As that becomes more developed, more enlightened, as new discoveries are made, new truths discovered and manners and opinions change, with the change of circumstances, institutions must advance also to keep pace with the times. We might as well require a man to wear still the coat which fitted him when a boy as civilized society to remain ever under the regimen of their barbarous ancestors.

—Thomas Jefferson, excerpted from a letter
to Samuel Kercheval, July 12, 1816

CONTENTS

INTRODUCTION

There's perhaps only one statement that virtually all Americans can agree on: our political system is broken. A historically low 20% now say they trust the government, down from nearly 80% in the early 1960s.[1] A historically high and equal number of both Democrats and Republicans (69%) believe that democracy is in danger of collapse.[2]

But what happens if you ask people *why* our politics is so broken? That's a question I've been asking since I first got involved in political reform fifteen years ago. I posed it to dozens of ordinary people I met in ten cities across the country while producing a short documentary for a group called Americans Elect. A few years later, I repeated it to Pennsylvania voters across fifteen counties, during my run for Congress as an independent candidate. Most recently, I added that question to a series of focus groups commissioned by the organization I now run, Unite America.

In all those settings, the three most common responses to "What ails American politics?" were strikingly consistent and roughly equal:

- *It's the bad guys.* Many are convinced that our problems stem from specific bad actors, whether they define them as MAGA conservatives or woke progressives, Trump or Biden, MTG or AOC.
- *It's the media and social media.* Another big group blames political dysfunction and cultural polarization on biased information sources. They see "fake news" or disinformation poisoning the country via some combination of Fox News, MSNBC, Facebook, conservative talk radio, the *New York Times*, and other outlets.
- *It's the rampant corruption in government.* This group points to systemic problems such as limitless dark money, shadowy lobbyists, and career politicians.

None of these concerns are necessarily wrong. But they all ignore the largest factor fueling our broken politics—one that has been hiding in plain sight for decades: partisan primaries. Most of us take these first-round elections for granted as a historically sacred or unchangeable aspect of politics, at every level from state house to president. But as you will soon see, they're neither sacred nor unchangeable.

The main idea of this book is that partisan primaries are not merely one problem among a long list of problems with our political system; they are (pun intended) the Primary Problem in our politics today. Abolishing partisan primaries is therefore the single most important thing we can do to improve representation in our government and hold it accountable to delivering better results.

If you're skeptical of this proposition, I don't blame you; so are most of your fellow Americans. A 2022 survey commissioned by Unite America found that while 45% of respondents believe our government is in need of "real, significant, and fundamental change," only 12% said the same about our election process. Significantly more believe that the biggest problem in our politics is the politicians running for office (72%) than the rules of our current election system (28%). And out of a long list of options for "What ails our democracy today?" 21% picked "corruption by the people in charge," but only 2% said partisan primaries, which came in dead last.[3] Changing this perception is why I wrote this book.

We have a government led by politicians most of us don't like ... because they say and do things that most of us don't agree with ... because that's the only way they can win the partisan primaries that keep them in power. That's the bad news. The good news is that the Primary Problem is surprisingly and entirely fixable.

WHY PRIMARIES MATTER

With so many alarming problems facing our country (and world) these days, you may wonder if it really matters whether we choose our leaders via partisan primaries or some other process. Don't we have bigger, more obvious issues to focus on?

First, primaries matter because elections matter. People around the world and here at home have fought and died for the principle of "one person, one vote." Our right to vote has gradually expanded to include all citizens over age eighteen. It doesn't matter how much money you have, what you believe, or whether your ancestors came here on the *Mayflower* or if you're a new citizen. When we show up at a polling place, we all get one vote. Elections are the mechanism by which we choose our leaders. It matters whether or not they truly reflect the will of the majority and accurately translate our votes into representation.

Second, elections matter because politics matters. Politics is supposed to be the process by which we identify problems, find agreement, and take action. It's the opposite of the "might makes right" ethos that dominated most of human history, and still dominates parts of the world today. In our constitutional republic, we give power to others, through elections, to act on our behalf. Politics is also the nonviolent means by which we decide how our shared resources are allocated and what laws we all live under—from how much money we invest in pandemic preparedness to what regulations should exist on new technologies.

And ultimately, politics matters because self-governance matters.

The purpose of government is summarized in the Declaration of Independence: to secure our inalienable rights to life, liberty, and the pursuit of happiness. Decisions made through our political system impact those fundamental rights in countless ways. Without a functional system of self-government, life in the state of nature would otherwise be, in the words of philosopher Thomas Hobbes, "solitary, poor, nasty, brutish, and short."

That's why the role primaries play in our elections, particularly whether they are advancing or undermining our great experiment of self-government, is vital for every American to consider. It impacts every other issue we care about. That's why this isn't just a book for political junkies. I wrote it for the millions of Americans in the so-called "exhausted majority"—reasonable people across party lines who are fed up with a system that no longer serves our country's needs. People who are tired of the loudest voices on the political fringes dominating our national debate. People who wonder not only if there's a reasonable fix to our political dysfunction but if there's one that can be enacted without the unlikely passage of new federal laws or constitutional amendments. (Spoiler alert: there is.)

How Just 8% of Voters Elect 83% of the House

One of my favorite quirks about the Constitution is that while it doesn't say a word about political parties or how exactly we should conduct elections, it does require a physical head count of every single American, once every decade. In 2020, the Census Bureau counted 331,108,434 of us,[4] and the state-by-state subtotals were used to reapportion the 435 seats of the House of Representatives. The average House district now includes about 590,000 people above the voting age of eighteen. How many of them would you expect to cast a ballot to choose their district's representative to Congress? Half? A quarter? A tenth?

Well, in 2020 the representative for Georgia's 14th district was chosen by just 43,813 people who voted in the Republican primary—only 8% of all eligible voters. And in 2018 the representative for New York's 14th District was chosen by just 16,898 people who voted in the Democratic primary—only 5% of all eligible voters. In both cases I'm only counting voters who cast ballots in the primary because both are landslide districts, respectively deep red and deep blue. In both cases the primary for the dominant party's nomination was the only election that really mattered.

Do these facts change how you think about Republican Marjorie Taylor Greene (MTG) and Democrat Alexandria Ocasio-Cortez (AOC), the candidates who won these districts? Since their initial victories with those slim primary totals, both have gone on to command tremendous media attention and political platforms. Both have significantly impacted the priorities and direction of their parties, pushing them toward more ideological extremes. Both are considered future contenders for higher office.

Love 'em or hate 'em, both MTG and AOC are beneficiaries of the current primary system, which strongly favors candidates who can appeal to a paltry yet passionate partisan base in a lopsided district. And they are far from alone. Unite America's research found that, nationwide in 2022, *only 8% of all voters cast ballots in the partisan primaries that determined 83% of House contests.*

How was that possible? First, 83% of congressional districts (359) are considered "safe" for one party or the other, including AOC's and MTG's. While some of this has to do with partisan gerrymandering, most districts are uncompetitive because of the increasing partisan divide between urban areas (which lean Democratic) and rural areas (which lean Republican). You might think we have a two-party system in America, but in reality we have two one-party systems in most parts of the country. In these places, primary elections are the only elections of consequence.

Second, very few voters participate in primaries and millions more are locked out entirely. In part, that's because fifteen states block independents from voting in primaries,* and another fifteen states prevent voters who are registered with one party from voting in the other party's primary. In 2022, those rules alone prevented roughly 30 million registered voters from casting a ballot in a primary that determined the outcome of a House election. Total primary turnout was just 21.3% nationwide.[5] However, the only primary votes that really mattered were those cast in the primary of whichever party had a lock on the district. And in the 129 House primaries in safe districts where the incumbent ran unopposed, voting was essentially meaningless.

That's how only 8% of voters nationally wound up casting ballots in partisan primaries that determined the outcomes of those safe seats. Primaries not only determine the winners of most elections but they also give disproportionate power to tiny factions of voters on the fringes who are most likely to participate and the special interests that aim to influence them.

The Impact of Partisan Primaries

In competitive elections, we often see the impact of partisan primaries on candidates who run far to the left or right to get their party's nomination and then reinvent themselves for the general election to appeal to a broader audience. They may change their tone or even their positions on hot-button issues. In 2012, an advisor to Mitt Romney's presidential campaign drew significant attention when he said the quiet part of modern campaign strategy out loud: "I think you hit a reset button for the fall campaign. Everything changes. It's almost like an Etch A Sketch—you can kind of shake it up and we start all over again."[6]

The less obvious but more pernicious impact of partisan primaries is how these same candidates, if elected, then govern. In 1974, political

---

*In four of these states, the Democratic Party has amended its party rules to permit independents to vote in their primary.

scientist David Mayhew's influential theory of congressional behavior asserted that members of Congress are "single minded seekers of reelection."[7] In short, they will act, speak, and vote in a way that is—first and foremost—necessary to keep their job, which nowadays means winning their next partisan primary. The problem is that what's required to win their primary often runs in the exact opposite direction of what's required to actually do their job, such as working across the aisle to solve problems.

In 1975, the renowned organizational theorist Steven Kerr published a paper entitled "On the Folly of Rewarding A, While Hoping for B."[8] He gives various examples of how misaligned incentives can lead to undesirable outcomes, such as: a company that wants to improve teamwork but only gives bonuses for individual performance; a university that wants to improve teaching but only evaluates professors based on their published research; a medical institution that wants to improve patient care but gets paid only based on services it provides. Our political system is no different. It rewards politicians who pander to their party's base with reelection, while hoping they will then come to Congress and work together to get things done. It is, to borrow Kerr's phrase, pure folly.

Think about the amounts of time, energy, and money we spend discussing and debating individual politicians. Now think about the relative amounts dedicated to examining the *process* that determines virtually everything about those politicians. We run our country like a company that scrutinizes its final products but entirely ignores its own assembly line. It's time we refocus our attention.

While general elections determine which party controls the government, primaries determine virtually everything else. In the chapters ahead, you'll see how primaries influence which candidates run for office and get elected; what they believe about specific policies; which voters, donors, and interest groups they are beholden to; and how they govern.

It's time to ask with an open mind: Are partisan primaries *really* the best way to elect our leaders?

MY JOURNEY TO REFORMING PARTISAN PRIMARIES

Before we get into the origins, consequences, and solutions to the Primary Problem, you might be wondering how I landed on primary reform as my calling.

During college I cofounded and led a student advocacy nonprofit called The Can Kicks Back. We were politically diverse and all sick of Washington "kicking the can down the road" on our country's long-term fiscal health, our $11 trillion national debt (which is now three times as massive), and the future of critical programs like Medicare and Social Security. (You know, totally normal things for college kids to obsess about.)

We were inspired by a 2010 bipartisan commission, led by former Republican senator Alan Simpson and Democratic White House chief of staff Erskine Bowles, that tried to get America's fiscal house in order with a reasonable compromise on spending and taxes. Simpson-Bowles was created by President Obama through executive order after a similar commission proposed by Congress had failed to pass. Eight Republican senators who had publicly supported that proposal, including Minority Leader Mitch McConnell, switched sides to vote against it, just days after Obama endorsed the idea. In other words, they were for it until they felt partisan pressure to oppose anything that Obama supported.

I happened to be on Capitol Hill when that Senate vote failed, and I felt visceral anger that this was not how our government was supposed to work. "No single vote by any single senator could possibly illustrate everything that is wrong with Washington today," wrote *Washington Post* columnist Fred Hiatt soon after. "No single vote could embody the full cynicism and cowardice of our political elite at its worst, or explain by itself why problems do not get solved. But here's one that comes close."[9]

After the GOP recaptured Congress in the 2010 midterms, divided government brought even more gridlock. In the fall of 2013, The Can Kicks Back organized a van tour across the country to visit college campuses—along with our mascot, a giant dented tin can named "AmeriCAN." Our goal was to build support for the Simpson-Bowles commission proposal, which had by then been abandoned by leaders in both parties, including Obama. Republicans would not agree to any kind of tax increases, while Democrats would not agree to any kind of entitlement reforms. Both seemed to be terrified of the wrath of their respective bases.

On the same day our tour arrived at the University of Wyoming for an event with Simpson himself, the government shut down over its inability to pass the annual budget. For the next seventeen days, Republicans—led by the attention-seeking senator Ted Cruz—unsuccessfully attempted to force Obama into defunding the Affordable Care Act. Amid the partisan rancor, any hope for a long-term budget compromise evaporated. By the end of 2013, it was clear to me that our country was going broke because our political system was broken and future generations would quite literally pay the price.

My own representative, Pennsylvania Republican Tom Marino, had voted for the shutdown and against the compromise that eventually reopened the government. He epitomized everything I thought was wrong with our politics. So I finished getting my master's degree at Georgetown University, left the nonprofit, changed my voter registration from Republican to independent, and launched an underdog campaign to replace Marino in Congress.

Mr. Troiano Doesn't Go to Washington

You might call it arrogant for any twenty-five-year-old to think he had a shot at winning a House seat—especially as an independent, without the support of either major party, and with no family fortune or wealthy patron. But I prefer to say that I ran to represent Pennsylvania's 10th Congressional District in 2014 out of idealism, not arrogance.

I campaigned seven days a week for ten months with the help of a scrappy, four-person team of fellow twentysomethings. We lived and worked out of a three-story house in Williamsport that, unbeknownst to us when we signed the lease, was adjacent to a drug den. Although

I was from a different part of the district, I knew we had to be based in the district's only city to have a chance at collecting the 7,500 signatures needed to qualify for the ballot. I collected nearly half of those myself, and when things got desperate I stood my First Amendment ground at a county fair, when police threatened to arrest me for soliciting.

During my campaign I had put out in-depth policy papers on topics where I thought Republicans, Democrats, and independents could find common ground, such as fiscal responsibility to reduce our debt, environmental sustainability to combat climate change, and economic mobility to fight inequality. But I quickly learned that my policy proposals didn't matter much. What resonated most with voters was a simple pitch: *I am running to represent you, not the party bosses or special interests.* I found that running without a party label gave me the opportunity to have clean-slate conversations with voters, without having to undo their preconceptions. I saw that most people aren't obsessed with politics and simply want leaders of good character, integrity, and judgment. But I also learned that it's hard to earn enough votes to win a seat in Congress one conversation at a time.

My used Toyota RAV4, a hand-me-down from my grandpa, logged over 30,000 miles crisscrossing our large district. There was always one more door to knock, one more call to make, one more thank-you note to write. Along the way we won endorsements from twenty-two mayors in the district, which gave us hope. Anything is possible in politics, right? But by late October, when we took the only automated telephone poll we could afford—a $2,500 hit to our tiny war chest—the writing was on the wall.

Those ten months are mostly a blur, but I will always remember Election Day clearly. I woke up early to vote, and just seeing that I could get my name on the ballot reaffirmed my faith in American democracy. I then got back in the Toyota to drive 3.5 hours across the entire district, one final time. Along the way I stopped at several polling locations to visit our volunteers. They included Harry, in Northumberland County, a Republican; Jerry, in Lycoming County, a member of the Green Party;

Randy, in Wayne County, a Democrat; Vince, in Tioga County, a Libertarian; and Karen, in Pike County, an independent. As I saw them all working the polls that day, it reassured me that some ideas can transcend party labels and loyalties.

Finally, I went home to Milford, the small town on the Delaware River where I grew up. After my loss became official, I drove to the local campaign office to thank our team, along with a crowd of friends I'd known as far back as preschool, extended family, and supporters from around and beyond the district. I told the group, "Today is a milestone, not an ending, along a journey to fix our politics. I promise you it is something I will remain committed and dedicated to." I meant it.

I ended up in third place with 22,734 votes. Still, my 13% share was the best performance by an independent House candidate running against two major-party candidates in more than two decades. Even the most cynical pundits were surprised. But the real question was *why* it was so hard for any candidate outside the major-party duopoly to gain traction.

It's the System, Stupid

"Congress has an 8% approval rating, yet 90% of members get reelected," I said during the only debate of my House race. "We find ourselves with a Congress that is both gridlocked and corrupt because we have failed to hold our leaders accountable." In hindsight I was right about the first part but not the second. It's not that voters fail to hold our leaders accountable; it's that the system prevents us from doing so.

Like many other states, Pennsylvania's congressional map was heavily gerrymandered. In 2012, the first election after new district lines were drawn, Democrats won 51% of the statewide popular vote for House seats, but only 28% of the actual seats (five out of eighteen).[10] My district was a "safe" seat, where Tom Marino beat his Democratic opponent in a 66% to 34% landslide in 2012. The results would have been roughly the same no matter who the candidates were.

Pennsylvania is also one of the fifteen states in which independent voters do not have a right to participate in partisan primaries. (At least, not yet!) In 2010, Marino won his first primary with just 41% of a three-way vote.[11] This meant that he didn't really represent a majority of voters in the district, or even a majority of Republicans. He merely represented *a plurality of GOP primary voters*—only 59,279 of them in a district with a total voting-age population of approximately 560,000, or about 10 percent. That's who controlled his fate. That's who he'd have to please if he wanted to stay in Congress.

And as I learned during my 2014 race, those GOP base voters were uncompromising. At the height of the Tea Party's influence, they weren't looking for a leader who would work across the aisle to solve problems. They wanted a fighter to take on President Obama. These dynamics meant that there was no path for a pragmatist like me in the Republican primary. I also knew that running as a Democrat would not fit me and would be pointless in my solidly red district. My only shot at blocking Marino's free pass to reelection, and giving voters another choice, was to run as an independent.

But every aspect of the system puts up extra barriers for independent candidates, turning that only shot into an extreme long shot. I was required to collect 3.5 times more signatures than either my Democratic or Republican opponents, just to qualify for the ballot. I was ignored by the media during the primary season, because I wasn't competing in either primary. And I heard concerns from many voters that they didn't want to "waste" their vote on an independent—or, worse, inadvertently help elect their least preferred candidate.

My campaign taught me that the only way to increase accountability and improve representation in our government would be to fix our broken election system. So that became my new focus.

A New Approach: Unite America

After my congressional run, I joined the founding board of a new non-profit called the Centrist Project, started by Dartmouth professor Charlie Wheelan, author of *The Centrist Manifesto*. It sought to elect a handful of independent Senate candidates who could form a "fulcrum" to control the balance of power and leverage their influence to advance bipartisan solutions. I became the executive director in the fall of 2016, at which point we had no office, no staff, and no long-term strategy.

One of my first undertakings was to head to Maine, where a group of reformers were working to establish "instant runoff" elections, also known as ranked choice voting (RCV), through a statewide ballot initiative. Under this system, voters have the option of ranking their candidates in order of preference, which ensures a majority winner, incentivizes broad coalition building, and levels the playing field for independent and third-party candidates. (I'll get into all of this in detail in this book.) I wanted to learn more about election reform and spent the days before the 2016 election knocking on doors in support of the initiative.

On election night 2016, while most of the country was either celebrating or despairing over Donald Trump's victory, my excitement was focused on Maine becoming the first state to adopt instant runoffs. It was a ray of hope for breaking the partisan fever that plagued America, as the bitterly divisive campaign between Clinton and Trump exemplified.

By 2019, the Centrist Project relaunched as Unite America, a philanthropic venture fund that invests in nonpartisan election reform around the country. Soon we had momentum and three dynamic cochairs: entrepreneur Marc Merrill, philanthropist Kathryn Murdoch, and former Fortune 200 CEO Kent Thiry. Our first grant from Unite America went to an upstart group of reformers in Alaska who were lobbying for the country's first top-four nonpartisan primary along with instant runoffs in the general election. The reform passed in 2020 and took effect in 2022, with dramatic results. It gave us confidence that big change is possible, and it inspired me to continue on my journey.

THE PRIMARY SOLUTION

My goal for this book is to illuminate how partisan primaries are the biggest solvable problem facing our democracy today and to inspire people just like you to get involved in the movement to reform them.

Part I shows how partisan primaries were invented in the first place (hint: not by the Founders!) and how they have become weaponized by fringe politicians and extreme special interests against the majority of our country.

Part II then digs deeper into the damage that partisan primaries are currently causing. You've probably heard of a win-win approach to conflict resolution, right? Our current primary system is lose-lose-lose: bad for voters, bad for the country, and even bad for the parties themselves.

Part III turns from understanding the Primary Problem to solving it. We'll explore several existing and new models for reforming primaries by giving all voters the freedom to vote for any candidate in every taxpayer-funded election, regardless of party. We'll dig deeply into Alaska, which demonstrated how primary reform gives more power to voters without advantaging or disadvantaging any particular party. And we'll explore solutions to the unique challenges of presidential elections, whose primaries often leave most voters frustrated at having to choose between "the lesser of two evils" by the time November rolls around.

Finally, part IV offers a state-by-state strategy for winning primary reform nationally and shows how advocates can respond to common objections along the way.

One big reason for optimism is that the road to primary reform doesn't require a constitutional amendment or federal legislation, and the path to transformational impact doesn't require winning in all fifty states. In fact, we can dramatically improve Congress if just six additional states abolish partisan primaries by 2026, which would bring the total to ten. With twenty senators and a few dozen representatives from these states freed from the grips of the political fringes and able to form new coalitions to actually govern, we can begin to address the major challenges that seem unsolvable today.

Of course, the political establishment won't go down without a fight. We need all the help we can get to make improving our elections a nationwide reality. I hope that after finishing this book, you'll be inspired to join our movement and help build a future in which every vote matters, our leaders truly represent us, and our democracy endures.

PART I

ORIGINS OF THE PRIMARY PROBLEM

Chapters 1 and 2 will show the strange and winding path that gave us America's primary system in the early twentieth century and what has changed over the last twenty years that has made it an accelerator to our growing political division and dysfunction. But before we get into any history, let's examine a recent example of what the Primary Problem looks like in action today.

"THE TWO LEAST QUALIFIED, LEAST COMPETENT CANDIDATES"

The 2022 Senate race in my home state of Pennsylvania was one of the most watched contests in recent years. Republican Pat Toomey was retiring, and partisan control of the fifty-fifty Senate was on the line in this competitive battleground. Ultimately, $374 million would be spent to compete for this one seat, making it the second-most-expensive Senate race in history.[1] Most of the attention came in the fall, but the race really took shape months earlier, when both major parties selected their nominees: Democrat John Fetterman and Republican Mehmet Oz.

Fetterman, the state's lieutenant governor, was an outspoken progressive and avid supporter of Bernie Sanders. Despite the fact that Fetterman had served as president of the state senate, not one of his twenty Democratic colleagues in that body endorsed his campaign. Nor did any of the ninety Democratic state house members.[2] Instead of endorsements, his great strengths were a talent for social media, a devoted online base of activists and small donors, and a unique personal style that included shorts, hoodies, and clever verbal barbs at Republicans. By contrast, Fetterman's main challenger for the Democratic nomination, Conor Lamb, was more politically mainstream and had a record of winning competitive elections. Lamb was a two-term member of Congress, a former assistant U.S. attorney, and a former United States Marine.

In endorsing Lamb over Fetterman, the *Philadelphia Inquirer* wrote: "Pennsylvanians deserve a senator who is more than just a plus-one vote for the Democratic caucus in the Senate; it's crucial that voters elect a candidate who would add value by representing the commonwealth."[3] In another setback, Fetterman had a stroke three days before the primary, which raised serious questions about his ability to serve in office. Nonetheless, his grassroots support and small-donor war chest led him to victory over Lamb and two other contenders, with a 59% majority in the Democratic primary.

Meanwhile, the GOP primary featured an even starker contrast between the top two candidates. Oz, the former celebrity TV doctor, had apparently moved to Pennsylvania just to run for Senate and had reinvented himself from a Hollywood liberal to a MAGA conservative. His campaign made many stumbles in trying to connect with working-class and middle-class voters, including a widely mocked viral video that Oz posted of himself shopping for "crudité" ingredients in a Wegmans supermarket, which he mispronounced as "Wegners."[4]

Oz's main opponent was David McCormick, a West Point graduate, former Army Ranger, and successful hedge fund CEO. Like Oz,

McCormick sought the highly influential endorsement of former president Trump, but he would only go so far to win it. He later described a meeting he had with Trump at Mar-a-Lago: "The former president looked me in the eyes and warned, 'You know you can't win unless you say the [2020] election was stolen.' I made it clear to him that I couldn't do that."[5] A few days after that meeting, Trump endorsed Oz.

In a supertight primary with seven contenders, Oz squeaked by with a 31.2% plurality, versus McCormick's 31.1%. The statewide margin was only 951 votes.

As Election Day approached, I wondered what my parents thought of this nationally significant race in a state where they had lived for several decades. They are classic independent voters who vote for the person, not the party, and usually focus on middle-class pocketbook issues. My mom stayed at home to raise my sister and me, while my dad commuted a few hours each day to his job in sales at a recycling company in New Jersey. They desired to see fundamental change in a political system they've increasingly grown disillusioned with. For them, that change looked like Ross Perot in 1992, Barack Obama in 2008, and Donald Trump in 2016. They were exactly the kind of voters who would ultimately decide whether Fetterman or Oz prevailed.

So when I asked my dad who he was backing, I was shocked by his reply: "Neither. Why should I?" At first I thought he was just trying to avoid a debate, but he was serious. He explained that, as an independent voter, he had no ability to participate in either party's "closed" primary in Pennsylvania, and he disliked both options that the major parties put forward. So he was planning to stay home.

In the end, Fetterman defeated Oz by about five points in the general election.

To help make sense of the result, I sought out Michael Smerconish, a Pennsylvania native and host of political programs on both CNN and SiriusXM. He told me, "I believe that the two least qualified, least competent candidates won their primaries, and I attribute that to our status as a closed-primary state. You run far left in a Democratic primary and far right in a Republican primary. Then you capture the nomination and pivot back toward the center. At least, people used to pivot, but elections today seem to be much more about motivation than persuasion."[6]

What Running in a Partisan Primary Is Really Like

To better understand the dynamics of Pennsylvania's Senate primary, I spoke to another candidate in that race: Jeff Bartos, a former Republican nominee for lieutenant governor who ran against Oz and McCormick in the GOP primary. Bartos stressed how different a primary electorate is from a general electorate. "It's a smaller audience you're speaking to. It's much more on the ground in diners, coffee shops, county parties, local township party meetings, and every barbecue, hog roast, and clambake you can think of."[7]

Bartos explained that, to win a primary, candidates need tailored strategies to appeal to two very different but equally important groups: party leaders who control the party apparatus, and grassroots activists who are the most consistent voters in low-turnout elections. The differences between those groups can pose a huge challenge to navigate. "Virtually everybody I met—the county committee people and the state committee people—they're local doctors, accountants, shopkeepers, manufacturing executives, farmers," Bartos said, describing the first group.[8] By and large, these leaders are focused above all on nominating a candidate who can win the general election. And Bartos won significant support among them, including five of six regional caucus straw polls in January and February 2022, leading up to the state convention.

In contrast, activists are not engaged in the official party apparatus, yet they tend to dominate the primary electorate and have very different priorities. "I was the devil incarnate to some of these folks," recalled Bartos. "They wanted to get angry and curse and yell, 'Let's go, Brandon!' . . . People would come up to me and say, 'What are you going to do about pedophilia?' And I'd say, 'Well, I really want to talk to you about agriculture policy.' . . . I define 'the extremes' as looking past all the present problems that are affecting the day-to-day of the Commonwealth and focusing on some boogeyman: *You don't get it, Democrats are evil!*"[9]

Bartos was hissed and booed at several events that featured "Stop the Steal" booths. He was repeatedly called a RINO (Republican in Name Only) and asked why he wasn't angrier at Democrats. He believes that these extreme elements of the party base are largely influenced by niche media. "Candidates, like businesses, go where the customers are, where the voters are. And if the voters are spending all day locked into this news source or that news source, online or on TV, the candidates are going to follow."[10] He warned at least one fellow candidate who was running for the first time about these dynamics. "The advice I gave them was, you're going to have consultants who tell you everything you need to do. If you just listen to them, you may be able to win. But if you listen to them *all* the time, you're going to wake up six months from now with a lot less money—wearing clothes, driving a vehicle, and shooting a gun you don't own today—wondering what the hell happened."[11]

Bartos stayed true to his beliefs as a pragmatic problem solver and was rewarded with 5% of the primary vote. Oz reinvented himself as a MAGA enthusiast and was rewarded with a 31% plurality to capture the nomination, though he ultimately lost a winnable Senate seat for the GOP. This doesn't seem like a very functional process, does it?

Why Were 1.2 Million Voters Left Out?

In Pennsylvania in 2022, 1.2 million voters unaffiliated with either major party were systematically disenfranchised from influencing which candidates made it to the general election, even though the partisan primaries were funded by all taxpayers at a cost of more than $75 million. We have good reason to believe that if those 1.2 million had been allowed to vote in either primary, the Senate race would have turned out differently. Polling found that both Fetterman and Oz were viewed unfavorably by a plurality of independents. Had those voters been given a voice in the primaries, we might have seen a general election between different candidates, like Lamb vs. McCormick. That may have resulted in far more serious (if less entertaining) debates about public policy, rather than about crudités and the propriety of wearing hoodies at political events.

Instead, in the final days before the general election, 17% of independents reported being still undecided or too frustrated to vote at all, compared to just 3% of Republicans and less than 1% of Democrats.[12] My dad was hardly alone.

"Pennsylvania politics, as long as I've been around, has been played between the forty-yard lines of the political football field," said David Thornburgh, the son of the former Republican governor and U.S. attorney general Dick Thornburgh. "Based on the 2022 election, that's not where we are right now."[13] Partisan primaries are a big reason why.

So why exactly are independents locked out of Pennsylvania's primaries? The answer goes back to the passage of the Pennsylvania Election Code in 1937. At the time, legislators were concerned about political trickery when new, similarly named parties would emerge to intentionally confuse voters about which primary to participate in. These parties were known as "mushroom parties" for their quick growth but short-lived nature. The solution legislators came up with was to restrict participation in each primary to only the registered members of that party. There were not many independent voters in the 1930s, so no one worried about locking such voters out of any primary altogether.[14]

Thornburgh pointed out that the same election code, still on the books to this day, also states in Section 1112, Section C, Sub-Section 1: "The county election board shall furnish a lantern, or a proper substitute for one, which shall give sufficient light to enable voters, while in the voting machine booth, to read the ballot labels."[15]

"The world of 1937 left us with both of these anachronistic provisions," observed Thornburgh, who is now leading a campaign called "Ballot PA" to open Pennsylvania's primaries to independent voters. We've long since substituted lanterns for a more modern replacement; it's finally time we do the same for partisan primaries.

ONE

THE INVENTION OF PARTISAN PRIMARIES

magine it's Election Day in 1824, which might be any time of the year in your state, since there's no national uniformity. If you are white, male, and over twenty-one, you can step up to the ballot box. Otherwise, of course, you have to stay home, or face being turned away, arrested, or perhaps something worse.

There's only a single voting location in your county. It's going to take you about a day to ride there by horse, so you'll require an overnight stay at a local inn while your transportation rests for the return journey. But don't worry, the election is scheduled on a Tuesday to ensure that you won't have to travel on the Sabbath and that you'll be back home by Wednesday, which of course is market day. (Some things, like Tuesday elections, never change.)

When you show up at the voting station, you won't be handed a ballot. Instead, you'll already have with you the preprinted "ticket" you were given by a representative from the party you support (almost certainly a faction of the Democratic-Republicans, since the Federalist Party collapsed a few years earlier, and the Whig Party hasn't been born yet). Your ticket lists the entire slate of your party's candidates, from local county offices through president and vice president. There's no candidate for the Senate on your ticket, since senators will be chosen by the state legislatures for another ninety years. And depending on your state, you might have already voted for the House of Representatives, or you might have to come back another day to do so. Your state might even elect multiple congressmen at large rather than district by district. And of course there aren't any ballot initiatives; that concept is decades in the future.

Most of your party's candidates were chosen months earlier by "party bosses" in your state and county. These local leaders met in literal smoke-filled rooms to debate who would best support their needs, including through jobs, contracts, and other favors known as patronage. Maybe the bosses also discussed the character and talents of the men they were nominating, and the commitment of those men to the well-being of voters like you. Or maybe those questions never came up. As a mere voter rather than a party insider, you have no idea. And you definitely had no say in whose names got on that ticket in your pocket.

As you drop your ticket into the ballot box, everyone in the room can see which party you support, thanks to the distinctive color and printing style of the ticket. You may also decide to support candidates from different parties by "splitting your ticket"—but that may draw attention. There's no privacy here. If you tell the men at the voting location that you'd like to cast a secret ballot, they will look at you like you came from another planet . . . or at least from another century.

I wish I could do this time-machine exercise with every American who assumes that our elections haven't changed very much over time, and that we are using a sacred process handed down to us by our almighty Founders. To the contrary, our elections have radically evolved since the early days. In fact, primaries were invented out of whole cloth in response to problems with the candidate nomination process, which got steadily worse in the mid- to late nineteenth century.

And just as partisan primaries were invented as a response to the urgent needs of an earlier era, they can and should be changed now, in response to the equally urgent needs of our own time. After all, if you're not riding a horse to vote, then perhaps other things can evolve, too.

THE ADVENT OF PARTIES AND CANDIDATE NOMINATIONS

One of the reasons our Founders never contemplated a party-driven nomination process is that they never desired to establish political parties in the first place. In fact, they feared the rise of parties. The framers tried to warn us that parties, representing competing groups of narrow interests, could become an obstacle to good government. In his 1796 Farewell Address, President Washington warned, "The alternate domination of one faction over another, sharpened by the spirit of revenge natural to party dissension, which in different ages and countries has perpetrated the most horrid enormities, is itself a frightful despotism."[1] Even John Adams, the future cofounder of the Federalist Party, wrote in a 1780 letter: "There is nothing which I dread so much as a division of the republic into two great parties, each arranged under its leader, and concerting measures in opposition to each other. This, in my humble apprehension, is to be dreaded as the greatest political evil under our Constitution."[2] Yet here we are.

Despite their fear of factions, deep policy disagreements between Hamiltonians and Jeffersonians quickly led to the emergence of two national parties—the Federalists and Democratic-Republicans. As early as 1796, the first presidential year without Washington as an option, nearly every candidate for Congress expressed his sympathies for one party or the other.

How did the parties nominate candidates at this early stage? There was no precedent yet for declaring a candidacy, either for national or state office. The initial nomination procedures that emerged, not surprisingly, were informal and varied considerably from state to state and within each state. Groups of people, often friends of potential candidates, would anonymously nominate men for office via local newspapers in order to promote them as capable leaders. In some states, candidates emerged from countywide general meetings. As the parties got stronger in states like New Hampshire, the power to nominate their candidates transferred to state legislative caucuses.[3]

By 1828, the two dominant national parties were the Democrats, led by Andrew Jackson, and the Whigs, led by Henry Clay. Parties established a grip on nominations through the "caucus and convention" system, which had emerged over the prior decade to become the dominant nomination method of the nineteenth century.[4] This was a two-phase nominating process. First, local party members nominated delegates at a caucus, and then those delegates assembled at a statewide convention to vote for their party's nominees. Technically, these delegates could vote for whoever they wanted at the convention and were not bound by any party rules. But in reality, there were limits on who delegates could support at the convention if they wanted to remain in the good graces of their local party leaders.

In smaller towns in the Northeast and some rural areas, caucuses were generally held face-to-face and featured significant public deliberation—the classic model of a New England–style town hall. But those were rare in other regions. It was more typical that caucuses resembled a traditional election, just with party members choosing delegates to represent them, rather than choosing candidates. Either way, regular voters who were party members rarely had a direct say in the selection of nominees.

Party committees would put out informal calls for conventions multiple times per year to choose nominees for open offices. Their main goal was promoting party unity by mobilizing voters behind a single candidate in the general election and avoiding factionalism. Committees didn't focus on the qualities of potential candidates but rather on "the fate of the party and its principles."[5] Overtly ambitious candidates were looked down upon because they might put their own needs ahead of the party's. As historian John F. Reynolds observes, "The convention system

surely had its drawbacks, but it did sustain the major parties throughout most of the nineteenth century. The many conventions required to
furnish candidates for numerous elective offices over multiple venues
renewed and reinvigorated the party organizations."[6]

GILDED AGE MACHINES MAKE NOMINATIONS MORE CORRUPT THAN EVER

After the Civil War, political corruption ran rampant, as did the inequality driven by the Industrial Revolution. That corruption extended
to party nominations, which became increasingly controlled by strong
party machines, especially in rapidly growing cities that had lots of
working-class immigrants. These newly naturalized citizens could be
enticed to support the local machines in exchange for jobs, favors, or
outright bribery.

By the Gilded Age of the 1870s, the spoils system of rewarding
friends of party bosses with nominations had become entrenched. As a
contemporary observer put it, "Under a debauched system of civil service the machinery for making nominations, or for finding out what the
will of the majority is, has fallen largely under the control of those who
hold or seek public office, as a consequence of the prevailing theory that
such offices are the proper reward of political services, and the spoil of
the victors in a political contest."[7]

Reformers and critics noted that party machines were using the
caucus and convention system to keep nominations under their tight
control, with little discussion or deliberation anymore. Booming urban
populations also meant less personal connection between politicians and
voters, while also making it easier to commit voter fraud.

Perhaps most ominously, the dominance of the machines made
elected officials increasingly beholden to the bosses who put them in
office, who essentially became their employers. The punishment for de-
viating from the party line would be a withdrawal of support at the next
nominating convention. As one account put it, "The machine eliminated

nearly all measures of accountability for those in public office. Instead of voting their ideology, or their pocketbooks, people voted for their employer."[8]

The most famous and influential machine boss of the Gilded Age was New York City's William "Boss" Tweed, who led the Democratic Party's political machine, Tammany Hall, from 1866 to 1871. His reign was the quintessential example of the corruption of machine politics, via an iron grip on nominations and the placement of loyal cronies in every available position of authority. One of his famous quips could be the motto of Gilded Age politics: "I don't care who does the electing, so long as I get to do the nominating."[9]

Tweed's corruption ran rampant. To ensure Tammany Hall's victory in the elections of 1868, Tweed's cronies arranged for a group of loyalists to vote over and over, as many as twenty times each, using fake names, disguises, and the names of dead people who were still on the registration rolls. Once in power, the Tweed Ring is estimated to have stolen or extorted from both the city government and private businesses between $75 and $200 million between 1867 and 1871 ($2 to $5 billion in today's money). Their methods included "padded bills, raised accounts, false vouchers, awards to highest bidders, inferior materials, unnecessary repairs wedded to defective workmanship, and outrageous kickbacks."[10]

How did he avoid consequences for so much corruption for so many years? As one historian notes, "His graft went unopposed for some time, because those who would have benefitted the most from a more fair and upright political system were the same people who were benefitting even more through Tweed's swindles."[11] But even Tweed couldn't hang on to power forever. In a criminal fraud trial in 1873, he was found guilty and sentenced to twelve years in prison. Amazingly, Tweed escaped from the Ludlow Street Jail in late 1875 and made it all the way to Spain. But he was arrested there when someone recognized him from an old editorial cartoon, went back to prison in New York, and died there in 1878.

Tweed's downfall didn't diminish his status as a role model for many other political machines around the country. For decades to come they would continue to emulate his methods, just with more restraint and caution to cover their tracks. In particular, machine bosses would continue to manipulate conventions and maintain an iron grip on nominations, making sure that only their loyal allies would have a shot at any political office.

CRAWFORD COUNTY INTRODUCES THE DIRECT PRIMARY

Although the caucus and convention system was coming under increasing criticism from reformers outside of the political parties for being conducive to corruption by party bosses, the first shift away from the system was actually catalyzed from within one of the major parties. In 1842, the Democrats in Crawford County, Pennsylvania, became the first local party in the nation to organize and implement a "direct primary"— giving every voter an opportunity to directly nominate their party's candidates.[12]

The Democrats were then the dominant party in Crawford, and receiving the party's nomination was tantamount to winning the election. So Democratic conventions had turned into political battlegrounds between intraparty factions. An unresolved nominating convention in 1835 resulted in two Democrats splitting the general election vote for governor in the county, enabling the Whig candidate to win statewide.[13]

Dissatisfaction with the convention system grew after that fiasco, and accelerated in 1837, when a change to the state constitution made more countywide offices elective and open to multiple candidates. At the 1839 Crawford County nominating convention, some rejected Democrats refused to accept the verdict of the delegates and instead ran as third-party candidates. The officially nominated Democrats won every office, but the dissident candidates performed surprisingly well, attracting some Whig votes as well as many Democratic votes.[14] Party cohesion was collapsing as tensions between the two factions worsened.

The next county convention, scheduled for June 1842, seemed destined to be contested if not hostile. A number of reforms to the delegate appointment process were proposed to bring down tensions between the "party regulars" and the "insurgents." But those rule changes weren't enough to stop the convention from deadlocking after multiple ballots and breaking up before nominees could be named for every office. Democratic leaders from towns across Crawford County worried that many candidates would be running in the general election without the approval of the party. In desperation they called a general meeting for that August to focus on nomination reform.[15]

At that meeting, a delegate named George Shellito presented a new plan to restore party unity through a direct vote of all eligible Democratic voters in the county. This would, in theory, eliminate distortions in representation and alleviate dissatisfaction among the underrepresented parts of the county. Shellito was no politician, just a farmer from Sadsbury Township with a strong interest in the party. But he must have been very persuasive, since his plan was adopted by a unanimous vote of the rules committee.

Some party insiders were highly skeptical of this newfangled primary because they couldn't assure nominations for their friends.[16] Some even encouraged a boycott of the primary to make it seem unpopular among ordinary voters.[17] But despite the efforts of these opponents, most party leaders saw the direct primary as a useful tool for resolving factional strife and promoting unity, not as a threat to their power over nominations.[18] And among voters, interest in the September primary seemed to grow as word spread across the county. One local newspaper explained its potential at the time:

> By this means every man's vote will act directly on the result—there will be no intermediate channels through which bargain and trickery can flow to prevent the will of the people from being honestly carried out. There will be no such thing hereafter as violating instructions— no "recruits" will be purchased to defeat the will of the majority. The people will now have the man of their choice nominated, without the

interference of brawling meddlers in town, who have nothing at heart but the accomplishment of their own selfish and disorganizing ends.[19]

In the end, turnout for the primary was quite high, everyone accepted the results, and the Democrats did well in the general election. The experiment was deemed a success, and direct primaries soon spread to other counties in Pennsylvania.

Ironically, the direct primary didn't endure in the county where it was born. The Crawford County Democrats struggled in the next few general elections, and in 1850 their leaders abolished the direct primary and returned to the previous system. They wouldn't have another direct primary for another half century.

ROBERT LA FOLLETTE BRINGS THE DIRECT PRIMARY TO WISCONSIN

While progressive reformers were pushing for direct primaries in numerous states around the turn of the twentieth century, including Ohio, Kentucky, and Minnesota, it's worth focusing in some detail on Wisconsin, where Robert "Fighting Bob" La Follette changed American politics forever by championing the first mandated, statewide use of the direct primary.

The caucus and convention system in Wisconsin served the needs of the railroad and lumber industries, whose wealthy elites were tightly aligned with the establishment ("Stalwart") GOP machine between the Civil War and 1890. But then the Democrats regained power with the support of working-class voters, winning the governorship and almost all offices on the state ticket in 1890. This led to a "great battle which raged in the late nineteenth century to prevent the dominance of American political and social life by the masters of wealth."[20]

La Follette was a GOP congressman who lost his reelection bid that year. But he broke with the Stalwarts in protest of their widespread corruption, including an attempt to bribe La Follette himself by a powerful senator. He was ostracized by the party elites and accepted his new role as an insurgent. He later wrote, "Out of the ordeal came understanding, and out of understanding came resolution. I determined that the power of this corrupt influence, which was undermining and destroying every semblance of representative government in Wisconsin, should be broken."[21]

The Panic of 1893 virtually ensured a GOP comeback in 1894, but La Follette hated the way the Stalwart machine crushed his preferred candidate for governor, Nils Haugen, in favor of a machine loyalist, William Upham. When Governor Upham chose not to run for reelection two years later, La Follette ran. He arrived at the 1896 GOP convention with enough delegates to take the nomination, but the Stalwarts bought off enough of his delegates to defeat him.[22] Their trickery only amplified his determination to lead the state to reform, which became his crusade for the next seven years.

La Follette spent 1897 giving speeches about the Crawford County plan, which he had only recently learned about. Direct primaries, he argued, could destroy the power of the machines (both Republican and Democrat); give power back to average workers and farmers; and foster the election of more honest and public-minded officials. Why shouldn't Wisconsin trust the intelligence of its own citizens to choose their own nominees?[23] The Stalwarts tried to stop his speaking tour (once even by having his train to a county fair leave an hour early, without him), and GOP-controlled newspapers turned against him, but La Follette persisted. In one of his most widely covered speeches, "The Menace of the Political Machine," he declared:

> Put aside the caucus and convention. They have been, and will continue to be, prostituted to the service of corrupt organizations. They answer no purpose further than to give respectable form to political robbery. . . . Go back to the first principles of democracy; go back to the

people. Substitute for both the caucus and the convention a primary election—held under the sanctions of law which prevail at the general elections—where the citizen may cast his vote directly to nominate the candidate of the party with which he affiliates and have it canvassed and returned just as he cast it. . . .

Then every citizen will share equally in the nomination of the candidates of his party and attend primary elections as a privilege as well as a duty. It will no longer be necessary to create an artificial interest in the general election to induce voters to attend. Intelligent, well-considered judgment will be substituted for unthinking enthusiasm, the lamp of reason for the torchlight. The voter will not require to be persuaded that he has an interest in the election. He will know that he has. The nominations of the party will not be the result of compromise or impulse, or evil design—the barrel and the machine—but the candidates of the majority, honestly and fairly nominated.[24]

La Follette was blocked again by the Stalwarts during his 1898 run for governor, but finally overcame them in 1900, when more Republicans were open to progressive goals. (At the time, governors in Wisconsin served two-year terms.) He easily won the general election, but still faced a daunting fight to pass direct primaries, with the state senate still controlled by Stalwarts. They complained that direct primaries for all offices would cost the state too much money and would infringe on the rights of the parties.[25]

Only after his reelection in 1902 did La Follette have enough assembly and senate support to pass a reform bill. And even then, getting it through the senate required a compromise with the Stalwarts, putting the question to a referendum that would require Wisconsinites to vote for or against direct primaries. The Stalwarts gambled that the referendum would fail, but an impressive 62% of voters supported it.[26] The state's long but ultimately successful battle for direct primaries became a role model for reformers nationwide.

Adoption of Direct Primaries

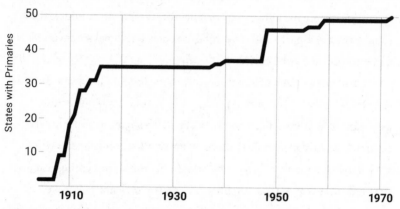

Note: In 1948, the Supreme Court ended the discriminatory practice of white-only primaries in eight southern states. Their adoption of direct primaries before this year is therefore not reflected in the chart.

Source: Adapted from Chapman Rackaway and Joseph Romance, Primary Elections and American Politics: The Unintended Consequences of Progressive Era Reform, (New York: State University of New York Press, 2022).

DIRECT PRIMARIES SPREAD STATE BY STATE

Thanks to La Follette and other leaders who called for the return and expansion of the Crawford County system, momentum toward direct primaries caught on. More than half of all states adopted the direct primary within eight years of Wisconsin's adoption.[27]

At the same time, there was no uniformity in who should be permitted to vote in party primaries. While most reformers touted primaries open to all voters as better than primaries only open to party members, others feared the potential for trickery and abuse. In 1900, a scandal-ridden Democratic three-term mayor of Minneapolis, Albert Alonzo "Doc" Ames, wound up winning a fourth term only after switching parties and bringing his supporters with him into the Republican Party primary. Leaders in both parties were furious and moved to close their primaries to only their registered members. Other localities and states followed after learning of Ames, who made national news after running from the law and getting arrested in New Hampshire. As late as 1928, only four states were using open primaries.[28]

It would oversimplify history to give all the credit for direct primaries to progressive reformers. The parties themselves also had self-interested reasons to accept direct primaries, as they gradually recognized. Both outsiders and insiders concluded that reform had to be better than the status quo.

For example, rural areas often embraced direct primaries before urban areas, as larger rural counties faced logistical issues that made it harder for bosses to exert tight control over caucuses and conventions. For parties, direct primaries simplified nominations and made them more efficient, while limiting the ability of a faction that opposed the party elite to gain power at a convention.[29]

On the other hand, western states tended to adopt direct primaries more quickly because their party organizations were younger and weaker, so residents were less attached to parties than their eastern peers. Additionally, western parties and governments were often directly entwined with big companies in industries like railroads and mining, which dominated the region's economy. For reformers, weak party loyalty and a desire to disentangle business and government helped them more easily galvanize support for the direct primary among the "common people."[30]

Finally, the primary reform movement got a boost from the nation's most popular politician of the Progressive Era. In 1912, former president Teddy Roosevelt tried to recapture the GOP nomination from his own handpicked successor, President William H. Taft. Roosevelt won nine of the twelve states that conducted primaries. Nevertheless, the GOP party bosses ignored those primary results and renominated Taft. Roosevelt and his supporters stormed out of the convention and started a new Progressive Party, nicknamed the Bull Moose Party. Part of their campaign message was that only direct primaries in every state could elevate the voices of ordinary people over the anti-democratic elites. As two historians put it, "His crusade made universal use of the direct primary a cause célèbre; assaulted traditional partisan loyalties; and championed candidate-centered campaigns."[31]

TAKEAWAYS FROM THE RISE OF THE DIRECT PRIMARY

The long journey from having no formalized candidate-nominating process at the time of our nation's founding, to the party-driven caucus and convention system of the 1800s, to the near-universal direct, partisan primaries by 1920 holds important lessons for reform efforts in our own time.

First and foremost, we shouldn't feel locked in by "the way we've always done it" because no such way exists. American political history is filled with experiments, false starts, and reversals of direction. The leaders of our early republic—of the Constitutional Convention, the early Congresses, and the first few presidential administrations—were all essentially winging it, relying on trial and error much more than precedent. History shows that there are many ways to choose leaders in a democracy, none of them perfect, all with pros and cons. Whenever our ancestors found that the electoral system of their time wasn't living up to its purpose, or was fostering too much corruption, they improved it.

Second, idealistic reformers and pragmatic politicians both have a key role to play in catalyzing any reform. Direct primaries solved pain points for both voters and party leaders during the Progressive Era, which is one reason why they spread so quickly. For voters, they provided a new way to be heard and participate, while cracking down on corruption. For parties, they provided a new way to manage the logistics of the nominating process, while mitigating intraparty division. Applying this history to today's primary reform movement means designing and positioning a win-win solution, a key strategy for mitigating knee-jerk opposition from both major parties. (We'll see how modern-day primary reform is in their own interest once again in chapter 5.)

Third, reform is contagious. It may seem futile to try to make elections more fair and democratic in just one county, city, or state, especially now that so much of American politics is nationalized. But look at the enormous long-term impact of local leaders like George Shellito in Crawford County and Robert La Follette in Wisconsin. Small, local actions toward worthy goals have a way of spreading beyond anyone's expectations, even if they take years to reveal their full effect.

Finally, history suggests that we shouldn't let setbacks overcome our optimism and determination. Imagine how discouraging it must have been for reformers when the Crawford County Democrats undid their own innovation, less than a decade after it began. Or when La Follette, a defeated politician in 1897, was slogging across Wisconsin for years on end, evangelizing for primary reform to any group that would listen to him. Or when even the great Teddy Roosevelt couldn't overcome the powerful political bosses of his time. Nevertheless, the direct primary ultimately prevailed, and so can essential reforms in our own time.

TWO

THE WEAPONIZATION OF PARTISAN PRIMARIES

During most of the century that partisan primaries have been widespread, our democracy has not been in crisis and our government has been able to function. Big majorities got big things done. In fact, many of the biggest pieces of twentieth-century legislation were passed with majorities of both the party in power *and* the party not in power, such as Social Security, the Interstate Highway System, and the Civil Rights Act. Throughout this period, partisan primaries were a rather innocuous part of our political system. They served their basic function of candidate nomination. The rare challenge to an incumbent in a primary usually only came if that incumbent became embroiled in scandal.

However, partisan primaries evolved into a major problem as a result of two realignments: in politics and in media.

For most of the twentieth century, our two major parties were composed of relatively diverse political coalitions, including conservative southern Democrats and liberal northeastern Republicans. America's two-party system was really a four-party system: liberal and conservative Democrats and liberal and conservative Republicans. As the political scientist Lee Drutman explains, "Coalitions were flexible, issue dependent, and thus multi-dimensional, with few permanent enemies and many possible allies on all issues."[1] The tectonic plates of our politics began to shift during the civil rights era as the parties began to realign around social and cultural issues, and as politics became both more nationalized and more closely contested. But since around the time of the 1994 midterm elections, which ended four decades of Democratic control of the House, partisan realignment neatly sorted liberals and conservatives into two "distinct, non-overlapping coalitions that offer extremely distinct alternatives to the American people."[2]

The second major realignment was the death of universal media. From 1961 to the early 1990s, there were just three major broadcast networks: ABC, CBS, and NBC. At its peak, an average of 29 million Americans tuned in nightly to watch Walter Cronkite anchor the *CBS Evening News*—an unimaginably huge audience today.[3] The network news shows, like the hundreds of local newspapers that gave most voters their other main source of news, had strong incentives to stress objectivity and appeal to everyone across the political spectrum.

Then came the rise of populist talk radio, conflict-driven cable news, and especially the internet and social media, which enabled anyone with a strong opinion to reach others who agreed with them. The media universe fragmented into countless niches and subniches, making it easy for people to get news and information that aligned with their political persuasions, while ignoring everything else. The concept of a singular "media" gave way to our current "choose your own news" environment. As a consequence, while 68% of Americans reported trust in the media in 1972, today that number has plunged in half to 34%.[4]

The combination of polarized parties and polarized media gradually transformed our political process. There was now a more narrow, nationally consistent definition of what an "ideal" Democrat or Republican would believe. Activists on both sides of the spectrum were absorbing a steady diet of information to reinforce their beliefs and bind them to their fellow partisans. As a result, partisan primaries started to become ideological purity tests through which candidates were screened for their adherence to the dogma of the increasingly far left and far right. These trends are also how the word "primary" went from being a noun to becoming a verb. In political slang, to primary an incumbent meant to challenge them from within the same party not for scandalous or negligent behavior, but for insufficient ideological purity and party loyalty.

Political scientist Robert Boatright found that the number of U.S. House primary challenges driven by ideology was about 3.4 times higher from 2010 to 2022 (seven election cycles), compared to 1990 to 2008 (ten election cycles).[5] "This trend is testament to the increasing polarization of our politics, the increasing strength of factions within each

FIGURE 2:

The Rise of Ideological Primary Challenges

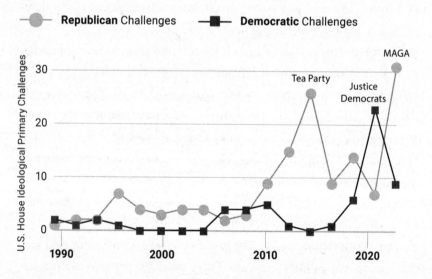

Source: Data from Dr. Robert Boatright, Clark University

political party, and the realization that contesting primaries was a very cost-effective way of changing political parties," writes Elaine Kamarck of the Brookings Institution.[6]

It's not that partisan primaries created our polarization out of thin air. Instead, they have been weaponized by the fringes as a way to advance their political agendas—magnifying and accelerating already polarizing trends in our politics.

HARBINGERS OF THE FUTURE: THE PURGING OF SPECTER AND LIEBERMAN

In retrospect, mid-2000s primary challenges to two longtime Senate incumbents, moderate Republican Arlen Specter and moderate Democrat Joe Lieberman, were the dawn of a new era that continues to this day.

Specter was first elected to his Pennsylvania Senate seat in 1980, when the GOP had a considerable number of moderates, particularly on social issues. Specter supported abortion rights and stem cell research, as well as President George W. Bush's education reform bill, No Child Left Behind. But he opposed the budget-busting Bush tax cuts, which got him attacked by conservatives as a RINO. Conservative House member Pat Toomey challenged Specter in the 2004 primary, with more than $2 million in backing from the Club for Growth. This conservative, pro-business organization, which Toomey would later lead, was founded in 1999 by economist Stephen Moore and remains one of the largest and most influential players in Republican primary politics.

Specter pulled out a narrow primary victory, 51% to 49%, and was easily reelected in the general election. As the GOP moved further to the right after 2004, Specter grew even further out of step with his base, though not with his state. In February 2009, he was one of only three Republicans to vote for the Obama administration's stimulus bill in response to the Great Recession. That April, Toomey announced that he would primary Specter again in 2010. Seeing the writing on the wall, Specter—a lifelong Republican—announced that he was becoming a Democrat.

But he wasn't enough of a Democrat for Democratic primary voters; they went instead for Representative Joe Sestak, 53% to 47%. In the general election, Toomey beat Sestak, 51% to 49%. Specter was punished by both parties despite representing the views of a majority of Pennsylvanians.

Meanwhile, the influential progressive group MoveOn.org saw the impact the Club for Growth was having in GOP primaries, and set out to do the same in Democratic primaries. After building a following of millions of voters and small donors to defend Bill Clinton during his 1998 impeachment, and then to promote social and economic justice issues, they turned their sights in 2006 on Senator Joe Lieberman of Connecticut. A moderate Democrat and Al Gore's nominee for vice president in 2000, Lieberman had supported the Iraq War and the Patriot Act, which became significant dividing lines within the Democratic Party between defense hawks and the anti-war left.

In late 2005, a year before his next election, a poll showed that Lieberman would be vulnerable in a primary. But on the bright side, it also showed he had strong support among independents and decent support among Republicans. His advisors suggested that he instead run as an independent. "I said, dammit, I am a Democrat. If these people want to defeat me in a primary, I prefer to have that happen than run away from the party," Lieberman told me.[7]

Sure enough, a wealthy businessman named Ned Lamont did challenge Lieberman, attacking his close working relationship with the Bush administration. MoveOn.org raised more than $250,000 from small donors to help Lamont, a major online haul for that era.[8] Lieberman also drew national attention as a target for progressives nationwide who wanted to push the Democratic Party toward more hardline opposition to the Bush agenda. "Anywhere I was doing a public event, there would be a pickup truck with two papier-mâché life-size figures, one of President Bush and one of me," Lieberman recalled. "And we were embracing and kissing each other on the cheek."[9] It was a scene from a State of the Union where President Bush and Lieberman embraced after the speech. Lamont's campaign turned it into a TV ad.

Lamont won the primary, 52% to 48%.

However, Connecticut is one of three states without "sore loser" laws that prevent candidates who have lost primaries from then running as independents in the general election. Lieberman had never heard of such a law until his campaign briefed him on it months earlier while suggesting he be prepared to launch an independent campaign if he lost the primary. As a result, the day after the primary, Lieberman's supporters turned in more than 7,500 signatures they had already collected to get his name on the general election ballot, under the banner of a new "Connecticut for Lieberman" party. Running against both Lamont and a weak GOP candidate, Lieberman drew the endorsements of many GOP leaders in the state and won the general election with 50% of the vote, compared to Lamont's 40% and Republican Alan Schlesinger's 10%. The state still wanted him, even though the system had conspired against him.

"The primary and my loss that night was the most personally painful experience in my whole political career," Lieberman told me. "But the win as an independent that November was the most thrilling, satisfying moment, even though I had been blessed to have many others."[10]

Unlike Specter, Lieberman continued to caucus with his original party during his final Senate term. But like Specter, Lieberman saw that his brand of politics was out of favor with his base. He opted to retire rather than run again in 2012.

More Extreme Partisans Smell Blood in the Water

The Club for Growth and MoveOn.org were both emboldened by these primary engagements, which increased their influence within their respective parties, even when they failed to topple an incumbent. Both groups claimed victory whenever incumbents changed their positions, or at least their voting behavior—including incumbents who hadn't been primaried yet, but feared the same fate as Specter and Lieberman.

So the primarying trend continued and accelerated. Michigan Republican representative Joe Schwarz, a moderate who opposed a constitutional amendment that would ban same-sex marriage, lost re-nomination in 2006 to conservative challenger Tim Walberg, who was backed by the Club for Growth. Schwarz told the press that his primary loss "just pushes the party farther to the right."[11]

Two years later, eight-term Maryland Democratic representative Al Wynn lost renomination to progressive challenger Donna Edwards, who was backed by MoveOn.org. Edwards attacked Wynn for his 2002 vote authorizing the Iraq War and promised to be a vocal advocate for more progressive stances on education, the environment, and other issues. In claiming credit for the victory, MoveOn.org told its supporters: "The race put other Representatives on notice: fail to listen to your constitu-ents, and you might be next."[12] And by "constituents" they meant only the most vocal minority who vote in primaries.

Then came the rise of the Tea Party movement, in response to the election of President Obama in 2008, the government's response to the financial crisis in 2009, and the passage of the Affordable Care Act in early 2010. Republicans rode conservative fury to a red wave in the 2010 midterms, picking up sixty-three seats in the House and seven in the Senate. They also turned their ire against alleged RINOs, who were seen as not aggressive enough in opposing the Obama agenda. Among the many prominent Republicans who got primaried during this era:

- Senator Bob Bennett (R-Utah) failed to even make the primary ballot because of organized opposition from the Club for Growth and Tea Party activists at the state GOP's convention, which at the time decided which candidates appeared on the primary ballot. Mike Lee went on to replace Bennett.
- Senator Lisa Murkowski (R-Alaska) lost her primary to Joe Miller. While a sore loser law prevented her from getting on the general election ballot as an independent, she became the first senator in more than a half century to get elected by a write-in vote, which is especially impressive considering that her supporters had to spell her name correctly.

- Representative Mike Castle (R-Delaware), his state's sole representative, lost an open-seat Senate primary to Tea Party–backed Christine O'Donnell. "Like Bennett and Murkowski, Castle paid for having been perceived as a bridge builder," reported NPR.[13] Dogged by strange rumors, O'Donnell then recorded a television ad in which she declared, "I'm not a witch"—leading to a *Saturday Night Live* parody and national humiliation. She lost the general election by seventeen points.
- Senator Richard Lugar (R-Indiana) lost his primary to State Treasurer Richard Mourdock, who then lost the general election to Democratic representative Joe Donnelly.

Over this same period (2010–2014), five House Republicans lost primaries to more conservative, Tea Party–backed challengers. These upsets brought about a sea change within the GOP and cemented primarying as a key dynamic in American politics.

The Left Follows Suit

Shortly thereafter, a resurgent progressive movement began to reshape the Democratic Party in similar ways. Self-identifying as a "democratic socialist" and promising a political revolution, Vermont senator Bernie Sanders won enough fans to mount a surprisingly strong challenge to Hillary Clinton for the 2016 presidential nomination. He captured about 40% of convention delegates and massive small-dollar donations by advocating for single-payer healthcare, free public college, a Green New Deal to combat climate change, more services for poor families, and much higher taxes on "millionaires and billionaires" to pay for it all.

Following Sanders's defeat, several organizations formed to continue promoting his platform within the Democratic Party, and to challenge the party's moderate/establishment wing. In 2018, Brand New Congress and Justice Democrats recruited or endorsed more than eighty candidates for local, state, and federal offices, two of whom successfully primaried House incumbents: Ayanna Pressley defeated Michael Capuano in Massachusetts, and Alexandria Ocasio-Cortez defeated Joseph Crowley (then the House Democratic caucus chair) in New York. Pressley and AOC became the nucleus of a group of progressive representatives known as the Squad. One polling firm found that if this group had its own political party, only about 8% of Americans would align with its views and values. But because of partisan primaries in our two-party system, that same small faction gets to exert significant influence over the entire Democratic Party.[14]

The trend continued in 2020, with seventeen Democratic House incumbents facing ideological primary challenges. Three succeeded: Cori Bush beat William Lacy Clay in Missouri, Jamaal Bowman beat Eliot Engel in New York, and Marie Newman beat Dan Lipinski, the last pro-life Democrat in Congress, in Illinois. Then, in 2022, another ten incumbent Democrats faced ideological primary challengers, with one losing.[15]

Reshaping any party's ideological identity can't be done solely through primarying incumbents, however. Like their counterparts in the Tea Party and then the MAGA movement, progressive groups also fought hard to win primaries for open seats in safe districts. In 2022, fourteen of the twenty-five safe Democratic seats without incumbents were won by candidates endorsed by at least one notable progressive group or elected official. As *FiveThirtyEight* reported, "Races . . . that pit a progressive against an establishment Democrat are watched closely as referenda on the future direction of the party."[16]

Ideology Isn't the Problem

To be clear, the problem with partisan primaries is not an inherent problem with any particular ideology, be it left, right, or anywhere in between. A wide spectrum of beliefs is necessary to sharpen our discourse, balance policy trade-offs, and shape laws to govern a large and diverse nation. The problem with partisan primaries is that the ideological fringes have *disproportionate* influence in our political system, which produces *unrepresentative* outcomes and leads to extreme polarization.

THE CONSEQUENCES OF EXTREME POLARIZATION

The ideological sorting of both major parties, the fragmentation of our media, and the weaponization of partisan primaries are some of the most important trends fueling polarization over the past three decades. Taken together, they make incumbents much more vulnerable to losing reelection to a more extreme candidate within their own party than to a candidate from an opposing party in a general election. The result: more politicians are winning who are less representative of America, and they are less willing to work with the other party to solve problems. (The people who used to do that are the ones getting beat.)

We all feel and hear about the growing polarization in our politics. But it's not just your imagination or media hype; we can measure it. Fifty years ago, if you lined each member of Congress up on an ideological spectrum from left to right, 196 members of Congress would fit somewhere between the most liberal Republican and the most conservative Democrat. Nearly half (45%) of the House would be standing on common ideological ground.[17] But that common ground began to erode until, by 2002 in the House and 2004 in the Senate, it outright disappeared: all the Democrats were to the left of the Republicans, and all the Republicans were to the right of the Democrats. Moderates have been hunted to virtual extinction. The Pew Research Center counted fewer than two dozen moderates in Congress by early 2022, down from 160 in the early 1970s.[18] Congress is now more polarized than at any time since the Civil War.

The change in the ideological makeup of both parties has not been exactly the same, on either the federal or state levels. Political scientists Norm Ornstein and Thomas Mann describe the "asymmetric polarization" of Republicans in Congress veering much more to the right than Democrats have to the left.[19] By one measure of ideology based on analyzing roll call votes, Republicans have become about four times more

FIGURE 3:
Growing Polarization in Congress

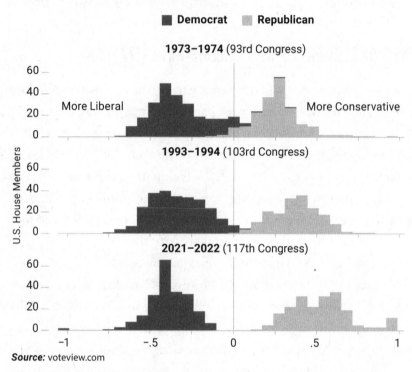

■ Democrat　　**■ Republican**

1973–1974 (93rd Congress)

More Liberal　　　　　　　　　　More Conservative

U.S. House Members

1993–1994 (103rd Congress)

2021–2022 (117th Congress)

Source: voteview.com

extreme than Democrats since 1971.[20] This picture looks different in state legislatures, however, where political scientists Boris Shor and Nolan McCarty find "the median Democratic state party chamber is polarizing 30% more than Republicans."[21]

Unlike the bipartisan breakthroughs on major issues in the twentieth century, nowadays very little gets done on a bipartisan basis. Major legislation, such as President Obama's Affordable Care Act and President Trump's Tax Cuts and Jobs Act, is jammed through Congress with party-line votes, followed by subsequent years of attempts at repeal after party control in Washington shifts. And because neither major party holds durable majorities in Congress, both sides have an incentive to hold out until they get back in power to get their way, rather than settle for any compromise—especially if such a compromise might help the opposition politically.

FIGURE 4:
Declining Bipartisan Support for Landmark Legislation

☐ **Party Members** in the house   ■ **Party Yea** votes

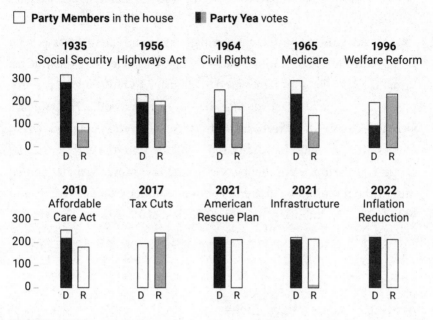

Source: GovTrack

How Extreme Polarization Undermines Democracy Itself

As both parties keep moving further apart, the political and policy stakes of losing an election keep rising; that's why we're told each election is the most important of our lifetimes. The huge consequences of gaining or losing power make it easier for both sides to rationalize not merely rejecting bipartisanship but even extracting political advantage by undermining (small-*d*) democratic norms and institutions.

After all, if we see our opponents as literal threats to the nation's survival, what lengths wouldn't we go to to fight them? Extreme partisanship is driven much less by the love of one's own party than by fear, hatred, and distrust of the other, a phenomenon known as "negative partisanship." Today, 62% of Republicans and 54% of Democrats view the other side "very unfavorably"—three times higher than thirty years ago. Just over 42% of Democrats and Republicans now view the other party as "downright evil."[22] This context explains the tit for tat and steady escalation of tactics that both parties have employed to maintain and exercise political power.

Consider the filibuster, a supermajority requirement that's part of U.S. Senate rules, but not mandated by law, let alone the Constitution. Prior to 1917, senators rarely used a filibuster to block a vote on proposed legislation. In fact, during the entire nineteenth century there were just twenty-three recorded filibusters.[23] Filibuster usage started to increase in the 1980s, but didn't truly explode until the early 1990s. By the end of the Bush presidency, the Senate saw more than 100 annual uses of the filibuster.[24] The trend continued under Obama, Trump, and Biden, with 252 filibusters in 2013–14, 328 in 2019–20, and a record 336 in 2021–22.[25]

FIGURE 5:
Animosity Across Party Lines

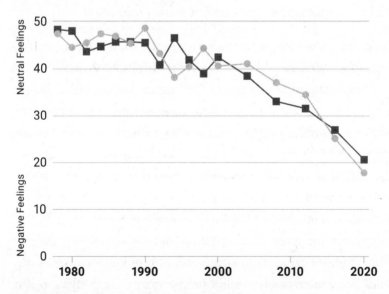

Republicans toward Democrats
Democrats toward Republicans

Source: American National Election Studies (ANES)

Or consider the Supreme Court. In 2013, Democrats invoked the "nuclear option" to go around the filibuster and confirm cabinet posts and federal judgeships with simple majority support. By 2017, Republicans employed the same tactic to confirm President Trump's Supreme Court nominee Neil Gorsuch—after refusing to even give President Obama's nominee, Merrick Garland, a vote in the last year of Obama's term. By 2021, Democrats were pressuring President Joe Biden to "pack" the Supreme Court and add more justices, since the number is established by law rather than the Constitution. Along the way, trust in the Supreme Court declined from 76% in 2009 to just 47% today, a problem for a branch of government that solely relies on its legitimacy to enforce its rulings.

"[T]he eagerness by both sides to thumb their nose at opponents is emblematic of what we might call total politics," writes the *Atlantic*'s David Graham. "Those in power use every legal tool at their disposal to gain advantage, with little regard for the long-term downsides. Total politics dismisses both the existence and value of neutral institutions; it (mostly) respects rules but not norms. All that matters is what's possible, not what's prudent."[26]

We are surrounded by total politics. Once largely ignored, judicial races are now attracting millions of dollars in donations to shift the ideological balance of what are supposed to be apolitical courts. Oregon Republicans and Texas Democrats have, at different times over the past couple years, brought their legislatures to a halt by walking off the job and literally leaving their state, causing a lack of quorum. In April 2023, two Black Democratic lawmakers in Tennessee led a protest on the state house floor on the issue of gun violence, disrupting the proceedings; in an unprecedented response, they were subsequently expelled—only to be reappointed to fill their own vacancies.

Ultimately, we can only have a democracy if some things matter more than winning an election or policy fight. The norm of political forbearance, as Steven Levitsky and Daniel Ziblatt explain in *How Democracies Die*, requires self-restraint on the exercise of political power even if one has the legal right to take a particular action. "The opposite of forbearance is to exploit one's institutional prerogatives in an unrestrained way," they write. "It is a form of institutional combat aimed at permanently defeating one's partisan rivals—and not caring whether the democratic game continues."[27]

The Rise of Election Rejection

The most important norm in our politics, upon which our entire democracy is built, is "losers' consent." That is, if you run for office and lose, you concede and move on. Maybe you can try again next time. But after the 2020 election, Donald Trump became the first modern presidential candidate to refuse to concede. As a result, only 22% of registered Republicans viewed Joe Biden's election as legitimate,[28] and 147 congressional Republicans (including eight senators) followed suit by objecting to the Electoral College vote.[29] Was this an aberration, or an escalation of prior trends?

The first time researchers found a major gap in voters' willingness to accept a recent presidential election result was actually in 2016, when Democratic voters in states won by Hillary Clinton were 19% more confident that their votes counted than they were in states won by Trump.[30] Fully 50% of Democrats incorrectly believed Russia actually tampered with ballots to help Trump.[31] Clinton herself told CBS News that Trump "knows he's an illegitimate president" because of "the many varying tactics they used, from voter suppression and voter purging to hacking to the false stories."[32]

Two years later, Georgia Democrat Stacey Abrams refused to concede her loss in the governor's race and filed a lawsuit against the state, alleging various violations of the Voting Rights Act. After a four-year trial, a federal judge rejected every claim and ordered Abrams's group to pay more than $230,000 in fees for costs incurred by the court.[33]

"The fact that Trump supporters in 2020 expressed a more virulent brand of election rejection than Democrats in 2016 should not blind us to the possibility that we have entered an era in which partisans of both sides are both unwilling to accept losses and willing to be overconfi-dent when they win," write MIT's Charles Stewart and Princeton's Jesse Clark.[34]

Historically, our leaders and candidates knew that if they disregarded the norms and institutions of American democracy, they would ulti-mately be punished at the ballot box. *But what if that isn't true anymore?* What if they owe their power to only a small faction of the most partisan voters on each side—who care only about winning, not principle? And what if those voters are electing ever more extreme candidates who, in turn, further polarize the electorate in a vicious, self-reinforcing cycle?

That is precisely where we find ourselves today, thanks in large part to partisan primaries.

THE GOOD NEWS AND THE BIG OPPORTUNITY

The good news, amid these dire trends of hyperpolarization, is that many Americans, of all parties and no party, have become engaged in the political process and are eager to get our politics back to something resembling normal. Instead of fighting each other, they want to help to fix the system. The big question is how best to do so.

Some are focused on addressing the problem of partisan news out-lets and social media that affirms our beliefs rather than informs them. Others are focused on addressing our cultural divisions, which leave us surrounded by people who think and vote like us, making it all the easier to caricature if not dehumanize our opponents. Both of these challenges are highly complex if not also generational in nature. That leads yet an-other group to focus on near-term, tangible changes we can make to the structure of our election system in order to improve voter representation and the political incentives of our leaders. Within this latter category, there has been no shortage of proposals, such as:

- Passing a constitutional amendment to overturn *Citizens United*
- Enacting congressional and Supreme Court term limits

- Reforming the Senate filibuster
- Expanding the size of the House
- Making Election Day a national holiday
- Abolishing the Electoral College
- Creating a system of public campaign financing
- Establishing proportional representation

All of these proposals—some of which I agree with, others I do not—seek to make our system work better. However, as the rest of this book will show, partisan primaries are *the biggest solvable problem* in our political system today, and therefore the one we should prioritize addressing. They're a *big* problem because they disenfranchise voters and incentivize our leaders to put narrowly partisan interests above the interests of the general public. And they're a *solvable* problem because nothing prevents us from abolishing them. Reforming primaries—such that every voter has the freedom to vote for any candidate in every election, regardless of party—doesn't require a constitutional amendment or even a bill passed by Congress; it can be done as a state-by-state campaign.

To be clear, I'm not suggesting that partisan primaries are the *only* major problem we face, or that fixing them will be a panacea. But, with limited resources, by focusing on the Primary Problem, we can slow the vicious cycle of polarization and give our country both more time and new pathways to reduce our toxic levels of polarization.

Consider the work of John Opdycke, one of the earliest and most respected leaders in the primary reform movement. He first got involved with Mayor Michael Bloomberg's attempt to open New York City's partisan primaries to independent voters in 2001, an effort that was squashed by the political establishment. At the time, there was no national movement to mobilize support, only one-off city and state efforts. So Opdycke launched a new group called Open Primaries in 2009. "I wasn't a lone wolf. I was a lone three-legged coyote," he told me, recalling how he was ignored and dismissed at the time. "But what you can't make go away is that there are citizens of the United States that are not allowed to vote in taxpayer-funded elections."[35]

Three major trends have propelled primary reform in the time since. First is the rapid rise of independent voters, which means more and more voters locked out of partisan primaries. A March 2023 Gallup poll found that 49% of Americans self-identified as independent;[36] independents outnumber *both* Democrats and Republicans in nine states that register voters by party.[37] Second is the collapse in political competition between the two major parties, which means partisan primaries are becoming more and more consequential in determining election outcomes. Finally, the growing dysfunction in our politics over the last decade has led to a federal government credit downgrading, policy gridlock on issues like immigration, and even a violent insurrection after a failed attempt to overturn a presidential election.

These factors have led an increasing number of thinkers, donors, and activists to identify partisan primaries as harmful to voters, our country, and the parties themselves, as the next part of the book will further explore. Diagnosing the disease, not just its symptoms, is the first step toward a cure for what ails our democracy.

PART II

A LOSE-LOSE-LOSE SYSTEM

The problem with partisan primaries is that they are doing the opposite of what they were designed to do when they were invented over a century ago. Rather than expand participation, they limit which votes matter. Rather than improve parties' nominating processes, they produce candidates who are less electable. And rather than clamp down on corruption, they have given more influence to special interest groups. As a result, partisan primaries are having a compounding impact on our democracy: they are bad for voters, bad for our country, and bad for the parties themselves. We'll explore each of those unintended consequences over the next three chapters.

But first, let's look at the Primary Problem through the lens of a single congressman: Kurt Schrader, a "Blue Dog Democrat" who represented Oregon's 5th district from January 2009 to January 2023.

KURT SCHRADER: BLUE DOG AND PROBLEM SOLVER

The same behaviors that earned Schrader a reputation as a problem solver on Capitol Hill also attracted the ire of his party. It's almost a law

of modern politics: for every bipartisan action there is an equal and opposite partisan reaction. These dynamics not only cost Schrader his job
when he was primaried out of office in 2022; they also cost the Democrats one of the five House seats they needed to keep the majority, after
Republicans defeated Schrader's more progressive primary challenger in
the general election.

An organic farmer and veterinarian before he entered politics,
Schrader presented himself as a pragmatist who focused on delivering
results for constituents. He told voters he was willing to buck his own
party or compromise with Republicans, if necessary, to deliver those
results—and he won majorities with that message in seven consecutive
general elections (2008–2020).

During his freshman term, Schrader joined the House Blue Dog
Coalition—a group of moderate Democrats from conservative-leaning
districts. The path to any Democratic House majority runs through
these suburban and rural districts, making these members of particular
political value to the party's leadership. The Blue Dogs' numbers have
been dwindling as the Democratic brand has fallen out of favor in these
geographies, from a peak of sixty-four in 2008 to fewer than ten today.[1]
The party's rural collapse since the mid-1990s is stark: Bill Clinton won
the popular vote in about half of the nation's rural counties in 1996, but
Joe Biden won just 10% of those counties in 2020.[2]

Much of the purging of both parties' moderates has been the result
of geographical sorting. Southern Democrats were replaced by Republicans, and Northeast Republicans were replaced by Democrats, as both
parties realigned around issues of race and civil rights. Yet many moderates have also fallen prey to purity tests within their own tribe. "Rather
than be celebrated as majority makers, Blue Dogs are viewed as disloyal
to the cause," explains former congressman Jason Altmire, a Blue Dog
who lost a Democratic primary following redistricting in 2010. "That's
how majorities are lost."[3]

Schrader was also a founding member of the House Problem Solvers Caucus—a bipartisan coalition that meets regularly to find common

ground on important issues. For many of the roughly fifty members who represent swing districts, affiliation with this group is politically advantageous because being seen working across the aisle is a plus, even if they legislate and vote as a partisan. Others, including Schrader, see the group mainly as an opportunity to, well, actually solve problems.

"The reason I ran for office is that I believe in our form of government, which is a representative form of government. It is not a party-driven platform. It's not a parliamentary system like they have in Europe and many other countries," Schrader told me in 2023. "So I'm supposed to represent my district—the Central Willamette Valley and Central Oregon coast. And I tried to do that."[4]

Problem Solvers Apply Leverage in a Divided Congress

After the 2020 elections left a narrow Democratic House majority, Schrader demonstrated his independence as one of two Democrats to initially vote against the American Rescue Plan, a $1.9 trillion pandemic relief bill that followed five previous pieces of COVID-related legislation totaling $3.4 trillion.

Schrader objected to the absence of any legislative process for the bill, as well as its overall size and scope.[5] He also opposed the inclusion of a minimum-wage hike, which would hit small businesses in the midst of the pandemic. After some changes were made by the Senate, he ultimately voted to help pass the bill on a party-line vote. The first response to his tweet announcing his vote warned, "Can't wait for your primary opponent in 2022."[6]

Democrats were also forging ahead with another massive $3.5 trillion spending bill, dubbed Build Back Better. Concerns about rising inflation gave many members pause, including Senator Joe Manchin. A bipartisan group of senators and House members, including Schrader, began to collaborate on legislation that would focus on "hard infrastructure" like roads and broadband. "The country was so divided at this point in time, we needed to bring it together and show Democrats and Republicans can actually get the job done on stuff that matters to you back home," Schrader said.[7] The group of ten senators—led by retiring Republican Rob Portman of Ohio and Democrat (later turned independent) Kyrsten Sinema of Arizona—eventually brokered a deal with the White House, and a $550 billion bill passed the Senate in early August, 69–30.[8]

Progressives had urged House Democrats to focus on Build Back Better, which could incorporate infrastructure spending and all of their other desired priorities, from paid leave to clean energy. But with the fate of the larger bill highly uncertain in the Senate, pragmatists in the House called for a vote on infrastructure first. Nine Democrats, including Schrader, went so far as to say they would withhold their votes on Build Back Better until after passing infrastructure, as the Senate had.[9] The backlash was immediate and severe. Progressive groups like Justice Democrats began running ads against the nine moderate Democrats, claiming they were obstructing the Biden administration's agenda.[10] "We were texting and emailing each other all the time," Schrader recalled about his group of fellow Blue Dogs, dubbed the Unbreakable Nine. "We kept together, against all odds, despite all the emoluments and intrigue and maybe a little bit of heavy-handedness, because we felt the country needed a win."[11]

I asked Schrader what he meant by heavy-handedness. He paused. "Well, there were things in our districts that might have a better chance of occurring, you know." He hastened to add: "Nothing illegal."[12] While I was left wondering what this may have meant for Schrader and his district, it was not altogether surprising considering the reputation Speaker Pelosi earned for her ability to keep her caucus in line.

On November 4, Schrader's Blue Dog group met upstairs at the Capitol while the progressives were huddling downstairs. A delegation of six members was sent up to see if they could secure a shared commitment for the respective groups to support both the infrastructure bill and a trimmed-down version of Build Back Better that had emerged from the Senate, now renamed the Inflation Reduction Act. All but one or two of Schrader's group signaled support. Apparently unconvinced, the progressive group sent another delegation back upstairs to confirm this was the case. The same response was given. Finally, the chair of the progressive caucus visited to look them in the eye and personally verify. "It shows that even within a party, the trust factor isn't that great, much less across party lines," Schrader reflected.[13] However, at that point, they shared a drink and agreed to move forward.

Three days later, Schrader and his colleagues succeeded in getting a vote on the Infrastructure Investment and Jobs Act, which passed the House with the help of thirteen Republican votes and was signed by President Biden. (The Inflation Reduction Act, a slimmed-down version of Build Back Better, followed in 2022.) In a body of 435 members, where most of the power is usually held by senior leadership, Schrader made his mark and helped get major laws passed. His reward was a primary challenger who ended his congressional career.

"It cost me my seat, but it was still a lot of fun because it was legislators representing their districts and their country unvarnished. There was no filtering. It was members doing their job, as folks back home would assume we do every day. But it almost never occurs except for these few signature moments."[14]

Schrader Gets Redistricted, Then Primaried

Due to population growth, Oregon gained an extra district in the decennial redistricting process, and it was one of the few states where Democrats would have the power to gerrymander—to redraw a map that would heavily advantage their own party.

The legislature's first proposed map sought to more than double the number of solid Democratic districts from two to five, leaving just one district safely in the hands of Republicans. Republicans responded to this extreme gerrymander by literally walking out of the legislature, denying the body the quorum needed to vote on the proposal.[15] Facing steep fines for their absence, Republicans agreed to return to vote on a marginally less tilted yet still gerrymandered map that would give Democrats four safe districts, Republicans one, and maintain one truly competitive district: Schrader's.[16]

That district became slightly more competitive between both parties and gave Schrader many new progressive constituents from Bend, Oregon, who would have no familiarity with him.[17] He maintains that he was personally targeted by the public employees unions, which carry enormous influence within the Democratic Party. "Folks have been gunning for me for a long time in activist circles. If you're not on the Bernie Sanders or Elizabeth Warren bandwagon, you're in big trouble. And I was never on that bandwagon."[18]

A month after the redistricting, a progressive attorney named Jamie McLeod-Skinner announced her bid to unseat Schrader in the May 2022 primary. She picked up endorsements from four of the five county Democratic parties, the Working Families Party, and Senator Elizabeth Warren. She highlighted climate change, college debt, affordable housing, and other needs of working families as issues she cared deeply about.[19] Some of those groups did so without inviting Schrader to visit, while others at least heard him out.

In one town hall, Schrader recalls an activist standing up in the back of the room to say: "God dang Schrader, I wish you wouldn't be so bipartisan! You're a Democrat." Schrader replied, "Well, I'm always going to be bipartisan. I'm supposed to be a representative, not just a Democrat."[20]

That may be true, but in Oregon's May Democratic primary, only registered Democratic voters in the district could participate. Oregon is one of fifteen states with closed primaries, which not only excludes Republicans but also independent and minor party voters. Of the 521,278 registered voters in the 5th district at the time, 33% were Democrats, 27% were Republicans, and 40% were neither. Turnout was 86,411—roughly half of all registered Democrats—and McLeod-Skinner won with 47,148 votes (55%). Ultimately, in a district of 521,278 registered voters, just 17% voted in the contest that ended Schrader's career, and only a third could have even had a say in the matter.

The result wasn't altogether surprising for Schrader, who reflected on the big difference between primary and general election voters. "Half to two-thirds of the primary electorate is a bunch of activists that eat, sleep, and breathe the latest social media blurb or their favorite cable channel. I would submit that most of America is too goddamn busy to do that. *I have a job, I got a family. My kids are in college. I have bigger issues.*"[21]

What happened in the general election was also not a surprise to him. "If the Left ends up replacing Rep. Schrader with a Republican, they will have done grave harm to the agenda they profess to care about," said a spokesman for Mainstream Democrats, a PAC that defended Schrader, following the primary.[22] And that is precisely what happened six months later, when McLeod-Skinner lost the general election by two points to Republican Lori Chavez-DeRemer. Democrats lost their House majority by five seats; Schrader's was one of them.

I asked Schrader if he thought the Democratic Party would learn its lesson. "No, no, no. They didn't learn the lesson. Just that Schrader didn't jump out and support the socialist candidate. If he had supported the socialist candidate all would have been good, you know?"[23]

Five other Blue Dogs also left the House at the end of 2022. Georgia's Carolyn Bourdeaux lost her primary, following redistricting, to fellow incumbent congresswoman Lucy McBath. Ten-term Tennessee representative Jim Cooper retired after his district was drawn to be much more heavily Republican. So did three-term Florida representative Stephanie Murphy, who told *Roll Call*: "It's hard to be a centrist because the party wants unity. . . . It's going to be [even] harder when there are less of them, because all of that firepower is going to be trained on a smaller number of people."[24]

Lose-Lose-Lose

To sum up: First, two-thirds of the registered voters in Kurt Schrader's district were disenfranchised from his primary. Then about 10% of registered voters, the most partisan and left-leaning Democrats among them, nominated a candidate who was out of step with the district's voters. Then that nominee lost an otherwise winnable general election, which contributed to the Democratic Party's loss of their House majority. And Congress as a whole lost a statesman who was willing to put what he believed was best for the public over his own political future.

Negotiation experts talk about striving for a win-win outcome, but this was a lose-lose-lose outcome: Oregon's voters, Schrader's party, and our whole country all emerged worse off. And that, as we're about to see in the next three chapters, is the Primary Problem in our politics today.

THREE

BAD FOR VOTERS

I n the last few years, we've heard the term "voter suppression" used with growing frequency and alarm. For example, when Georgia Republicans passed a law to roll back some of the more expansive COVID-era voting provisions, such as large numbers of ballot drop boxes and online absentee ballot applications,[1] Major League Baseball moved its All-Star game out of the state in protest, and President Biden visited the state to denounce what he referred to as "Jim Crow 2.0."

Even though some Republicans were motivated to make it harder to vote, the impact of this 2021 law was actually modest. In fact, Georgia voters still had easier access to the ballot box than those in several blue states, including Delaware and New York. In 2022, Georgia set a state record for the total number of ballots cast in a midterm election.[2] Further, a January 2023 poll commissioned by the *Atlanta Journal-Constitution* found that 73% of the state's registered voters reported being very or somewhat confident that the November 2022 election was "conducted fairly and accurately." This represented a 17-percentage-point increase in voter confidence from the year prior, and both liberals and conservatives reported an increase in faith.[3]

Now consider a different kind of voter suppression: in the same 2022 midterm cycle, as we saw in the introduction, only 8% of voters nationally cast ballots in partisan primaries that effectively decided 83% of U.S. House races. About 30 million voters in "safe" districts across thirty-one states were legally prohibited from voting in the taxpayer-funded primary that effectively determined the winner.[4] It wasn't merely harder or more inconvenient for them to vote; *they literally were not allowed to cast a ballot.*

If you missed seeing outrage from leaders in either party about this second type of voter suppression, you are not alone. There is no definition of democracy I am aware of that provides for an election system with this kind of systemic voter disenfranchisement.

As we saw in chapter 1, direct primaries were originally designed to democratize the party nomination process, with the hope of catalyzing more participation and giving voters better representation. What we see today is the opposite. Primary turnout is anemic, in part because of the intentional exclusion of voters based on their party affiliation, and representation is distorted through a bifurcated series of elections that, by design, produce candidates who best reflect the fringes rather than the mainstream.

Let's dig deeper into the reasons why party primaries are bad for voters.

PARTICIPATION: WHO VOTES AND WHICH VOTES MATTER?

Imagine you were a voter in Massachusetts in 2022.

If you were a Republican, voting in the general election for your preferred House candidate was like showing up to the varsity football championship with a middle school team. The candidate nominated by your party in the primary was toast in each of the state's nine congressional districts, where the narrowest margin of victory for Democrats in

2022 was 9%. In one district, Republicans didn't even bother to field a candidate.

If you were a Democrat or independent voter, conversely, the Democratic primary (which is open to independents) was the only election of consequence. Your excitement about being able to cast a meaningful vote for Congress probably disappeared, however, when you saw that there was only a single candidate on your primary ballot. There was literally no choice in all nine of the state's districts.

I suppose we can still call this an election, technically. But not one in which a single voter's ballot—Democrat, Republican, or independent—actually mattered in determining the outcome.

Now imagine you were a voter in Oklahoma in 2022.

If you were a Democrat or independent, you might as well have been a Massachusetts Republican. In all five of the state's congressional districts, the Republican primary was the only election that mattered—and you were not allowed to participate.

If you were a Republican, at least there was a contested congressional primary in four of the five districts. Across these contests, 287,862 Republican voters cast a ballot. And these voters—a mere 9.5% of the state's voting-age population—elected the state's entire congressional delegation. Sure, 9.5% is more democratic than 0%, but not by much.

Massachusetts and Oklahoma are far from outliers: twenty other states did not feature a single competitive congressional race. Uncompetitive congressional districts and exclusionary primary rules have combined to dampen voter participation and outright disenfranchise millions of voters across the country from a process that was originally meant to empower them.

UNCOMPETITIVE DISTRICTS

Beginning in 1997, the nonpartisan *Cook Political Report* adapted an analytic tool developed by the nonpartisan election reform organization FairVote to rate how far each U.S. House district leaned Democratic or

Republican, based on how the district voted in the prior two presidential elections compared to the national average. What emerged was a shorthand familiar to most political observers today, known as the Partisan Voting Index: "A Partisan Voting Index (PVI) score of D+2, for example, means that in the 2016 and 2020 presidential elections, the state or district performed about two points more Democratic in terms of two-party vote share than the nation did as a whole, while a score of R+4 means the state or district performed about four points more Republican."[5]

In 2022, districts ranged from D+40 in Oakland, California, to R+33 in rural Alabama. These ratings tell us not only which party is favored to win, but how competitive the district itself is. They also allow us to see how districts have evolved over time. Cook's first set of ratings in 1997 found 160 seats between D+5 and R+5, which it defines as a swing seat that could reasonably be won by either party. By 2022, the number of swing seats collapsed by nearly half, to 82. And the number of "hyper-competitive" swing seats—those between D+3 and R+3—fell from 105 to just 45.

That means that in the vast majority of congressional districts, we can predict the winner before a single vote is cast, based on the district's partisanship alone. Each cycle, well in advance of the election, FairVote does just that in its *Monopoly Politics* report. These projections only factor in incumbency and presidential and congressional results from the two preceding elections without any attention to challengers, campaign finance, or voting records.

In 2020, FairVote projected the outcomes in 357 of 435 congressional seats, and got 356 of them right, for a 99.7% success rate.[6] They actually improved their prediction record since 2018, when they had a 97% success rate. If elections in each of these districts had been a true coin toss, the odds of calling them all correctly would be .000000068% . . . with one hundred more zeros right after the decimal point. That means that "safe" districts really are safe enough to bet on, with increasingly rare exceptions.

FIGURE 6:
Decline in Competitive House Districts

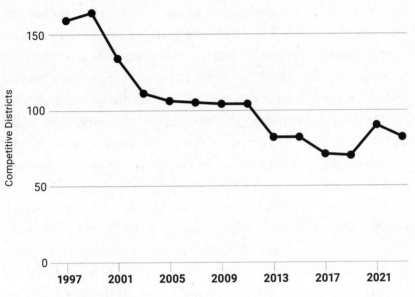

Source: Cook Political Report

As FairVote observes: "The ability to project more than four out of five seats without knowing anything about the candidates, their campaigns, or the nature of the year, with a high degree of success, is a powerful demonstration of how winner-take-all elections have effectively removed most representatives from any sort of accountability to the general election voters."[7] In February 2023, nearly two years before the next House elections, FairVote projected 367 safe seats, noting that even incumbency is now barely a factor compared to partisan affiliation.[8]

Why are so many districts uncompetitive, and why is the number increasing? There are three major trends.

Partisan Voting Habits

First, a growing number of Americans now vote straight party line, not necessarily because they love their own party but because they increasingly dislike the other one. In 2022, the Pew Research Center found that record percentages of both Democrats (68%) and Republicans (76%) reported that a "major reason" for their partisan affiliation was their belief that the other party's policies are "harmful to the country."[9] Thus a district with a majority of Democratic voters will almost always vote for a Democrat—regardless of whoever the Democrat may be—and the same for Republicans.

It didn't used to be like this. While individual ballots are secret, we can track vote totals between Democratic and Republican candidates for different offices within the same district or state. In presidential years, analysts typically compare the votes for a presidential candidate with those for a congressional candidate of the same party. The difference represents the number of split-ticket voters, harkening back to the era when such voters literally had to cut and clip together ballots (or "tickets") handed to them by the parties to deposit in the ballot box.

In 1992, the party of the winning U.S. House candidate differed from the party of the winning presidential candidate in 116 congressional districts, more than a quarter of all seats.[10] By 2020, that number fell to just 16.[11] On the Senate side, in the last two presidential elections, only one state elected a senator from a different party than that of the presidential candidate who won the state (Susan Collins in Maine in 2020). Political scientists have found that polarization is a root cause of the decline of split-ticket voting, specifically the increasing alignment of the two parties into distinct ideological camps. When individual voters' partisan and ideological identities are both strong and in alignment, they are significantly less likely to split their tickets.[12]

Partisan Gerrymandering

The second reason so few House districts are competitive is because they are literally being drawn that way, through partisan gerrymandering. While the practice goes back to a redistricting plan signed into law in 1812 by its namesake, Massachusetts governor Elbridge Gerry (and well before him), technology has enabled partisan leaders to draw congressional district lines to maximize their advantages with much more precision. Today's gerrymanderers predict voters' preferences based not only on their registered affiliation but also on mountains of demographic and consumer data.

After each decennial census, states must redraw their state and federal district boundaries to adjust to gains or losses of House seats. While the original objective of redistricting was to ensure all citizens have equal representation, politicians have manipulated the process to their own benefit by maximizing the number of districts that would reliably elect a candidate from their own party and minimizing the number of districts for the other.

Neither party shows any shame in the process when they control both a state legislature and governorship, often producing districts that look more like a Rorschach test than a map. For instance, in Illinois, which lost a seat in Congress in 2022, Democrats got rid of two Republican districts and added a new one of their own, leaving just one toss-up district among the state's seventeen. In Florida, which gained a seat in Congress, Republicans added four new GOP districts—leaving just one toss-up district among the state's twenty-eight.[13]

Much ink has been spilled about which party benefited more from the post-2020 round of redistricting. Democrats gained a net of six Democratic-leaning districts (ranging from D+5 to D+15).[14] On the other hand, Republicans employed a different strategy to make their already Republican-leaning districts even safer, gaining sixteen "solid" red districts (at least R+15 each).

Republicans benefited in this cycle from controlling the districting process in eighteen states (171 districts) compared to Democrats' five states (32 districts)—with the balance of districts being redrawn by divided legislatures or redistricting commissions. Republicans also slightly benefit from a congressional map that tilts in their favor simply by means of how the population is distributed between urban and rural areas.[15]

In the end, it was the voters who lost rather than either party. Across all the states, Congress now has eight fewer competitive districts as a result of partisan gerrymandering.[16] That's eight more seats that will be determined by *some* voters in primary elections, rather than *all* voters in general elections. Six million Americans will have worse representation in Congress.

Self-Sorting

The third reason so few districts are competitive is that voters have increasingly been sorting *themselves* geographically to live near others who share their political and cultural perspectives. In 1976, only 26% of voters lived in a "landslide" county, defined as one where the vote margin between both candidates was at least twenty points. By 1992, 38% of all counties were landslide counties, and by 2004 the total was over 48%. Following 2016 and 2020, roughly 60% of Americans now live in a landslide county.[17] County boundaries have not changed, but who lives in them and how they vote have.

Some research has found that "many Republicans and Democrats apparently do prefer to relocate in areas populated with co-partisans."[18] Other studies, however, have concluded that partisans who are relocating do not do this intentionally. Rather, the types of neighborhoods and communities that they find appealing also happen to be largely populated by people who support their party.[19] Regardless of the motivating factors, the outcome is the same: an increasing number of Americans living among people who largely share their political views.

To use a more gut-level metric, consider the growing gap in presidential election outcomes in rural counties with a stereotypically conservative Cracker Barrel compared to urban counties with a stereotypically liberal Whole Foods. In 1992, Bill Clinton won the presidency while winning the popular vote in 60% of counties with a Whole Foods and 40% with a Cracker Barrel, a 20-percentage-point gap. In 2020, Joe Biden won 85% of the Whole Foods counties and just 32% of the Cracker Barrel counties, a 53-percentage-point gap.[20]

We can also express our stark political divisions as gray versus green, rather than blue versus red. After the 2016 election, the *New York Times* analyzed aerial images from the National Agriculture Imagery Program and indexed them based on precinct-level presidential outcomes. The result is a visualization of our geographic sorting. "Gray" areas (developed, urban, with more pavement and buildings) were largely won by Hillary Clinton, while "green" and "sandy" areas (less developed, rural, with more grass, trees, or sandy deserts) were largely won by Trump.[21]

This is why gerrymandering alone cannot explain the decline of swing districts. *Cook*'s David Wasserman found that of the seventy-seven swing seats that have vanished since 1997, 58% of the decline resulted from natural geographic sorting of the electorate from election to election, while only 42% of the decline resulted from changes to district boundaries.[22]

Adding It All Up

The bottom line is that over 80% of House races lack real competition in the November general election, which means that the primary election is the only election that matters in those districts. And this lack of general election competition is not just a problem for the House but for every layer of government. Only about fifteen states typically have competitive senatorial and gubernatorial general elections.* That's

---

*Based on the number of "swing states," according to the latest *Cook* PVI.

why about two-thirds of all states get relatively little campaign advertising in September and October of election years, while purple states like Pennsylvania, Arizona, and Georgia are bombarded with nonstop ads.

The lack of general election competition at the state legislative level is even worse. Nationally, in 2022, one major party or the other did not even bother to put up a candidate in over 40% of state legislative elections.[23] Think about that. In more than a third of all elections for state legislature, voters had only a single option on their ballot. And even when there are multiple candidates, most races are not at all competitive. Between 1992 and 2020, only about 20% of all state legislative general elections were decided by fewer than twenty points.[24]

This lack of general election competition is foundational to the Primary Problem, because it shifts the only election of consequence to the primary, where the electorate is skewed toward the fringes and influenced by special interest groups—creating perverse incentives for candidates and elected officials.

WHO VOTES: EXCLUSIONARY RULES

Even though primary elections are the only elections that matter in a majority of states and districts, very few voters participate in them. And those who do look almost nothing like the electorate as a whole.

Primaries Fly Under the Radar

If most voters were aware that the primaries are where their votes usually matter most, recent turnouts don't reflect it. In the 2022 midterms, states in which the dominant party's primary was the only election of consequence for governor or Senate saw a total primary turnout of just 19.5%, which is actually *0.55% lower* than the primary turnout in states where competitive general elections ultimately determine the outcome. Across all states, general election turnout, however, was more than twice as high (43.2%).[25]

During the 2022 general election, as another example, Massachusetts voters elected 254 people to federal, state, or county offices. These
offices included high-profile positions like governor and U.S. representative as well as lower-profile offices like state representative, county commissioner, and Register of Deeds (but not dogcatcher, alas). Of these 254
elected positions, just 18 featured a candidate who won by a margin of
less than ten percentage points. That's just 7% of all general election contests in the state that could reasonably be considered competitive. You
might expect that the primaries would therefore attract a relatively high
number of voters. Not so. Only 18% of eligible voters cast ballots in the
primaries (which effectively determined the outcome of 93% of all offices), compared to 45% of eligible voters who turned out in the general
election.[26]

In reality, many voters (wrongly) believe the general election is the
"real" contest—since it features a head-to-head matchup between both
political parties—and leave the decision in the primaries to others who
they assume know more about each of the candidates. A 2017 Yale study
concluded that, "Compared to general elections, we find that for U.S.
House primary elections sizable segments of the electorate consider the
stakes lower and the costs of voting greater, feel less social pressure to
turn out and hold exclusionary beliefs about who should participate, and
are more willing to defer to those who know and care more about the
contests."[27]

A contributing factor to low turnout in primaries is that they get
less media attention, and the attention they do get is diluted across six
months. While there is a single day on which all states hold the general
election, in 2022 there were eighteen days on which states held primary
elections for Congress, between March 1 and September 13.[28] The reason
is not because someone decided there ought to be eighteen different primary days, but because Congress never took action to standardize and
narrow the primary calendar.

Primaries also get less attention because the media thrives on conflict.
Intraparty primary skirmishes are much less interesting than the partisan

trench warfare of general elections, which determine the party that ultimately controls the legislature. Further, much of the media coverage that primary elections do receive isn't informative or useful to potential voters. A 2016 analysis found that two-thirds of articles covering non-presidential primaries mentioned at least one campaign issue (such as public safety or education), but the number of articles mentioning key issues declined as the primary election approached.[29] In other words, just as Election Day approached and more potential voters became aware of the upcoming primary, it was less likely that they would be exposed to issue-driven news coverage that could inspire or inform their participation.

The Strongest Partisans Show Up in Metaphorical Face Paint

It's a cliché to compare politics to sports, but think about different types of NFL fans attending a game. One group shows up in normal clothes, shortly before kickoff. Another shows up a few hours early to tailgate and hang out with other fans, all wearing team colors. A third group isn't merely wearing team colors, but also sports *face paint*, and maybe even *body paint*, and waves signs at the cameras while hooting and dancing around for all four quarters.

Similarly, you know who shows up to vote in a primary? People who *really* like politics. Sure, you get some very committed voters who believe in their civic duty. But generally, you get the most engaged partisans on both sides ready to cheer their team on to victory—including some belligerent ones who have clearly had too much to drink.

Partisans on the fringes are much more motivated to be politically active. "Many of those in the center remain on the edges of the political playing field, relatively distant and disengaged, while the most ideologically oriented and politically rancorous Americans make their voices heard through greater participation in every stage of the political process," noted the Pew Research Center. Pew found that voters who held consistently liberal or conservative views were

FIGURE 7:
Primary Participation by Ideology

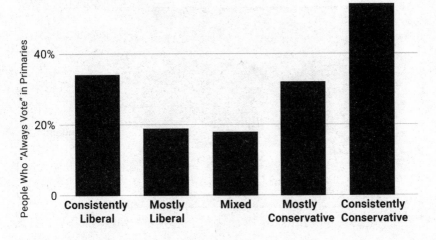

Source: Pew Research Center, data from 2014

nearly twice as likely to vote in a primary than voters who held mixed political views.[30] In Pew's 2021 political typology, the far-left "Progressive Left" (6% of the public) and far-right "Faith and Flag Conservatives" (10% of the public) were not only much more likely to vote than "Stressed Sideliners" (15% of the public) in the middle, but also more than twice as likely to make a contribution to a candidate or support a candidate on social media.[31]

Primary voters tend to be much more partisan than the electorate as a whole. The Brookings Institution conducted the largest-ever exit poll of primary voters, in 2016 and 2018, and found that independents comprised only about 20% of voters in both parties' primaries.[32] Gallup, on the other hand, which regularly asks voters about their partisan identification, has consistently found in recent years that more than 40% of Americans identify as independents, while the percentage of voters who identify with each major party is in the high 20s or low 30s.[33] And this gap only continues to grow as more Americans leave both parties.

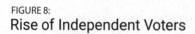

FIGURE 8:
Rise of Independent Voters

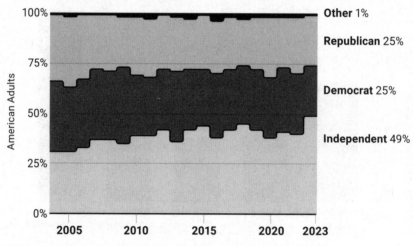

Source: Gallup, data from March 2004 to 2023

Clearly, the ideological wings of both parties are vastly overrepresented in partisan primaries, which have evolved into litmus tests by which base voters of both parties judge whether their candidates are not only sufficiently progressive or conservative, but also to what extent they are willing to fight the other side.

In 2020, Unite America conducted our own exit poll of Republican voters in Colorado's 3rd Congressional District. Compared to all general election voters, we found that GOP primary voters were more than twice as likely to consider themselves "very conservative" (60% vs. 25%) and tune into Fox News (59% vs. 24%). On issues, GOP primary voters were thirty-five points more likely to believe in accelerating the deportations of undocumented immigrants and twenty points less likely to believe that the right to bear arms should be balanced with commonsense gun safety regulations.

The Republican incumbent in that district, Scott Tipton, had a congressional voting record that was scored to be in the middle of the Republican conference—not as conservative as some, but no RINO (Republican in Name Only). In short, he was a good ideological fit for his district, but not for GOP primary voters. He lost his 2020 primary by less than ten thousand votes—to Lauren Boebert, who on the morning of January 6, 2021, tweeted "Today is 1776" before voting to overturn the results of the 2020 presidential election.

Primary Rules Keep Certain Voters Away

The rules determining who can vote in primaries are the biggest factor affecting who actually participates. The design of primary elections varies state to state, consistent with our Constitution, which gives states the power to set "the time, place, and manner of their elections." (With the exception of situations where Congress steps in to pass federal election laws.)

The invention of direct primaries, as chapter 1 detailed, was a function of individual state actions, not Congress. States adopted different variations of direct primaries and subsequently revised them—giving rise to today's complex web of rules that vary from state to state, including which voters can even participate.

African Americans, in particular, were discriminated against by the parties in setting rules for their primaries. Following the adoption of the Fourteenth and Fifteenth Amendments, which were supposed to guarantee the citizenship rights of former slaves and their descendants, southern states erected barriers to voting, such as literacy tests and poll taxes. And for about fifty years, the most effective barrier employed by southern states was the so-called "white primary," which accomplished something states were unable to do in general elections: explicitly bar African American participation.

The Democratic Party operated a political monopoly in the post-Reconstruction South. As political scientist V. O. Key Jr. noted of that era: "Nominally in the South 'candidates' are chosen in the Democratic 'primary.' Such is the formal language. In fact, the Democratic primary is no nominating method at all. The primary is the election."[34] By denying African Americans the ability to participate in the primary, southern Democrats found a loophole in the Fifteenth Amendment.

When these restrictions were challenged, the Supreme Court, in *Grovey v. Townsend* (1935), found that political parties were private organizations and could therefore determine their own rules and membership qualifications. This decision stood for nearly a decade until it was overturned by *Smith v. Allwright* (1944), in which the court asserted: "The right of a citizen of the United States to vote for the nomination of candidates for the United States Senate and House of Representatives in a primary which is an integral part of the elective process is a right secured by the Federal Constitution, and this right of the citizen may not be abridged by the State on account of his race or color."[35] So began decades of jurisprudence that has wrestled with balancing the right of free association for political parties with the fact that primaries have become "an integral part of the elective process."

Fast-forward to today. No court has yet established a constitutional right for voters to participate in partisan primaries regardless of their party affiliation. Thus, in forty-five states with partisan primaries, the states and parties themselves get to decide who can cast ballots—even if the primary is taxpayer-funded and the only election that truly matters.

Restrictive primary rules disproportionately impact independent voters, who make up the largest and fastest-growing segment of the electorate today. There are as many Americans overall who self-identify as independent as there are who identify as Democrats or Republicans combined. Independents outnumber either Democrats or Republicans in eighteen of the thirty-one states that register voters with a party affiliation.[36]

Of the forty-five states with partisan primaries, fifteen hold "closed primaries," meaning that they're exclusively open to those who are registered with the party, and independents are banned from voting. In these states, the parties themselves can amend their rules to allow independents to participate; currently, the Democratic Party in just four of these states has done so (Idaho, Oklahoma, South Dakota, Utah).[37] In the eleven closed primary states in which neither party allows independents to participate, over 14 million Americans are completely disenfranchised during primary elections.[38]

An additional fifteen states use a "semi-open" primary system that allows independent voters to choose which party's primary they would like to vote in. However, party-affiliated voters must still only vote in their own party's primary. While this offers some degree of flexibility for independents, a Democrat in a red district or a Republican in a blue district does not have a voice in the election of consequence.

Finally, fifteen states hold "open primaries" in which all voters can pick which party's primary they would like to participate in. (In fourteen of these states, voters are not registered by party, so there is no way for the state to restrict participation based on party affiliation.) While this offers the greatest degree of flexibility in a partisan primary system, voters may only pick one party's primary ballot—they cannot, for example, vote in a Democratic primary for state legislature and a Republican primary for Senate in the same election.

The remaining five states have either replaced partisan primaries with nonpartisan primaries (Washington, California, and Alaska for all offices, and Nebraska for its state legislature) or have eliminated primaries altogether (Louisiana).

At this point, I can almost hear defenders of the status quo proffering a "simple" solution to the Primary Problem: if you want to have a real voice, you should simply register for whichever party dominates in the general elections where you live.

Tell that to the nearly half of all veterans who are independents,[39] many of whom have never registered with a party because they swore allegiance to our country without wanting to belong to any political faction. Or tell it to the nearly 30% of African Americans who identify as independents,[40] and whose families have already faced a long history of disenfranchisement after being "guaranteed" the right to vote. Or tell it to any taxpayer who helps foot the bill for administering elections (more than $400 million nationally in presidential years),[41] yet may not be able to cast a ballot in one.

Indeed, it's not so simple.

FIGURE 9:
Primary Rules by State

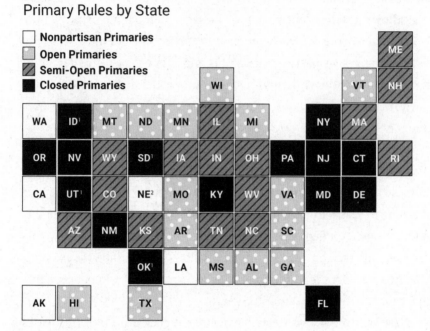

- ☐ Nonpartisan Primaries
- ☐ Open Primaries
- ▨ Semi-Open Primaries
- ■ Closed Primaries

Note 1: The Democratic Party in the following states allows independents to vote in their primarie ID, OK, SD, UT

Note 2: NE uses top-two nonpartisan elections for state legislative elections only; all other primaries are closed (R) and semi-open (D)

Source: Adapted from Open Primaries and the National Conference of State Legislatures analysis (primary systems

POLARIZATION AND THE CREATION OF PARTISAN ECHO CHAMBERS

Partisan primaries are corrosive for our political culture and society, well beyond the exclusion of millions of voters in closed elections. They erect even bigger barriers between Democrats and Republicans as well, fueling polarization. Candidates are only going to spend time and money talking to voters who are likely to vote for them. The rise of data-driven microtargeting enhanced a candidate's ability to direct a higher volume of communication to an even smaller universe of likely supporters. That means the only thing partisan voters hear about the other party is likely to come indirectly from their own side and their own news sources, whether Fox News, MSNBC, or otherwise.

"Campaigning to Republicans in Iowa is completely different than campaigning to Republicans in Nebraska, even though the states share a border," explains John Opdycke, the president of Open Primaries.[42] At the state legislative level, Iowa has a closed partisan primary, while Nebraska has a fully nonpartisan top-two system. "In Iowa, if you're a Republican, you never, *ever* hear from a Democrat for any reason at any time. In Nebraska, they're used to having their door knocked on by Democratic candidates and getting mailings and phone calls from Democrats that are like 'Hey, I'm not an AOC Democrat, I'm a Nebraska Democrat, vote for me.'" It doesn't make Nebraska Republicans any less conservative, but it creates an ecosystem in which the two sides do not inhabit completely different political realities and therefore have an easier time coexisting. "The analogy one local operative gave to me to the difference in political culture between both states was the Galápagos Islands—like how a species of iguana on this one island will look completely different because it has never had any interaction with these other iguanas."

You don't need to be Charles Darwin to see the impact this dynamic has had on our political divisions. You may have experienced it within your own family at Thanksgiving. The research group More in Common set out to measure both parties' misperceptions of the other. They asked Republicans to estimate how many Democrats agreed with the statement "Police are bad people." They guessed, on average, 52%. The reality? Just 15%. Similarly, they asked Democrats to estimate how many Republicans deny that "racism exists." They guessed, on average, 49%. The reality? Only 21%.[43] While there are many factors fueling this perception gap, a political system that is designed to isolate voters from any kind of interaction or engagement with the other side certainly does not help.

REPRESENTATION: WHO RUNS AND WHICH CANDIDATES WIN

So far we've been looking at the "input" side of the Primary Problem: unfairness in who votes and which votes matter. But it's equally important to look at the "outputs" side of the equation: who runs in primaries, and which candidates tend to win.

The Majority Does Not Rule

Let's start with the problems caused by "plurality winners," and an example from a high-profile House district.

New York's 10th Congressional District, which spans Lower Manhattan and the west side of Brooklyn, is the second-smallest district by geographic size in the country. In 2022, after redistricting changed its boundaries, the district's Democratic primary attracted one of the largest fields of candidates for any House primary in the country. Thirteen candidates threw their hats in the ring, including former New York City mayor and ex–presidential candidate Bill de Blasio (who America loves to hate and who dropped out two months after entering). All but four of the candidates were women or people of color.

The unusual size of the field meant that support was likely to be fractured among similar candidates. As *Politico* reported, "The city's institutional left split their support among several of those candidates."[44] A day before the election, two female rivals held an unusual joint press conference to plead with voters: vote for a woman to champion reproductive freedom.

Ultimately, a white male lawyer worth an estimated $253 million named Daniel Sachs Goldman (no apparent relation to Goldman Sachs) prevailed against sitting representative Mondaire Jones, one of the first openly gay Black members of Congress, and Yuh-Line Niou, a Taiwanese American state assemblymember. Goldman put over $4 million of his own money into the primary, and won with just 16,686 votes, which put him 1,306 votes ahead of Niou and 4,909 votes ahead of Jones. His total was just 25.8% of votes cast, meaning that nearly 75% of primary voters preferred a different candidate. More notably, Goldman's voters were a mere *3.5% of registered voters* in the district.[45] But they were all he needed to go on to win a general election landslide in his deep blue district. Goldman's title may now be "Representative," but the 10th district's election outcome was anything but representative.

"Majority rules" is a common phrase we associate with our democracy, but in virtually all American elections, the winning candidate only needs to have the most votes—not a *majority* of votes.*

In general elections, which are usually a two-way contest between a Democrat and a Republican, the winner usually has a majority. Even if there is a third-party candidate, he or she is unlikely to get more than a single-digit percent of the vote. In contrast, primary elections typically see crowded fields whenever there's no incumbent on the ballot. This is especially true in "safe" districts, where the primary election will effectively determine who gets elected.

In 2022, thirty congressional districts held partisan primaries for open seats that were in safe districts.[46] These contests averaged nearly 6.5 candidates in the dominant party's primary. Ultimately, in eleven of those thirty districts the winner had just a plurality of support.

Across House, Senate, and statewide offices, FairVote found that 41 million Americans live in jurisdictions currently represented by a leader who did not win a majority of votes in a partisan primary that determined the election.[47] In many cases this means an elected leader isn't ideologically or demographically representative of their own party, let alone their whole district or state. They don't just represent the minority, but a *minority* of the minority. All thanks to party primaries in which a *plurality rules*.

---

*Two states, Georgia and Louisiana, hold runoff elections if no candidate receives a majority of votes cast during the general election. Nine states hold runoff primary elections if no candidate receives majority support in the initial primary (or, in the case of North Carolina, at least 30% support). Alaska and Maine (for federal elections) use ranked choice voting to ensure winning candidates have majority support.

Unorthodox Contenders Opt Out and "Sore Losers" Are Kicked Out

Three minutes and one obscure law made all the difference for Republican-turned-Libertarian presidential candidate Gary Johnson in Michigan in 2012.

Johnson dropped out of the Republican primary to instead seek the presidential nomination of the Libertarian Party, which he won. His platform of advancing civil liberties, ending the War on Drugs, and reining in foreign intervention was unorthodox within the GOP and did not resonate among its conservative base. "We rode bikes 500 miles across the state, we scheduled town halls—for whatever reason, nobody's really coming out to hear what I have to say," lamented the former New Mexico governor to reporters.[48]

After his decision to drop out, Johnson's campaign submitted an affidavit to the Michigan secretary of state's office at 4:03 p.m. on December 9, 2011, requesting that his name be removed from the Republican primary ballot for president. Unfortunately, the deadline was 4:00 p.m., and the state GOP wasn't interested in cutting him any slack. As a result, his name would still appear on the GOP ballot—which *also* meant his name could *not* appear on the general election ballot as an independent or as the nominee for any other party, including the Libertarian Party.[49]

This prohibition, known as a sore loser law, is intended to prevent candidates who lose partisan primaries from running against their party's nominee in the general election. In this case it meant that voters in Michigan who wanted to support Gary Johnson in 2012 would have to write in his name, as 7,774 eventually did. Let's just say, that wasn't enough.

You may not have heard of sore loser laws, but if you've ever been disappointed at having to vote in November for "the lesser of two evils," you've certainly felt part of their impact. While there are many inherent obstacles to independent and third-party candidates, the inability of major-party candidates to qualify for the general election ballot after losing a primary is a big reason why most elections are binary choices.

Sore loser laws are a relatively new phenomenon. Nearly half of all states (twenty-one) adopted these laws between 1976 and 1994. Today, all but three states have them, at least for all non-presidential contests.

In addition to reducing competition in the general election, sore loser laws also severely narrow the field in the primary itself, because there is little point for any candidate with a low chance of winning to run. There is no plan B available after a long-shot candidate loses a primary, and as a result, that candidate has no leverage to nudge the party in a new direction by threatening to run as an independent. One 2014 study found that, because of these dynamics, sore loser laws alone could explain as much as one-tenth of the polarization in Congress.[50]

Pragmatists Fail the Purity Tests

Partisan primaries have become like exams in which every candidate is scored (sometimes literally) based on their partisan loyalty, ideological purity, and political temerity. Especially in a safe district, the dominant party's primary is the eye of the needle through which any candidate who hopes to be elected must pass.

In a contemporary Republican primary, virtually any viable candidate must be pro-gun, anti-abortion, anti-Obamacare, skeptical (at best) that President Biden won the 2020 election, and culturally traditional (if not rabidly anti-woke). In a contemporary Democratic primary, virtually any viable candidate must be anti-gun, pro-choice, pro–single-payer health-care (but fine with Obamacare in the short term), pretty certain Russia pulled the strings in the 2016 election, and comfortable with the politics of personal identity (if not able to brag about representing a minority group).

While extremely partisan base voters love these kinds of candidates, more average voters wonder where all the "normal" candidates have gone by November. One explanation is that they lost their primary, which automatically ended their candidacy. A more likely explanation is they did not run in the first place.

"Ideological moderates also see no point in entering contests that naturally push them out to the extremes," explain Chapman Rackaway and Joseph Romance in *Primary Elections and American Politics*. "Moderate voices tend to opt against running in partisan races specifically because they know that they will not be competitive in primary elections that intrinsically favor extreme candidates and viewpoints."[51]

In this context, "moderate" may mean anything in between "split-the-difference centrist" on one hand to "party ideology is not my religion" on the other. We are not only talking about ideological moderates, but also about leaders who may not fit neatly into either party's box and want to retain some capacity to exercise independent judgment. Examples could include a Democrat who supports school choice, much to the ire of the teachers' unions, or a Republican who supports making corporations pay higher taxes, much to the ire of those corporations. (By the way, either hypothetical candidate would be espousing a belief shared by the majority of Americans—Democrats, Republicans, and independents!)[52]

Danielle Thomsen tested this hypothesis by surveying over five hundred state legislators who did and did not run for Congress between 2000 and 2010 and analyzing their ideology based on voting records. She found that "party fit" strongly affected their decision to run or not. For example, according to her statistical model, a one-unit decrease in a Republican's conservatism (as measured by their self-reported ideology) correlated with a four-point decline in their confidence in winning a GOP primary.[53] Ideological moderates in both parties were less likely to believe they could win a congressional primary, less likely to run, and even less likely to value a House seat to begin with. (On the latter, I suppose, why covet something you can't have?)

"The quality of political representation is compromised when only a narrow ideological subset of individuals is willing to engage in electoral contests," Thomsen concluded. "If the only candidates who are willing to run for office are as extreme as the rascals in office, this has serious consequences for the representation of those in the ideological middle, which includes the majority of the American people."[54]

Whether you happen to like extreme rascals or would prefer more heterodox alternatives doesn't really matter, because the primary process denies voters those options. Voting in most places in America is like showing up to the local Baskin-Robbins and finding they only have one flavor. You can either pick that flavor or leave. Chances are, you wouldn't come back. In our elections, it's no wonder why over 100 million eligible voters stay home.

UNREPRESENTATIVE BY DESIGN

In an oversimplified yet still instructive model of the electorate, imagine that all voters within a particular district exist on a one-dimensional left-to-right ideological spectrum. Most would agree that the best representative of this district is the one who comes closest to matching the ideology of the median voter—with about half of the district on one side of that voter and half on the other. That's the exact right position to be closest to the greater number of voters. In political science, the "median voter theorem" suggests that, in a healthy two-party system, both parties have an incentive to compete for the median voter in order to win elections.

FIGURE 10:
An Illustration of Median Voter Theorem

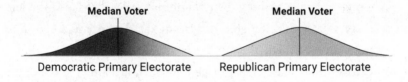

Median Voter   **Median Voter**

Democratic Primary Electorate   Republican Primary Electorate

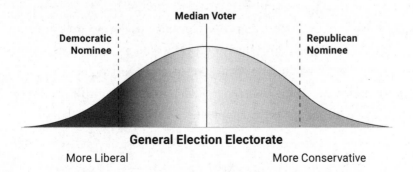

Median Voter

Democratic | | **Republican**
Nominee | | **Nominee**

General Election Electorate

More Liberal   More Conservative

This does not equate to a representative being a "moderate." In a very Democratic district, the median voter may be quite progressive, and so should that district's representative. In a very Republican district, the median voter may be quite conservative, and so should that district's representative.

Unfortunately, our election system isn't healthy enough to favor this kind of representative. The candidates who survive partisan primaries and make it to the general election are, almost definitionally, incapable of representing the median voter of the district. Instead, they represent the median voter of their party's primary electorate. The general election then becomes a question of which party's nominee represents the median voter the least worst.

Because of all the barriers to participation and restrictive rules in primaries, the most partisan and ideological voters end up selecting the most partisan and ideological candidates. Leaders who don't fit that category rarely run in the first place. Winning candidates don't even need a majority of primary voters, merely the largest plurality. And because of uncompetitive districts, party nominees are all but guaranteed to win the general election in more than 80% of elections. In the other 20% of districts, voters are left with an unappealing choice between two relatively extreme options.

When Democratic-leaning districts nominate leaders far to the left of the median voter, and Republican-leaning districts nominate leaders far to the right of the median voter, the result is a Congress that is much more polarized than the American people. Such an outcome is not an aberration; it is the logical outcome of elevating the voting power of the fringes, while effectively disenfranchising tens of millions of voters. And this dysfunctional outcome further drives the polarization, discontent, and cynicism of the American people, in a vicious downward spiral.

John Adams envisioned that Congress would be "a portrait, in miniature, of the people at large."[55] Today, in large part because of partisan primaries, our Congress is more like a funhouse mirror. And most American voters aren't happy about what they see in that mirror.

FOUR

BAD FOR THE COUNTRY

To its practitioners, politics is about power: getting it, keeping it and using it. But for the nation, the basic purpose of politics is to concili- ate. If everyone agreed on everything, politics would be unnecessary. So would democracy and elections. A dictator could govern by uni- versally accepted preferences and policies. Without consensus, poli- tics is how we resolve our differences short of resorting to violence. One reason so many Americans are unhappy with politics today is that it has abdicated its central role. It doesn't narrow our differences; it exaggerates them.

—*Robert Samuelson,* Washington Post *columnist, 2010*[1]

love this quote because it succinctly nails the fundamental problem with American governance: too many politicians are incentivized to exaggerate our differences in order to maintain and build their own power. Many Americans throw up their hands and call our system dys- functional, but it is actually functioning exactly as we should expect— because our elections reward this kind of behavior. The biggest tragedy in our politics today is not that the American people are divided on many issues; it's that our Congress remains bitterly divided *even when we agree.*

A major reason for the disconnect between the politicians and "We the People" is the partisan primary. Primaries have become a leading weapon used by activists, extremists, and special interest groups to punish politicians who care more about the national interest than about beating the other side. They have become both an obstacle to effective governance and a threat to democracy itself.

Let's start with one of the most polarizing issues of the past decade, in which the destructive impact of partisan primaries is on full display.

WHY OUR IMMIGRATION SYSTEM REMAINS BROKEN

At the start of 2014, Congressman Eric Cantor (R-Virginia) was riding high. He was the powerful House majority leader, after winning seven consecutive terms and rising through the GOP leadership on his way to become speaker. It's unlikely that he was worried when he found out about a primary challenge by David Brat, an economics professor and former legislative assistant to a state senator. In his previous primaries, Cantor had only ever attracted a single challenger, whom he beat with 79% of the vote. Brat, in contrast, had never won any kind of election. And Cantor enjoyed an overwhelming 26:1 fundraising advantage; he would soon build a $5 million war chest against Brat's paltry $120,000.

So when Brat defeated Cantor in the Republican primary, it was reported nationwide as "shocking" and "stunning." The *Los Angeles Times* called it "one of the greatest political upsets of modern time."[2] What could possibly explain this outcome? Two words: immigration reform.

To understand what happened, we have to start a year earlier, when a bipartisan group of senators known as the "Gang of Eight" negotiated a comprehensive immigration reform bill. (Congress might be the only place where gangs are actually a good thing.) This compromise bill would increase border security, offer more visas to high-skilled workers, and provide a path to legal status and eventual citizenship for millions of undocumented immigrants. It passed the Democratic-controlled Senate in a 68–32 landslide, winning the votes of every Democrat, both independents, and fourteen Republicans. It offered both parties significant progress on their top priorities: border security for the Republicans and bringing the undocumented out of the shadows for the Democrats.

The bill then went to the Republican-controlled House, where Speaker John Boehner (R-Ohio) called instead for a piecemeal approach that prioritized border security, rather than a comprehensive bill that included a path to citizenship. In response, other Republican leaders called on the House majority to embrace the Senate's compromise. As former Florida governor and presidential hopeful Jeb Bush wrote in a *Wall Street Journal* op-ed, "No Republican would vote for legislation that stifled economic growth, promoted illegal immigration, added to the welfare rolls, and failed to ensure a secure border. Yet they essentially will do just that if they fail to pass comprehensive immigration reform—and leave in place a system that does all of those things."[3]

Bush concluded that while Democrats and Republicans had different priorities, the worst possible outcome would be to do *nothing* and see the immigration problem compound. But his argument was unpersuasive. Speaker Boehner would not even bring the Senate bill to the House floor for a vote. He insisted that any bill would need to have the support of not just a majority of the House, but a majority of the GOP caucus—a procedural threshold known as the Hastert Rule.

Such a rule is neither in the Constitution nor the rules of Congress. It's an operating norm that began under Speaker Newt Gingrich in the 1990s and was named after his successor, Dennis Hastert, who continued the tradition. The Hastert Rule's overriding priority is to consolidate power for the majority party. As Boehner remarked, "When you have to get Democrats to pass the legislation, you are not in power anymore."[4]

Cantor Cracks the Door for Dreamers

Cantor was a conservative who advocated for dealing with immigration issues one at a time, beginning with economic and security challenges and then addressing what to do about the roughly 12 million undocumented immigrants then living in the country.[5] "We in the House really do want to make progress on this issue," he told the *National Review*'s Ramesh Ponnuru at the Aspen Ideas Festival in June 2013, three days after the Senate bill passed.[6]

Cantor specifically addressed the issue of the 2.1 million undocumented immigrants who were brought to our country as children— sometimes accompanied by their families, but other times sent alone by desperate parents with the hope of giving them a better life.[7] These individuals became known as Dreamers, after the DREAM Act, introduced in 2001 by Democratic senator Dick Durbin and Republican senator Orrin Hatch, which aimed to give them a path to legal permanent residency and eventual citizenship. The DREAM Act failed on several occasions when brought up for a vote, including in 2007, when bipartisan immigration reform was championed by GOP senator John McCain and President George W. Bush.

The DREAM Act did not pass when Democrats controlled the House, Senate, and White House from 2009 to 2010. Some might say that some issues are better left unresolved so they can be used on the campaign trail, especially if solving them would give one's opponents credit. Eric Cantor advocated giving it another shot. He told that 2013 Aspen audience: "We ought to have the compassion to say these kids shouldn't be kids without a country, and we ought to allow them the life that they deserve."[8]

The Tea Party Throws Immigration Reform Overboard

But the comprehensive bill was a nonstarter for the Tea Party, which had effectively become the new base of the Republican Party and was exercising its growing power in GOP primaries.

"You certainly had 20% of the Republican conference that identified themselves as being on the far extreme ideologically to the right," Cantor explained to me.[9] "When I was leader, we passed the Obamacare repeal fifty-six times. Why? Even though we knew that President Obama was not going to repeal the bill that basically had his name on it, nor was the

Senate controlled by [Democrat] Harry Reid at the time going to pick that up, they needed to go back and say to their primary electorate they were trying to fight. The same thing happened with raising the debt ceiling. A lot of people would come to me and say, 'I can't vote for this.' And I said, 'Do you understand that this is a risk that the country has never, ever seen before?'"[10]

The same hard-line dynamics extended to the issue of immigration, where Cantor found himself under attack by both sides for his more pragmatic approach. Cantor recalled one point during his primary campaign where there was a clash of activists at Capitol Square in Richmond—from both the pro-immigration, progressive group La Raza and the anti-immigration Tea Party—protesting him for either not going far enough or for going too far. "All of a sudden I'm trying to get resolution between two sides and find myself caught in the middle," Cantor said.[11]

David Brat, Cantor's GOP challenger, built much of his early support by attending Tea Party events, which Cantor himself largely ignored. He attacked Cantor as an out-of-touch Washington insider who was insufficiently conservative, especially on immigration. Brat referred to immigration as "the most symbolic issue that captures the differences between myself and Eric Cantor in this race."[12]

John Pudner, Brat's campaign consultant, identified 23,000 conservatives on the voter rolls who had not voted in the last few primaries, but who he believed were prime targets. With the campaign flat broke, Pudner personally paid $2,800 to produce a rudimentary thirty-second ad attacking Cantor on immigration. The first cut featured stock footage of Cantor walking through Congress while the narrator said, "Cantor's next deal with Obama is amnesty and citizenship for illegal immigrants."[13] But it wasn't hard-hitting enough. "I told the guy, 'You're fired if the next cut of this doesn't show immigrants coming over the border,'" Pudner recalled to me.[14] The revised ad was targeted online to those 23,000 conservatives and caught fire. Fox News aired it nationally, after which Fox host Laura Ingraham came to Cantor's district for an event.

Feeling the heat, Cantor backed away from his openness to

immigration reform, stopped talking about the Dreamers, and put out campaign mailers and commercials about his opposition to the Senate's immigration bill. "Conservative Republican Eric Cantor Is Stopping the Obama-Reid Plan to Give Illegal Aliens Amnesty," blared the headline of one mailer from Cantor's campaign.[15] But it was too little, too late.

36,105 Voters Change the Trajectory of a Major National Issue

On June 10, 2014, Brat won 55.5% of the Republican primary vote in Virginia's 7th district; his 36,105 votes represented just 7.6% of all registered voters in the district.[16] "It was a real surprise to us," Cantor recalled. "We had had internal polls that had us significantly up."[17] Cantor resigned from Congress on August 18 rather than finish out his term.

To this day, Cantor believes Democrats—who are able to vote in Republican primaries in Virginia—raided his primary and were a difference-maker in costing him the election. However, a post-election analysis by the Upshot found: "Turnout was still far, far higher in Republican precincts. Democratic areas did not contribute a large number of votes. . . . Since Mr. Brat ran so strongly in Republican territory, it's hard to see that he needed Democratic votes to push him over the top."[18]

The shock of the defeat of the House majority leader sent a loud and clear message to every Republican in the country. Immigration reform was now the third rail of GOP primaries: if you touch it, your career may die. "I don't think there's been any serious attempt to do anything on immigration since my primary defeat," Cantor reflected. "People pointed to my defeat and said, 'Don't start working with the other side because it's treacherous.'" Cantor referred to his "unscheduled departure" as a "canary in a coal mine."[19]

"For the vast majority of Republicans—who don't have to worry about losing in the general election—support for comprehensive immigration reform amounts to something that could needlessly complicate an otherwise simple reelection bid," explained the Washington Post's Aaron Blake. "It's a risk—and politicians are notoriously risk-averse."[20]

"Build the Wall" vs. "Abolish ICE"

The gap between the parties on immigration reform has only widened since Cantor's defeat. It became a chasm in June 2015, when Donald Trump announced his presidential campaign, calling for a crackdown on illegal immigration and slurring Mexicans in crude language: "They're sending people that have lots of problems, and they're bringing those problems with them. They're bringing drugs. They're bringing crime. They're rapists. . . . I will build a great, great wall on our southern border. And I will have Mexico pay for that wall."[21]

"Build the wall" became a rallying cry for Trump supporters and later for the Republican Party after he won the nomination. In office, Trump's sharp rhetoric quickly turned into controversial policies, such as when the Department of Homeland Security began separating families at the border to deter other potential immigrants.

The GOP's lurch to the right caused an opposite reaction among Democrats. In 2015, before Trump's announcement, the Pew Research Center found that 63% of Democrats agreed with this statement: "Immigrants strengthen our country because of their hard work and talents." By 2017, agreement was up to 83%.[22] Such a dramatic swing in public opinion demonstrates the power of "negative partisanship": *If they're against it, we must be for it, because they're bad people and we're the good guys.*

Alexandria Ocasio-Cortez of New York made immigration a centerpiece of her 2018 House campaign, becoming one of the first Democratic primary candidates to propose eliminating the Immigration and Customs Enforcement agency. "Abolish ICE" soon became a progressive rallying cry. AOC's surprise defeat of longtime incumbent representative Joe Crowley, the chairman of the House Democratic Caucus, pulled her party to the left on immigration, just as Brat's defeat of Cantor pulled the GOP to the right.

As *The Hill* reported, abolishing ICE was "fast becoming a litmus test for Democrats."[23] Barely a week after Ocasio-Cortez's primary victory, two progressive senators and aspiring presidential candidates,

Kirsten Gillibrand and Elizabeth Warren, also came out for abolishing the agency. By July, six House Democrats introduced a bill in Congress to abolish the agency and create a commission to deal with the details. (You know, minor things such as figuring out what agency would become responsible for addressing human trafficking.)

These Democrats were acting with rational self-interest. Support for abolishing ICE among Democratic voters doubled from 21% around the time of Ocasio-Cortez's victory in July 2018[24] to 42% by August 2019.[25]

As a slogan, "Abolish ICE" became a "shorthand to signal a new brand of a more aggressive Democrat," according to the *Huffington Post*. But as a policy, it was not embraced by immigration reform groups, which focused instead on cultivating bipartisan support to pass legislation. "They view the push as mostly coming from white-dominated progressive groups, not Latino organizations."[26]

The Real Human Suffering Caused by Partisan Primaries

According to one poll, 80% of all Americans support creating a path for Dreamers to earn citizenship, including 93% of Democrats, 74% of independents, and 71% of Republicans.[27] Yet, more than two decades after the DREAM Act was first introduced, and a decade after comprehensive reform passed the Senate with bipartisan support, we are no closer to a solution. Consensus between the parties has become harder to find as primary-driven fissures within the parties have grown larger.[28]

Meanwhile, millions of real people continue to suffer, and not merely the 4 million Dreamers or the roughly 12 million total undocumented immigrants, who can't join the mainstream economy.[29] There are also hundreds of thousands of new people attempting to cross the border illegally every month, peaking at 200,000 intercepted by U.S. officials in November 2022.[30] And there are another 1.5 million asylum seekers in the U.S. legally while they await hearings regarding their claims, the largest number of pending applications on record.[31] The status quo is the worst possible option, yet that is what continued gridlock produces.

THE CONSEQUENCES OF PRIMARYING

I've gone into detail about immigration because it's such a powerful example of the polarizing and paralyzing impact of partisan primaries on what our government does—or doesn't do—day to day and year to year.

Primaries have become a key tool for activists and interest groups to push extreme political goals that may appeal to a majority of primary voters, but not to a majority of the general electorate. For incumbents, both actual primarying and the mere threat of primarying can be terrifying. Rather than suffer the same fate as Eric Cantor or Joe Crowley, many resist compromising across the aisle, even on important issues they care deeply about. In races for open seats, more ideological candidates are advantaged and less ideological candidates opt out from even competing.

The ultimate result is leaders who are unable (because they are so extreme) or outright unwilling (because they are so afraid of extremists) to work with each other to solve the nation's problems. Division and dysfunction replace collaboration, compromise, and progress. In any private sector enterprise, it would be unthinkable if the people who try hardest to fulfill their actual job description got fired instead of promoted. Yet that's where our political system is today: the more likely a politician is to do their job, the more likely it is for them to lose it.

In addition to immigration, America faces a host of other challenges that Congress has failed to meaningfully address because of the polarization and partisan gridlock made worse by the Primary Problem. It's worth considering a few more to gauge the true impact of how governing dysfunction fueled by the Primary Problem is hurting our country and our future.

Climate

Each year, the Climate Change Performance Index ranks countries based on their actions to bring down greenhouse gas emissions and increase their production and use of renewable energy sources. In 2023, the U.S.

ranked fifty-second out of sixty-three countries included in the index.[32] A report from the consulting firm Deloitte projected that current congressional inaction on climate change will lead to devastating direct consequences to our country—including an estimated $14.5 *trillion* in lost GDP over the next fifty years due to disruptions in agricultural production, the impact of extreme weather events and rising sea levels, and costs of heat-related illnesses.[33] One of the most obvious, bipartisan, and impactful policy solutions—a revenue-neutral tax on carbon emissions that would be offset by an equivalent amount of tax reductions or rebates elsewhere—has stalled out multiple times in Congress as the parties fight over bumper sticker positions like the Green New Deal or whether climate change even exists.

Education

The U.S. continues to underperform in global education rankings, especially in math, where we placed thirtieth out of seventy-nine countries tested in 2018 by the Organization for Economic Cooperation and Development (OECD). The U.S. has made virtually no progress on K–12 math scores since 2003.[34] In addition, costs of higher education are soaring and leaving millions of Americans saddled with crushing college debt. While both parties either elevate culture war issues like books bans and bathrooms, or pursue popular Band-Aid solutions like debt forgiveness, they largely ignore ways to leverage federal education funding to incentivize greater cost containment, transparency, and accountability. Meanwhile, countries that compete with us economically continue to adapt and improve.

Healthcare

Research from the Commonwealth Fund concluded that the U.S. has the worst health outcomes among eleven high-income countries, despite spending the most on healthcare.[35] The COVID pandemic exposed deep disparities and deficiencies with our country's healthcare system. Yet even the tragedy of 1.2 million deaths has not been enough to drive Congress to meaningfully address the issue. For example, the CDC reports that individuals with obesity may have faced triple the risk of hospitalization due to infection; the U.S. obesity rate (41.9%) is the highest of any OECD country.[36] Supporting a healthier society extends well beyond how we treat illness and pay for that treatment—including to how we expand access to healthy foods, infrastructure for physical activity (sidewalks, bike routes, etc.), and preventative care. Congress has largely spent the last decade debating whether to keep or repeal the Affordable Care Act, rather than work on how to improve and build upon it. Further, addressing crises such as the rapid rise of opioid overdose deaths and the shortage of rural doctors should not be partisan issues.

Budget & Economy

The national debt is now more than $33 trillion, which represents a larger share of GDP than at any time since World War II.[37] This staggering number makes the famous 1950s quip by Senator Everett Dirksen—"A billion here, a billion there, and pretty soon you're talking real money"— seem quaint. It also gives the U.S. the twelfth-highest debt-to-GDP ratio in the world.[38]

The nonpartisan Committee for a Responsible Federal Budget noted that our overall debt and high annual deficits can lead to higher inflation and threaten the country's long-term economic strength and global competitiveness.[39] Yet Congress isn't able to hold bipartisan negotiations in good faith on a package of potential revenue increases and spending cuts to put America on a more sustainable fiscal path. It's easier for one side to call the other an evil mob of tax-and-spend socialists, while being attacked in return as monsters who want to steal Grandma's hard-earned Social Security and Medicare benefits. If Congress continues to kick the can down the road, retired Americans and future retirees will soon lose out: Medicare will not be able to cover full benefits as soon as

2031, while Social Security benefits will see an across-the-board cut of 20% by 2034.[40] That translates into an annual reduction of Social Security benefits of $17,400 for the typical retiring couple.[41] The longer we wait to make any changes, the more dramatic and painful they will be. That is the price of partisan gridlock we all pay.

Rejecting Compromise

"If you got seventy-five or eighty percent of what you were asking for,
I say you take it and fight for the rest later."

—*Ronald Reagan*[42]

Politics is the art of compromise; without it we wouldn't have a country at all. At the Constitutional Convention in 1787, big states wanted legislative representation to be proportional by population, while small states wanted equal representation for each state. Only the so-called Great Compromise, creating both the House and the Senate, avoided a deal-breaking deadlock.*

In the modern era, compromise has been at the core of nearly every major legislative achievement. Consider the Americans with Disabilities Act (ADA) of 1992. Until the ADA, millions of disabled Americans were routinely discriminated against in employment, public accommodations, and access to government services. Companies had no obligation to provide assistance such as closed-captioning for TV shows or wheelchair ramps for restaurants. No one could sue an employer for being fired simply for contracting a disease like HIV.[43]

The ADA was championed by Republican senator Bob Dole, who had lost the use of his right arm during World War II and spoke about his own experiences of facing bias against the disabled.[44] Though a staunch

---

*It is important to acknowledge that the Great Compromise also included the profoundly problematic provision that enslaved individuals would be counted as three-fifths of a person for the purposes of representation and taxation.

conservative Republican, Dole believed strongly in compromise. After his retirement he even cofounded the Bipartisan Policy Center with three other former Senate majority leaders from both parties.

The ADA had critics on both sides. Some Republicans claimed it went too far in its regulations, with the Chamber of Commerce warning that it would have "a disastrous impact on many small businesses struggling to survive."[45] Some liberal groups, like the National Council on Disability, feared that the ADA's language about protections was too vague and its penalties were too limited. Legislators worked through these and other issues with a series of trade-offs. For instance, the final version of the ADA exempted private businesses with fewer than fifteen employees; delayed the imposition of penalties by two years to give companies time to make adjustments; capped the potential damages individuals could win in discrimination lawsuits; and included some but not all mental illnesses under the act's protective umbrella. It passed the House by a margin of 377–28 and the Senate by 91–6 and was signed by President George H. W. Bush.

Dole faced no backlash for compromising with Democrats, winning his Senate reelection primary that year with 80% of the vote and the general election with 63%.[46] Four years later, he had no trouble winning the 1996 Republican presidential nomination. But today, the incentives run in the opposite direction.

Speaking at a ceremony that marked the ADA's twenty-fifth anniversary, Dole remarked on the congressional compromises of that bygone era: "Sometimes we'd vote with Democrats, sometimes they would vote with us. In some cases you can't agree and you just vote. But I think in most cases you can work it out. . . . We worked together because it was the right thing to do."[47]

Before we conclude that primarying is the main reason for today's absence of bipartisan laws like the ADA, let's consider other possible reasons why our senators and representatives might refuse to compromise. They may simply feel so strongly about a bill that any compromise would be an unthinkable breach of their principles, values, or morals. Or if their party is in the minority, they may feel it's too risky to give the majority party a victory that could be used as a talking point against them in the next election.

Three political scientists tested those and other possible explanations in 2014 through 2017, conducting multiple surveys of hundreds of state legislators. They asked legislators to respond to hypothetical compromises in which they would receive half of their ideal outcome, such as a 2% increase in the gas tax, rather than their stated goal of a 4% increase. The only statistically significant factor preventing compromise turned out to be electoral self-interest, i.e., whether the legislators believed voters would punish them. Respondents who believed compromise would hurt their reelection were 21 percentage points more likely to reject a compromise. And of those who believed compromise would hurt them, 58% specified that their concern was primary voters, while only 26% were mainly concerned about their next general election.[48]

The researchers conclude, "We find that legislators exacerbate gridlock by rejecting compromise proposals because they fear being punished in primary elections. In this way, legislators' electoral interests can cause them to act in ways that hurt their policy interests and may lead to representation of the uncompromising positions held by a subset of their voters at the expense of the broader electorates' preferences."[49]

Changing Members and Changing Behaviors

There are two ways Congress changes over time: by replacement or by adaptation. The Primary Problem impacts both: by influencing what it takes to fill an open seat, and by influencing how far one has to toe the party line to avoid a primary challenger. Combined, these forces make it harder and harder for anyone in Congress to find common ground.

Let's consider the impact on new members. An analysis by the *Cook Political Report* after the 2022 primary season identified 53 Republican House primaries that were won by nonincumbents; 24 of them (45%) were associated with the MAGA movement or the Freedom Caucus.

On the Democratic side, 41 primaries were won by nonincumbents; 13 of those (32%) were won by self-identified progressives. *Cook* concluded that both House caucuses are continuing to become more ideological, but the GOP is doing so at a quicker rate, perhaps due to Trump's influence.[50]

A similar analysis by the Brookings Institution found that in GOP primaries without an incumbent, 86% of Trump-endorsed candidates won. Brookings also found the leftward shift in the Democratic Party significant, though less dramatic. About 27% of Democratic primary candidates addressed "left-wing issues" such as "Defund the police" or "the Green New Deal" on their campaign websites, and nearly 40% of those candidates won.[51]

The other way Congress changes is when incumbents change their behavior out of political self-interest. For the vast majority who represent safe districts or states, that means staying in line with their primary electorate.

Consider Utah's Orrin Hatch, who won seven consecutive Senate terms beginning in 1976. He earned a reputation as a Republican who would work across the aisle—at least until 2010, when his fellow Utah senator Bob Bennett lost renomination to a more conservative challenger, Mike Lee. After that, Hatch began to align himself with Lee, voting the same way 78% of the time on roll-call votes (excluding unanimous votes). That earned him a rating of 99% from the conservative Club for Growth. But after Hatch successfully navigated his 2012 primary and reelection, his voting alignment with Lee dropped to 64% and his Club for Growth rating dropped to 44%.[52] He retired at the end of his term in 2018.

One reason old-fashioned politicians like Hatch worry about being primaried is how random the risk seems. "However rare, primary upsets are important because of the psychological impact they have on incumbents," wrote Elaine Kamarck of the Brookings Institution and James Wallner of the R Street Institute, a center-right think tank. "Upsets shape the expectations members have about the future. They have an outsize psychological influence on members precisely because they are so unexpected."[53]

Eric Cantor confirmed as much when he told me, "The fear of being confronted by a more extreme candidate who would throw bombs and burn the house down would cause the majority of members to be first and foremost concerned about getting through their primary." The consequences are clear. "The incentives in place for people in public office right now is never, ever to back down and to never, ever compromise or find common ground, because if you are seen to do that, you are necessarily not fighting hard enough."[54]

Political scientist Richard Barton researched how the threat of being primaried affects the willingness of members of Congress to work across party lines. He developed a model to estimate the vote share an ideological challenger could be expected to win in any given district based on past election outcomes, which in turn represented the threat level each incumbent would face from such a primary challenger. Analyzing 1,360 members of Congress from 1980 to 2016, he found that higher primary threat levels disincentivized bipartisan behavior: "The increase in competitive ideological primary challenges explains about one-quarter of the drop in bipartisan bill cosponsorship since the 1980s." He also found this effect was about equal in both parties.[55]

Even Popular Things Don't Get Done

Perhaps the most frustrating impact of our current primary system is that it blocks compromise on issues where compromise is not only possible, but would be popular with a large majority of the electorate.

A joint study by the University of Maryland's Program for Public Consultation and Voice of the People found more than 150 proposals that won more than 50% approval from Democrats, Republicans, *and* independents. Consider just a few of these proposals for two of the gridlocked issues mentioned above: the federal budget and immigration.

FIGURE 11:

Proposals to improve the federal budget:	Democrats support	Republicans support	Overall support
Raise taxes on capital gains and dividends by treating them as ordinary income for individual incomes above $1 million	80%	69%	75%
Gradually raise the retirement age to collect Social Security to 68 over a 10-year transition period	78%	81%	79%
Reduce Social Security benefits for the top 25% of lifetime earners	81%	72%	76%
Proposals for immigration reform:	Democrats support	Republicans support	Overall support
Require that employers use E-Verify to establish the legal status of current employees and all new applicants	68%	80%	73%
Provide undocumented immigrants eligible for DACA status with legal status and a path to citizenship	92%	69%	80%
Increase the number of visas for skilled workers in high-tech industries	86%	72%	80%
Increase the number of visas for low-skilled workers in industries that need them, such as agriculture	87%	66%	77%
Hire more federal workers to process the claims of asylum seekers faster	96%	90%	93%

Source: The University of Maryland's Program for Public Consultation and Voice of the People, data from 2020

Another study looked at polling data on 1,779 proposed policy changes over a twenty-year period. After controlling for the preferences of affluent Americans and organized interest groups, which have undue influence on Congress, the researchers found that a policy preferred by the public became law only about one-third of the time. That was the case regardless of whether 20% supported it or 80% did. The two Princeton researchers concluded: "It makes virtually no difference whether an overwhelming majority or only a small minority of average citizens favors a policy change."[56]

A political system in which the views of most Americans are virtually irrelevant can only be described as fundamentally broken.

PARTISAN PRIMARIES ENDANGER DEMOCRACY ITSELF

It's bad enough that partisan primaries inhibit progress on so many important challenges facing our country. An even bigger problem is that these same polarizing forces now threaten our democracy itself by opening the door to anti-system demagogues and undermining our shared commitment to bedrock democratic principles such as free and fair elections, peaceful transfers of power, and the rule of law.

Historically, most authoritarian populists rise to power by exploiting divisions and attacking a political establishment that has failed to adequately address major problems. "Democracies that are unable to solve national problems tend to fall apart as citizens turn on each other and often support deeply polarizing demagogues who promise that they alone can solve the nation's ills," writes Miguel Schor, a Drake University law professor.[57] Further, as a joint report by the conservative American Enterprise Institute and the progressive Center for American Progress warns, "In the United States, the appeal of authoritarian populism has gone hand in hand with a decline of trust in government and a rise in partisan polarization. Increasingly . . . the government is seen as unresponsive to citizens' concerns and captured by well-organized special interests."[58]

Such were the conditions in 2016, when Donald Trump executed a hostile takeover of the Republican Party in the primaries and then vanquished Hillary Clinton in the general election. His campaign hammered at the failures of "the swamp" (referring to Washington, D.C.) to help ordinary Americans. When the Economist Intelligence Unit downgraded the United States from a "full democracy" to a "flawed democracy" for the first time in 2017, they wrote: "By tapping a deep strain of political disaffection with the functioning of democracy, Mr. Trump became a beneficiary of the low esteem in which U.S. voters hold their government, elected representatives, and political parties, but he was not responsible for a problem that has had a long gestation."[59] In the time since, Trump has severely accelerated our democratic decay.

Not only did our primary-driven polarization create the conditions for Trump's rise to power, but partisan primaries also gave Trump a powerful tool to exercise his grip over the Republican Party and, eventually, assist in his unprecedented effort to overturn the results of the 2020 presidential election.

Partisan Primaries Fuel the Big Lie

Why did so many Republicans—147 of them—object to the Electoral College result on January 6? Most voted to overturn the election out of fear. Not fear of the angry mob that had invaded the Capitol hours earlier, but fear of who might threaten their reelection—specifically in their next primary.

Trump ruthlessly deployed the threat of primarying to coerce candidates into asserting that the 2020 election was stolen from him. He explicitly thundered that message on the National Mall, on the morning of January 6: "You have to get your people to fight. And if they don't fight, we have to primary the hell out of the ones that don't fight. You primary them. We're going to let you know who they are."[60]

Over the next several months, he followed through by viciously attacking Republicans in Congress who did not go along with his plot, in particular the seventeen Republicans who voted to impeach or convict him for his role in the January 6 insurrection. Of the thirteen members who were up for election in 2022, six decided not to run rather than face election-denying primary opponents. Of the seven who ran, four were successfully primaried out of office by Trump-endorsed challengers, including Representative Liz Cheney (R-Wyoming), the vocally anti-Trump vice chair of the Select Committee to Investigate the January 6th Attack. After winning her 2020 primary in Wyoming with 73.5% of the vote, she lost her 2022 primary with just 28.9%. A few weeks before the primary, Cheney acknowledged the political risks she had taken on principle: "If I have to choose between maintaining a seat in the House of Representatives or protecting the constitutional republic and ensuring the American people know the truth about Donald Trump, I'm going to choose the Constitution and the truth every single day."[61]

These results were not surprising considering that 71% of Republicans saw Joe Biden's 2020 victory as definitely or probably illegitimate a full year after January 6.[62] One study found that GOP voters preferred election-denying candidates over their opponents in Republican primaries by a margin of 5.7%—a more significant margin than differences based on gender, race, or profession.[63]

Of the 552 Republican nominees running for any federal or statewide office in 2022, 36% fully denied the legitimacy of the 2020 presidential election and only 14% fully accepted it. Election deniers made up a much greater portion (60%) of candidates running in safe GOP House districts than in more competitive districts (36%), underscoring the role of political incentives in their positioning.[64] Ultimately, 97% of Trump-endorsed candidates won their primaries in 2022.[65] Engaging in primaries was a main way he wielded his power over the party.

Only three Republicans who voted to hold Trump accountable advanced to the 2022 general election and won reelection: Dan Newhouse from Washington, David Valadao from California, and Lisa Murkowski from Alaska. They shared one huge advantage: their states have replaced partisan primaries with nonpartisan primaries, so they could build support across the whole electorate—not just the base of their party.

True Believers or Opportunists?

How many election-denying candidates were lying for political advantage in 2022, as opposed to sharing their sincere beliefs? We'll never know for sure, but as an example let's consider retired general Don Bolduc, who ran for the Senate in New Hampshire. During a debate on August 14, he said, "I signed a letter with 120 other generals and admirals saying that Trump won the election, and, damn it, I stand by my letter. . . . I'm not switching horses, baby. This is it."[66] (The letter suggested election irregularities but actually stopped short of saying Trump won.)[67]

Bolduc prevailed in the ten-way GOP primary with 37% of the vote, less than two thousand votes ahead of New Hampshire state senate president Chuck Morse. Just two days after winning the September 13 primary, according to the *New York Times*, Bolduc reversed his position "like a driver making a screeching U-turn."[68] He told Fox News: "I've done a lot of research on this, and I've spent the past couple weeks talking to Granite Staters all over the state from every party, and I have come to the conclusion—and I want to be definitive on this—the election was not stolen."[69] But by that point many voters already saw Bolduc as antidemocratic, and he lost the general election by nine points.

Imagine the power a partisan primary must have to cause a retired U.S. Army brigadier general to debase himself, and our democracy, in such a public way.

The Impact of Election Denialism on Our Democracy

The proliferation of election denialism made previously lower-profile races for secretary of state, the office that oversees elections in most states, hotly contested—and GOP primaries gave a fast-track to the most dangerous candidates in the country. For instance, Arizona secretary of state candidate Mark Finchem had attended the Capitol protests on January 6 and, while serving in the state legislature, introduced a bill that would allow the body to overturn future election results.[70] Finchem won his four-way primary with 41% of the vote.[71] In Nevada, Secretary of State Jim Marchant promised to get rid of both mail ballots and voting machines in favor of counting all election results by hand.[72] Marchant prevailed in a seven-way primary with 38% of the vote.[73]

In the 2022 general election, unwavering election deniers fortunately paid a political price in competitive elections, especially among independent voters. Every election-denying secretary of state candidate in a battleground state, including Finchem and Marchant, lost their election (albeit by slim margins); only ten out of forty-seven election deniers won competitive races in the House or Senate. However, election deniers in safe districts and states nearly all prevailed, including 147 members of the House, four members of the Senate, seven governors, six attorneys general, and two secretaries of state.[74] For example, Chuck Gray won his secretary of state race in bright red Wyoming, where the Democrats didn't even bother to field a candidate. Gray was so extreme that he hosted screenings of the discredited documentary *2000 Mules* and claimed that "the woke, big tech left has stolen elections with ballot drop boxes."[75]

In terms of impact, it doesn't matter if the election deniers were true believers or opportunists, or whether they won or lost, in terms of the damage they did in eroding public confidence in election outcomes. Between 2018 and 2022, according to the Pew Research Center, Republican voter confidence that elections would be administered properly plunged from 87% to 56%.[76]

Many election deniers who won their elections subsequently helped enable widespread efforts by state legislatures to restrict voting access or interfere with the nonpartisan administration of future elections. Hundreds of such bills have been introduced since 2020, and by the end of 2021, nineteen states passed thirty-four laws that changed the voting process, often to make it more difficult for citizens to cast ballots.[77] For example, three states reduced the length of voting hours and/or the number of voting locations.[78]

The Danger in Meddling in the Other Party's Primaries

All of this makes it deeply irresponsible that the Democratic Party spent more than $50 million during the 2022 primaries to prop up Republican election deniers, on the theory that they would be easier for Democrats to defeat in the general election.[79] In one of the most egregious examples, the party spent nearly $500,000 to help election denier John Gibbs defeat pro-impeachment representative Peter Meijer in the GOP primary in Michigan's 3rd district. The Democrats ran an ad that technically attacked Gibbs, but its message was clearly meant to increase his appeal among pro-Trump voters who would make up most of the district's primary electorate.[80]

Meijer, a member of the Problem Solvers Caucus, was the Republican candidate in this race who more closely approached the Democratic Party's stated commitment to democracy. But Democratic operatives apparently decided they were willing to do anything to increase their chances of winning the seat, including backing someone who believes the January 6 insurrection was carried out by antifa or other far-left groups.[81] The Democrats' meddling in Michigan achieved its narrow objective: Gibbs defeated Meijer in the primary by about 3.5 points before losing to Democrat Hillary Scholten by double digits in the general election.

But no party that claims to stand for democracy should be actively working to help election deniers get an inch closer to high office. "Our democracy is fragile, therefore we cannot tolerate political parties attempting to prop up candidates whose message is to erode our dedication to fair elections," wrote thirty-five former Democratic members of Congress in a joint statement published by Issue One denouncing the tactics.[82] Partisan primaries make this kind of election meddling and manipulation all too easy.

To recap, partisan primaries prevent our leaders from doing the jobs we hire them to do by fueling extremism and discouraging compromise. In turn, as a country, we fail to address the challenges facing the lives of everyday Americans. A populist authoritarian not only exploited this environment to get elected in 2016 but also further weaponized the primary process to attempt to stay in office against the will of the people in

2020. In the time since, Trump has used primaries to cast out of the party any conservatives who defended the Constitution and rule of law, which cynical elements of the Democratic Party have been eager to assist with by meddling in those same primaries. It is uncertain to what extent the 2024 elections may accelerate our democracy's current dystopian direction, but one thing is abundantly clear: partisan primaries are bad for our country.

FIVE

BAD FOR THE PARTIES

One of the most fundamental and important functions of a political party is to put forward candidates who are capable of winning general elections. Today, both major parties are less capable of doing so because of the influence that activists and special interests have in partisan primaries. Although it may seem counterintuitive, the primary system that many partisan leaders now defend is actually hurting their own interests.

THE DEMOCRATS' PRIMARY PROBLEM

We saw this dynamic in the introduction to part II, with Representative Kurt Schrader being primaried by a more ideological candidate, who went on to lose the general election, in a seat Schrader had previously held for six terms. His race was no anomaly. "Democrats are benefitting from a perception among voters that Republicans are extreme, but they cannot fully reap the gains of this view, as voters think Democrats are extreme as well," notes Third Way, a center-left think tank affiliated with the Democratic Party.[1]

According to a Third Way study conducted in 2022, on a left-to-right ideological scale of 1–10, the average swing voter self-identified as a 5.4— slightly right of center. Such voters were then asked to place candidates of both parties on the same spectrum; they perceived Republicans (6.5) to be closer to them, on average, than Democrats (3.6). The Democrats must reduce this gap if they hope to win future congressional majorities, Third Way concluded.[2] That will be hard to do as long as partisan primaries are pushing the party and its candidates to their left flank.

Another good example of this problem for Democrats was the 2022 Wisconsin Senate race, in which Republican incumbent Ron Johnson was extremely unpopular with swing voters. Johnson downplayed the January 6 insurrection, calling the crowd at the Capitol "jovial" and "friendly."[3] By early 2022, polling found that 56% of Wisconsin independents disapproved of Johnson's job performance, up 14 points from late 2020.[4] But then Democratic primary voters nominated progressive Mandela Barnes, the state's lieutenant governor, after several more mainstream challengers dropped out. The progressive Working Families Party spent more than $1 million to support him.[5] Barnes had a difficult time responding to Johnson's focus on growing crime in the state, despite attempting to walk back his previous support for reducing police funding.[6] Barnes narrowly lost the general election to Johnson, 50.4% to 49.4%.

THE GOP'S PRIMARY PROBLEM

The Republican Party's Primary Problem is arguably more severe at this point, though the Democrats may be catching up soon enough.

During the first ten months of 2022, most pundits were predicting a "red wave" of Republican victories to wash ashore in the midterm elections, which would determine all 435 House seats and 35 Senate seats. Both chambers were narrowly controlled by the Democrats as the year began. But historically, the party that controls the White House loses an average of twenty-eight House seats in the midterms, as voters signal a desire for a different direction or, at least, a balance of power. This trend is even stronger when the same party controls the trifecta of the presidency, the Senate, and the House.

Even more ominous for the Democrats, President Biden's approval rating was hovering around 40% to 43% most of the year,[7] and the inflation rate remained over 8% from March to September—higher than it had been since January 1982.[8] Some pundits suggested that Republicans would not only win back the House but would pick up as many as thirty seats.[9] Others even predicted a repeat of the red wave of 2010, when the GOP won a net gain of sixty-three seats in the backlash to President Obama's first two years. These dynamics extended to the closely divided Senate, where the Democrats were barely clinging to control, 50–50, with Vice President Harris serving as the tiebreaker for every party-line vote. There were several seats opening up in red or purple states, giving the GOP multiple paths to recapturing a majority.

But all the historic, economic, and demographic trends didn't take into account the growing impact of the Primary Problem on the parties and, especially in 2022, the GOP. Republican voters nationwide nominated many extreme candidates who continued to litigate the legitimacy of the 2020 election and either were endorsed by former president Trump or declared their fierce allegiance to him. These included the Senate nominees in five highly competitive swing states: Blake Masters in Arizona, Mehmet Oz in Pennsylvania, Herschel Walker in Georgia, Adam Laxalt in Nevada, and Don Bolduc in New Hampshire. Those races alone could determine control of the Senate. Similar MAGA-aligned nominees also won primaries for many competitive House seats, often against the wishes of local party leaders.

Complicating the election further, in May 2022 there was an unprecedented leak of the Supreme Court's upcoming decision to overturn *Roe v. Wade*, ending forty-nine years of federal protection for abortion rights. Many conservatives were thrilled, with some calling for their congressional candidates to endorse severe restrictions or outright bans on abortion at the state and federal levels. Both the Supreme Court's decision and the GOP's reaction drove a significant boost in Democratic voter enthusiasm, while making far-right nominees seem even more out of step to swing voters, many of whom believe in balancing the rights of pregnant women with some restrictions on late-term abortions. In Pennsylvania, for example, Oz took the position that abortion should be illegal at any stage of pregnancy, telling a tele–town hall: "It's still murder if you were to terminate a child whether their heart's beating or not."[10]

In mid-August, Senate Minority Leader Mitch McConnell took a thinly veiled but unmistakable swipe at his own party's primary process for producing nominees who would alienate swing voters. "I think there's probably a greater likelihood the House flips than the Senate. Senate races are just different—they're statewide, candidate quality has a lot to do with the outcome."[11] The phrase "candidate quality" became a short-hand for what ailed the Republican Party in 2022.

Sure enough, in November all five of those swing-state GOP nominees lost their Senate races, and Democrats picked up one net seat, for a 51–49 majority. And while the House did flip, the anticipated red wave turned out to be a trickle. The GOP gained only nine seats, leading to a very thin majority of 222–213.

As the *Cook Political Report*'s Dave Wasserman observed, "MAGA adherents who triumphed in primaries by running to the right proved easy prey to Democratic attacks [that] they were too extreme, particularly on abortion. Gibbs [MI-03] had once questioned women's suffrage, Kent [WA-03] had called for murder charges against Anthony Fauci and Majewski [OH-09] was caught vastly exaggerating his military service."[12]

Using data from *Cook*, Nate Cohn of the *New York Times* calculated that, on average, "MAGA Republicans" nominated for the U.S. House performed about 5 percentage points worse than other, more traditional Republicans. In competitive districts, MAGA Republicans were 6.6 points worse off.[13] Democrats wound up winning twenty-five of the thirty-six districts considered toss-ups. Significantly, in at least nine of these districts that Democrats won, the Republican nominee had won his or her primary with just a plurality of votes, not a majority.

"Trump remains quite popular among Republican voters, and his endorsement was decisive in plenty of House primaries this summer," noted the American Enterprise Institute's Philip Wallach. "But close association with the twice-impeached president was a clear liability in competitive 2022 House races, turning what would have been a modest-but-solid Republican majority into (at best) a razor-thin one."[14]

As GOP leaders processed these disappointing House and Senate results, many privately blamed Trump for his damaging endorsements. But the far more determinant factor in these outcomes was low-turnout primaries that were captured by the most partisan and passionate voters. They were the main reason the Republican Party became less popular and less powerful in 2022 than it otherwise might have been.

A Speaker in Name Only

The GOP's Primary Problem is not limited to the races it lost in 2022; it extends directly to the party's challenges in governing with a small majority in the House and a conference that includes a significant faction of hard-core partisans.

After paying his dues in the House for sixteen years, Kevin McCarthy was finally on the verge of becoming Speaker, his ultimate ambition. Although the vast majority of the 222 newly elected Republicans supported him for Speaker, a handful of GOP holdouts threatened to block him. The election of a new Speaker—usually a quick formality on January 3, at the start of each new term—turned into the longest and most contentious such contest since before the Civil War. All 435 House members had to cycle through fifteen different ballots over four days, with some sessions stretching late into the night.

In the midst of those endless revotes for the speakership, McCarthy lamented, "We have 90% of the votes. I've never seen a body where 10% is going to control the 90%. It just doesn't happen."[15] (The irony was apparently lost on him that that's precisely how Congress operates—with roughly 10% of eligible voters nationally effectively determining nearly 90% of all House seats, via partisan primaries.)

Of the twenty members of the Republican caucus who withheld their votes from McCarthy at least once during those four days, eighteen held safe seats, where the primary was the only election that mattered; an average of 6% of eligible voters in their districts put them into office.[16] And of the five members who voted "present" on the final ballot (thus allowing McCarthy to win by lowering the majority threshold, but without casting an affirmative vote), two reached Congress by primarying an incumbent from their own party: Bob Good of Virginia and Lauren Boebert of Colorado.

In between each round of voting, McCarthy and his allies tried to entice or pressure the holdouts. During these private negotiations, McCarthy gave away seats on the powerful Rules Committee, which controls which bills make it to the House floor, to several members of the far-right Freedom Caucus. He also lowered the threshold required to make a motion to vacate the chair, which would empower a single disgruntled member to force a vote on stripping him of his speakership.* Finally, a super PAC affiliated with McCarthy struck a deal with the conservative Club for Growth, promising not to spend in open-seat primaries in safe Republican districts. If they followed through, this would open the door for the Club for Growth and its allies to have even greater influence on primaries. Content with these and other concessions, the holdouts finally relented on January 7.

As the price of achieving his dream, McCarthy had ceded much of the power of his new office to the most extreme elements of his conference. In the process he also lost a great deal of his credibility and influence, making it much less likely that he could shape the legislative priorities of his party. On key issues, he would be riding in the front seat of the bus but not driving it. And if he complained about where the extremists were driving the bus, they now had the power to banish him to the back row. As the *National Review*'s Philip Klein put it, "He is a speaker in name only."[17]

---

*This came to pass on October 3, 2023, when McCarthy was ousted by a motion to vacate despite still having the support of the overwhelming majority of the GOP caucus.

A far-right faction of House members, kowtowing to fringe primary voters, now held all the cards. These representatives seemed to put most of their energy into getting attention from conservative media and social media, often via extreme statements and symbolic votes. And because of their outsize influence—won via all those concessions from McCarthy— they had the power to drive the official GOP agenda even further out of step with a majority of the national electorate, compounding the party's electoral challenges.

This dynamic was a dramatic shift from prior decades, when any representative who defied the party leadership would lose prestigious leadership posts and other perks. But by 2023, McCarthy's opponents would publicly trash-talk the Speaker without fear of reprisal, if doing so could raise their national profiles and influence with the base. As Florida representative Matt Gaetz told *Politico*, "In today's world of social media, digital communication and wall-to-wall cable television, the leadership no longer has a stranglehold on the brand or the messengers."[18]

Such unrestrained politicians no longer even need their party leadership for help with fundraising, which used to be one of any party's strongest tools for controlling rogue members. Online small donations are now driven by media coverage and high visibility on social media. With the ability to control their own destiny in partisan primaries, why should any Republican fear the disapproval of party leadership

COMPOUNDING TRENDS

To varying degrees, both parties face the same problem: the path to winning national elections runs through a relatively small number of competitive districts and states that are decided by swing voters, yet both parties are largely steered by primary voters who take their cues from more extreme politicians from safe districts and states. This paradox keeps nudging both sides toward their respective ideological corners— making it harder to win durable majorities that are capable of advancing their agendas.

For this reason, party leaders themselves have begun to reevaluate the utility of partisan primaries. Jeff Bartos, a Republican candidate for U.S. Senate in Pennsylvania in 2022, told me, "To win an election we need to get the most votes. It seems to me that the easiest way to get the most votes is to appeal to the widest group of people. But right now, the system is geared towards appealing to the people you know are going to turn out consistently, which is a small group. I think it's bad for the party."[19] And in the words of Senate Majority Leader Chuck Schumer, in a 2014 *New York Times* op-ed advocating for top-two primaries: "The partisan primary system . . . has contributed to the election of more extreme officeholders and increased political polarization. It has become a menace to governing."[20]

For both parties, time is of the essence. The political and governing challenges they face because of the Primary Problem will only get harder over time, for a few reasons. First, as we've seen, there are fewer competitive districts in virtually every election cycle, leading to partisan primaries having even greater influence within both parties. More safe districts equals more legislators who are likely to pander to primary voters.

Second, both parties are losing their remaining ability to influence the outcome of those primaries, particularly to advance more mainstream candidates. Recall McCarthy's concession to the Club for Growth that he would avoid taking sides in contested Republican primaries in safe districts; in 2022, before that deal, McCarthy's super PAC spent tens of millions of dollars in such primaries.[21] Likewise, the Democratic Congressional Campaign Committee tried to crack down on the primarying of Democratic incumbents by blacklisting any consultants and vendors who worked for insurgent primary challengers. But that policy by party leaders looked hypocritical in 2020, when Speaker Pelosi endorsed a primary challenger, Representative Joe Kennedy, against incumbent Massachusetts senator Ed Markey. "No one gets to complain about primary challenges again," tweeted Representative Alexandria Ocasio-Cortez in response to the Markey vs. Kennedy race.[22] The DCCC rescinded its policy in 2021.[23]

The final trend is that Congress is becoming increasingly narrowly divided, giving disproportionate power to small factions of members—especially those on the ideological edges who have proven to be the most willing to use such leverage. Control of the House has been determined by fewer than twenty seats only eight times in the last century; five of those times have happened in the last twenty-five years.[24] The close division in our politics also means that just under 60,000 votes in a handful of states decided the 2016 and 2020 presidential elections. To the extent the partisan divide is largely driven by demographics and levels of education, these divides are quite stable.

"Neither party appears well positioned to break into a clear lead in the House," noted the *Atlantic*'s Ron Brownstein in early 2023.[25] "The two sides look more likely to remain trapped in a grinding form of electoral trench warfare in which they control competing bands of districts that are almost equal in number."

Such narrow majorities wouldn't be a big deal if both parties were broadly representative of the public and willing to negotiate with each other. But the opposite is increasingly true. The net result: unless something dramatic changes, we're heading toward a long-term stalemate in which neither party can function as an effective governing coalition when in power. Instead, what we are left with are hardly true political parties at all—merely two empty vehicles whose only unified purpose is to win power and whose only chance to do so is being seen as the least unappealing of the two options.

HOW DID WE GET HERE?

As we saw, reformers during the Progressive Era rightly targeted party machines as pernicious, corrupt forces that used government resources to maintain and build their own political power. Where those reformers took a wrong turn was in conflating the party machines with political parties as a whole. Rather than focusing on narrow efforts to root out corruption of the machines, such as by promoting merit-based government jobs instead of patronage, reformers took away the parties' most essential function: to choose the candidates that would represent them in elections. They transferred that power from party leaders to a direct, popular vote. In short, they got the problem right, but the solution wrong.

Giving citizens a more direct say in candidate nomination sounds like a good idea on the surface, but the fundamental error of Progressive reformers was believing that a more direct democracy would lead to a more participatory and therefore more representative one. In other words, if Americans were given more opportunities to get involved politically, then in theory more of them would participate, and election outcomes would better reflect the popular will. This theory proved true for some Progressive Era reforms, such as giving women the right to vote and allowing citizens (rather than state legislatures) to directly elect the Senate. But the same logic turned out to be deeply flawed when it comes to candidate nomination.

While well-intentioned in their goal of cracking down on corruption and democratizing elections, the reformers who made direct primaries the new norm accidentally threw the baby out with the bathwater. "No exogenous shock has been more damaging to the political parties than the introduction of the direct nominating primary election," write political scientists Chapman Rackaway and Joseph Romance.[26] "The scope of the Progressive reforms was so great that they affected the entirety of the political party structure, not just the machines. The spillover effect did achieve its intended results of marginalizing the party machines, but it did so at the larger cost of weakening parties themselves for the long term."[27]

A few observers at the time predicted that removing influence from party leaders would not lead to a more noble version of democracy. Henry Jones Ford, a politics professor at Princeton University, wrote in 1909: "One continually hears the declaration that the direct primary will take power from the politicians and give it to the people. This is pure nonsense. Politics has been, is and always will be carried on by politicians, just as art is carried on by artists, engineering by engineers, and business by business men. . . . The direct primary may take advantage and opportunity from one set of politicians and confer them upon another set, but politicians there will always be so long as there is politics."[28]

Determining what a party stands for and who should represent it were once centralized and professionalized activities that were the domain of party leaders, party members, and elected officials. Under the old caucus and convention system, each aspiring candidate made a case to party leaders about their ability to be a standard-bearer for their party. If chosen, candidates lined up unequivocally behind their party, and the party lined up with equal enthusiasm behind the selected candidates. There was very little daylight between the two.

However, as Ford predicted, removing that power from parties did not automatically confer it to the people at large. "Rather than disenfranchising political elites, primaries shift power from one set of elites (insiders who serve the party organizations) to another set (ideologues and interest groups with their own agendas)," writes Brookings fellow Jonathan Rauch and political scientist Ray La Raja.[29] In other words, the party bases became the new party bosses. Over time, the newly empowered activists, ideologues, and special interests skillfully manipulated direct primaries to their own ends. As a result, political parties have lost a significant amount of control over their brands, policy agendas, and standard-bearers.

Direct primaries reinvented not just how candidates were chosen but also how campaigns would be waged, elevating individuals and diminishing the parties. Under the new system, candidates began focusing their communications to voters more on their own personalities and personal policy agendas rather than on the platforms of their parties. Today, party nominations are totally up for grabs. There is zero friction for any individual to run for office in a partisan primary, campaign directly to voters, and potentially win the election to carry the party's banner into the general election and into office. In fact, many candidates seek to distinguish themselves from their party—or even run *against* their own party.

Parties have ceded their influence to other actors with their own agendas. For instance, in the 2022 U.S. Senate primary in Pennsylvania, the state GOP committee—composed of some three hundred officials—decided to forgo making a candidate endorsement at the state convention. Many wanted to avoid getting crosswise with Trump, who would soon issue an endorsement of his own. "At that point, this is basically just a social club without the alcohol," said Bartos, who had won the party's endorsement for lieutenant governor in 2018. "The party has given up. The party used to exist to help winnow through electable candidates."[30]

Direct primaries also opened the doors to various interest groups. "Over the last couple of years, we've let PACs and big money crucify fellow Republicans. We've seen PACs dominate who gets elected," said Billy Nungesser, the Republican lieutenant governor of Louisiana.[31]

WHY SHOULD THE REST OF US CARE?

I suspect at least some independent-minded readers may be wondering why they should care if the Primary Problem is hurting the major parties. And those who aren't enamored by either Democrats or Republicans may be feeling more schadenfreude than sympathy for the woes of congressional leadership. My response is that the negative impact of partisan primaries on the parties should matter to all of us, because strong parties *as institutions* are actually important to a healthy democracy—even if we don't happen to care much for the current two.

As the Founders and their successors discovered during the first few decades under the Constitution, parties are necessary organizing mechanisms for running a republic. They function as important intermediary institutions that oil the gears of self-government by recruiting candidates, mobilizing voters, and organizing coalitions within legislatures to advance policy agendas. As brands, parties signal to voters what affiliated candidates generally stand for, which is important when most voters don't have hours upon hours to research every individual candidate. We rely on such shortcuts as consumers every day. Imagine trying to buy a car if each vehicle were individually designed and manufactured. You wouldn't have the time to test-drive each one. You rely on the brand to give you some sense of price, safety, durability, and so on. Direct primaries didn't strip parties' brands from our ballots, but they did strip the parties from being able to ensure any kind of quality control over their candidates.

Parties used to have the power to prevent radical leaders from claiming their nominations and getting to the general election—even if those candidates enjoyed support from upward of 30% to 40% of the public. For example, leaders in both parties prevented the presidential nominations of extremists and bigots like Father Charles Coughlin, Huey Long, Joseph McCarthy, and George Wallace. In *How Democracies Die*, Steven Levitsky and Daniel Ziblatt explain, "Backroom candidate selection had a virtue that is often forgotten today: It served a gatekeeping function, keeping demonstrably unfit figures off the ballot and out of office. To be sure, the reason for this was not the high-mindedness of party leaders. Rather, party 'bosses' . . . were most interested in picking safe candidates who could win. It was, above all, their risk aversion that led them to avoid extremists."[32] In other words, parties' gatekeeping powers were good for both them and our country.

Well-intentioned, good government reforms subsequent to direct primaries further put the parties at a disadvantage. For example, various campaign finance reforms and the *Citizens United* Supreme Court decision made it harder for the parties to raise money and easier for political action committees—often representing narrow and extreme special interests—to raise enormous sums. When such PACs focus on low-turnout primary elections, relatively modest investments can pay off for candidates sympathetic to a PAC's causes, even if those candidates don't align with the platform of the party's leaders.

The combination of these reforms has severely weakened political parties in both their ability to win elections and to pass policy. This weakening has generally been hard for ordinary voters to notice because it coincided over the past few decades with a strong upswing in partisanship. It may seem counterintuitive, but these trends are related:

in the absence of strong parties that have a consistent vision, identity, and platform, the single greatest defining characteristic for both
has simply become: *We're not the bad guys. If you hate the other side,
you have no choice but to vote for us.* This zero-sum, binary division
of American politics is at the core of our democratic dysfunction and
anti-democratic extremism today.

Even though parties' excesses can undermine good governance,
well-functioning parties serve a vital role in organizing politics. That's
why no democracy in the world has endured for long without some kind
of stable party system to mediate engagement in a complex society and
political system.

THE DISTINCTION BETWEEN NOMINATING AND ELECTING CANDIDATES

While direct primaries have been harmful for political parties, I am not
proposing a return to the old system in which party leaders were able to
determine the only options for all of the voters. Gone forever are the days
of party bosses handpicking candidates for each office and tightly controlling voters' options in the general election, and we should be grateful
for that. Instead, I am arguing for disentangling the process of *nominating
candidates*, which should belong to the parties, from the process of *electing candidates*, including primaries, which should belong to the public.
Taxpayers should not run or subsidize the parties' nomination process,
nor should the government interfere with however parties would like to
nominate their own candidates. Party nomination processes should have
a single purpose: to formally endorse which candidate a party backs.
Likewise, primary elections should have a single purpose: to winnow a
potentially large candidate field down to a smaller number of candidates
in the general election.

What could this look like in practice? That can be left up to the
parties themselves to decide, in a nod back to the earliest traditions of
American politics. Who knows what innovations might emerge as the

parties experiment with new ways of endorsing candidates. We can let party leaders combine their professional judgment with any vetting process they consider appropriate. "Members of Congress, governors, and party officials could . . . rate candidates on measures such as political experience, ability to work with others, ethics, and so on," suggest Jonathan Rauch and Ray La Raja. "While not dispositive, insiders' judgments would encourage the news media and the public to focus on characteristics that matter for governing."[33]

Such ratings could also be solicited from a larger group of party members and voters, if the parties transform twentieth-century conventions into twenty-first-century online town halls. In addition to endorsing a candidate, participants could also engage in real-time deliberation of issues and priorities, at scale. Imagine if the definition of participating in a party nominating process went from spending an hour simply casting a ballot to spending an hour in a participatory online meeting, with the chance to help shape the direction of one's party. The only thing stopping us is our own imagination.

It's Already Happening

In four states that have replaced partisan primaries with nonpartisan primaries, along with dozens of cities that have adopted fully nonpartisan elections, the parties have adapted to remain active in candidate recruitment, endorsement, and support. For example, the California Democratic Party organizes a pre-primary endorsement process within the state's top-two nonpartisan primary system. Candidates pay a small filing fee to access a list of party leaders who will vote in that process, such as county central committee members. A candidate who secures over 50% of that vote may be endorsed at the state convention, but if no candidate reaches that threshold, the party will not endorse in the race. These endorsements are marketed to voters by both the endorsed candidates and the party itself. Further, party leaders and their large networks mobilize campaign donations to endorsed candidates.[34]

Such tactics are effective; in general elections that feature two candidates of the same party, according to one study of California's top-two nonpartisan primary system, the party-endorsed candidate won about 70% of the time.[35] In future designs of nonpartisan primaries, it is possible that the ballots themselves could indicate which candidate has been endorsed by which party. The ballot distinction can be as simple as "Joe Smith, Republican" versus "Jane Doe, Republican Nominee."

In at least eight states with partisan primaries, parties hold local caucuses and statewide conventions that can, in part, determine which candidates advance to the primary ballot.[36] For example, in the Colorado Republican Party, statewide candidates who reach a 30% support threshold at the state convention automatically advance to the primary ballot. (Other candidates can still run in the primary by gathering signatures from registered voters instead.) In 2023, the GOP's new state chair, Dave Williams, urged the party to opt out of the state-run primary process, specifically because it is open to independent voters. Regarding potential alternatives, he told *Colorado Politics*, "It's really only limited to our imagination and funding and logistics. . . . If we wanted to, as a party, just mail every registered Republican and say, 'Hey, vote on our own ballot,' we could do that. . . . It doesn't have to be the caucus and assembly."[37] He's correct; it's the party's prerogative.

Ideas from Abroad

We can look almost anywhere in the Western world for other examples, as the United States is the only country that has a system of government-funded, popular elections to decide candidate nominations for political parties. In all other democracies, the parties administer their own processes, almost always incorporating the judgment of party leaders and almost always separate from the country's formal legal frameworks. The way each party designs and administers its own selection process reflects its distinctive values.[38]

Consider our neighbor to the north. Like our House of Representatives, Canada's Parliament is composed of legislators from single-member districts, chosen via first-past-the-post (plurality) elections. But Canadian political parties set up committees to vet potential candidates, who must first meet established criteria, such as not having a criminal record. Then each aspiring candidate must interview with the committee to demonstrate core competencies, such as being familiar with the Constitution and the party's platform. Only then will the party decide which candidates become "qualified nomination contestants."

When Canadian citizens register to join any party, they gain the opportunity to vote on the party's leadership, participate in policy conventions to help shape its platform, and take part in nomination meetings to select its candidates. In some cases, these nomination meetings take place by mail or even online (imagine that!). Notably, for both the Liberal and Conservative parties in Canada, candidates are required to win a majority of members' votes to be nominated. Both parties voluntarily use a form of instant runoffs to ensure that no one is nominated with a mere plurality of votes. The result is a rational system for presenting voters with a range of qualified, reasonable candidates from multiple parties.

There is an obvious tension between supporting open, participatory elections and allowing party leaders to influence candidate nominations. However, if the goal is producing more representative outcomes, there ought to be a role for both party insiders and everyday voters. As Rauch and La Raja point out, "When party insiders evaluate candidates, they think about appealing to overworked laborers, harried parents, struggling students, less politicized moderates, and others who do not show up on primary day—but whose support the party will need to win the general election and then to govern."[39]

We can reform partisan primaries in a way that both restores the parties' control over how they nominate their candidates and restores all Americans' control over how we elect our leaders. Doing so can go a long way toward strengthening the parties as political institutions, in addition to better serving all voters and our country. The big question, of course, is how to do so. In part III, we'll see how improving our system doesn't require a constitutional amendment or even federal legislation. It can happen state by state.

PART III

THE BETTER ALTERNATIVE

N ow that we've seen the interlocking, self-reinforcing problems caused by partisan primaries, it is time to explore options for reform, and how adoption of reform is currently playing out, from Louisiana to Alaska.

Attempts to improve or replace partisan primaries began almost as soon as they became the dominant means of choosing nominees. While the inclusion of voters in the party-nominating process made candidate selection more democratic and reduced the influence of party bosses, reformers were still agitated by how polarizing, corrupt, and dysfunctional the process and its results remained. Thus, the roots of the modern primary reform movement were planted—specifically the goal of removing parties from the primary process altogether.

Diverse experimentation with new models took place from coast to coast, at every level of government, starting in 1909. It's worth taking note of some key moments during this century of research and development. They offer more evidence that the states truly can be "laboratories of democracy," as Supreme Court Justice Louis Brandeis famously put it.

San Diego, 1909: Nonpartisan Municipal Elections

The corruption of party machines was felt most acutely at the municipal level, where party bosses had much greater control over smaller
geographic areas. In many cities, reformers advocated going beyond
adopting direct primaries and removing the influence of political parties
from the election process entirely by removing all party affiliations from
government offices—and the ballots that elected them.

San Diego was one of the first cities to toss out the party machines,
and political parties themselves, from elections, beginning in 1909. Reformers were intent on breaking the grip of the Republican machine,
led by "Boss" Charles Hardy. In the prior election in 1907, Hardy was
successful in getting his handpicked candidate, John F. Forward, elected
with just 40% of the vote in a three-way contest.

Through a city charter amendment, reformers established fully nonpartisan elections—a single primary in which all candidates would be
listed *without* party labels and in which all voters could participate. The
top two finishers would advance to the general election, ensuring that
the eventual winner had majority support. Boss Hardy, confident in his
ability to control any system, did not oppose the plan. In the 1909 election, Forward once again pulled 40% of the vote. However, that was only
enough to get him to the general election, where he lost 53% to 47%.

San Diego reformer Edgar Luce remarked at the time: "The machine
was powerless to whip their followers into line for the 'ticket.' . . . The
new system left the machine helpless and without its old weapons with
which to 'lineup' its forces. The new system therefore is a great boon to
independent good government politics."[1]

The new system caught on at the municipal level across the country.
Today forty-two of our country's fifty largest cities, from Albuquerque to
Wichita, hold nonpartisan municipal primaries.

The Rise of Ranked Choice Voting in the 1910s

As the electoral experimentation of the Progressive Era continued during the 1910s, at least eighty-eight municipalities adopted some version of what we now call ranked choice voting, which at the time was often called "preferential voting." Rather than selecting just one candidate, voters had the option of ranking all the candidates. While there were different methods of tabulating the ranked ballots, they all produced electoral outcomes that were more representative than the status quo of candidates only needing to earn a plurality of the vote in a district with a single representative.

Preferential voting was both ahead of its time and a victim of its own success. In general, cities that adopted it experienced increased minority representation. For instance, three Ohio cities (Cincinnati, Hamilton, and Toledo) all elected their first African American city council members following adoption of this reform, while a fourth, Cleveland, achieved proportional representation of African Americans on its city council for the first time. Other minority groups, including Irish-, Italian-, and Polish-Americans, also benefited from preferential systems, as did women of all backgrounds. These gains in representation led to backlash from white leaders, who had previously held nearly all local political power. They exploited racial tensions and spikes in immigration to build opposition to preferential systems and ultimately succeeded in repealing all but two of them by 1962.[2]

Ranked choice voting has recently made a comeback. As of this writing, two states and fifty-one U.S. municipalities used a ranked choice voting system in their most recent elections, while about a dozen are awaiting implementation in upcoming elections.[3]

Nebraska, 1934: Nonpartisan State Elections

The push for fully nonpartisan elections rose to the state level when Nebraska senator George Norris pushed for their inclusion in a 1934 ballot initiative to replace the state's assembly and senate with a single "unicameral" legislature.

Norris was a prominent, independent-minded Republican statesman, featured by future president John F. Kennedy as one of eight "profiles in courage" in his famous book with that title. In arguing for nonpartisan elections, Norris wrote: "[State legislators] would not be subject to the influence of political bosses and party machines. They would not be responsible to any party on a false issue, but would be responsible to their own people upon issues which have a direct bearing upon the official duties of the members of the legislature."[4]

Norris barnstormed the state throughout the spring and summer of 1934, and that November the initiative passed by a 60% to 40% margin. It did not hurt that the proposal was presented to voters alongside two others that legalized gambling on horse racing and repealed prohibition (two proposals that Norris, a straitlaced, good government reformer, strenuously opposed).

However, unlike nonpartisan elections at the municipal level, Nebraska's legislative innovation did not catch on at the state level. To this day, it remains the only state in the country with either a unicameral or nonpartisan state legislature.

Washington, 1935: The Blanket Primary

Members of the Washington State Grange, a fraternal organization that promotes the interests of farmers and rural communities, pursued a variation of Nebraska's reform in 1934.

When Washington had established its direct primary in 1907, voters had to publicly declare which party they belonged to in order to receive that party's primary ballot. (In other states, like Wisconsin, voters were given multiple ballots and could decide in private.) The Grange took exception to this practice, because it left the door open to coercion and corruption.

The Grange's leaders would have preferred a nonpartisan state government similar to the system then being debated in Nebraska, but they did not believe it would be viable as a ballot initiative in Washington. Instead, they sought to create a single, "blanket" primary ballot that featured all candidates with their party labels.[5] Voters could select, in private, any candidate they desired for each office—regardless of party affiliation. The top candidate from each party would be nominated and advance to the general election.

Fred J. Chamberlain, the chairman of the Grange's legislative committee, told a local newspaper that the measure would "end the evil of employers and politicians 'checking up' on how their subordinates voted."[6] Over 115,000 people signed the ballot petition, more than what was required to force the legislature to either adopt the proposal as written or send it to the ballot for a vote of the people. After much deliberation, the legislature adopted the measure the following year and no referendum was necessary.

Louisiana, 1975: No More Primaries

Like much of the South, Louisiana was a one-party, Democratic-dominated state after the Civil War, and this trend persisted for more than a century. Each party held closed primaries, but the GOP was so weak that Democratic primaries were the only elections that really mattered. The primaries required a majority winner, so a runoff was held if no candidate won a majority in the first round. This system came under pressure in the 1960s, as the national Democratic Party began to support civil rights, and conservative white voters began to consider Republican candidates more seriously. In 1964, the GOP took a surprisingly high 38% of the vote for governor, by nominating a pro-segregation former Democrat who had switched parties.

Four years later, the race for governor was even closer, with Democrat Edwin Edwards (who first had to win a primary that included seventeen candidates) defeating Republican David C. Treen by just 57%–43%. Edwards resented the fact that he had to get through three hard-fought

elections (primary, primary runoff, and general), while his GOP opponent was essentially handed his nomination without opposition. So the
new governor lobbied for an "open election" system that would eliminate
partisan primaries and allow all candidates who met ballot qualification
requirements to go directly to a general election. All voters, regardless of
party registration, would vote, and any candidate with a majority would
immediately win. If no one got a majority, the top two finishers would
advance to a runoff election.

Edwards argued that this would shorten and simplify the election
cycle, with two possible elections at most, not three. The Louisiana legislature enacted the open election system for state elections in 1975 and
expanded it to federal elections (excluding president) in 1978. Although
this reform was pushed by Edwards for largely self-interested reasons, it
has nonetheless had a positive impact on the state's quality of representation and policy outcomes, as we'll see in the next chapter.

Washington, 2008: The Nonpartisan Primary

Alaska and California copied Washington State's blanket primary system. Prior to 1947, the territory of Alaska held party primaries open to
all voters, until a blanket primary was adopted by referendum, with more
than 80% of Alaska voters in favor.[7] California, on the other hand, had
closed partisan primaries prior to its implementation of the blanket primary in 1998, which passed two years earlier at the ballot box with support from 60% of California voters.[8]

But in 2000 the blanket primaries in all three states came crashing
down, thanks to a 7–2 Supreme Court decision that California's system
violated a political party's First Amendment right to free association. The
blanket primary "forces political parties to associate with—to have their
nominees, and hence their positions, determined by—those who, at best,
have refused to affiliate with the party, and, at worst, have expressly affiliated with a rival," wrote Justice Antonin Scalia in the majority opinion.[9]

Advocates in Washington State quickly pushed the legislature to amend their blanket primary to a *nonpartisan* blanket primary (which I refer to simply as a "nonpartisan primary"), in which all candidates are listed on a single primary ballot with their preferred party labels, and the top two finishers advance to the general election, *regardless of party affiliation*.[10] Now the purpose of the primary was no longer to nominate a candidate from each party, but to winnow the field down to two—whether that meant one Democrat and one Republican, two Democrats, a Republican and an independent, or any other combination. This kind of primary is considered "nonpartisan" not because the candidates lack party labels, but because the primary does not serve a party nominating function.

After Washington's governor vetoed a bill to establish a nonpartisan primary, the state's voters adopted the reform by ballot initiative in 2004, following another successful petition drive led by the Washington State Grange. It was again immediately challenged in court, and implementation was put on hold until the Supreme Court, in another 7–2 opinion, upheld the law as constitutional in 2008.[11] Justice Clarence Thomas wrote in the majority opinion that, unlike the old system, the new primary does not produce party nominees and therefore does not infringe on the rights of the parties to do so.[12]

The nonpartisan primary—and the template for future primary reform—was born. Washington used the top-two nonpartisan primary for the first time in 2008. California followed suit by adopting the policy in 2010 and using it for the first time in 2012. And Alaska established a top-four nonpartisan primary in 2020, as we'll explore in chapter 7.

The history of election reform is still being written.

SIX

THE PRIMARY SOLUTION

The most powerful solution to the Primary Problem is, quite simply, to abolish partisan primaries. As well-intentioned as they were during the Progressive Era and as harmless as they may have been throughout the twentieth century, they have now become a clear and present danger to our democracy. It's time for the next evolutionary phase of our election system, continuing the tradition of periodic improvement since the Founding.

The long arc of election reform has always bent toward democratization—toward expanding the definitions of who can vote and the methods of how they can vote. What could be more democratizing today than taking the power to decide who represents us out of the hands of the 8% who decide primaries and putting it into the hands of a majority of all voters?

Abolishing partisan primaries will ensure that candidates have to earn majority support from all of their constituents, beyond relying on the most passionate voters in their party. It will give all voters an equal voice and level the playing field for all candidates, regardless of party affiliation. Most important, it will provide greater accountability and better incentives for our leaders by rewarding, rather than punishing, them for doing what we elected them to do.

There are several options to replace partisan primaries. All potential reforms come with trade-offs, including between political viability and policy impact, just like other matters of public policy. Ask an environmentalist the best ways to end carbon-based energy consumption, or a fiscal hawk the best way to eliminate our budget deficit, or a healthcare advocate the best way to minimize the number of uninsured. There is no silver bullet. But that's okay, because the states can still serve as laboratories of democracy.

To show the potential power of such reforms, let's start in Louisiana, the first and so far only state that has abandoned primaries altogether, beginning in 1975.

HOW LOUISIANA EXPANDED MEDICAID

Louisiana and Mississippi share a lot in common, beginning with a border. They have the two highest poverty rates of any state in the country (about 19%).[1] They have roughly the same demographics, with close to a third of their populations being Black.[2] They vote similarly for presidential candidates, with Joe Biden winning about 40% of the vote in both states in 2020.[3] They both hold statewide elections off-cycle, in odd-numbered years.

But they have very different election systems. Mississippi holds open partisan primaries; voters can choose whichever primary they prefer to participate in, without needing to be registered to that party. On the other hand, beginning in 1975, Louisiana abolished partisan primaries and implemented its two-round, "open elections" system. The state holds a general election in which all candidates are listed on the same ballot with their party label. All voters can participate, regardless of party affiliation. A candidate who wins a majority of the vote (i.e., one vote more than 50% of total votes cast) is elected. If no candidate wins a majority, a runoff election follows weeks later between the top two candidates.

In 2015, these different systems led to radically different election outcomes and governing incentives, which, in turn, led to radically different policy outcomes—specifically on healthcare and the question of whether to expand Medicaid to hundreds of thousands of uninsured people under the Affordable Care Act. This makes Louisiana a perfect case study of the impact of primary reform, with a natural control group next door.

A Lawyer, an Ob-gyn, and a Truck Driver Walk into a Primary

In 2015, incumbent Mississippi Republican governor Phil Bryant saw an easy path to reelection. Nonetheless, three Democrats sought to defy the electoral odds and tossed their hats in the ring: an attorney, an ob-gyn, and a truck driver. (That sounds like the setup for a joke, but it's just Democratic politics in Mississippi.) The attorney, Vicki Slater, had a staff of a half dozen and spent $230,000 on her campaign.[4] The ob-gyn, an Air Force veteran named Valerie Short, campaigned across the state on an even more modest budget of $50,000.[5] And the truck driver, Robert Gray, raised just enough to pay the $300 filing fee to get on the ballot. In fact, he didn't even bother to tell anyone he was running, let alone do any campaigning. When Gray's mom saw her son's name on the ballot, she called her daughter to remark on the perceived coincidence: "I voted for him because he has the same name."[6]

So did another 152,086 Democratic primary voters, giving Gray the nomination. "Mr. Gray, now Mississippi's Democratic nominee for governor, gave some interviews and then set off with a truck full of sweet potatoes for a potato chip factory in Pennsylvania," reported the *New York Times* on this strange upset.[7] Did he win because his name was listed first on the ballot? Or because he was the only man running in a state that has never elected a woman governor? Or because voters knew it didn't matter, so they picked a name at random? I'd bet on all of the above.

In any event, Robert Gray lost the general election in a landslide, with just 32% of the vote.[8]

A Moderate Democrat Prevails in a Red State

Meanwhile, on the Louisiana side of the border, incumbent Republican governor Bobby Jindal was term-limited and running for president, and both parties saw several serious candidates running to replace him. Republican contenders included the lieutenant governor, a public service commissioner, and a sitting U.S. senator, David Vitter. Democratic hopefuls included an attorney, an Army veteran turned entrepreneur, and the state's House minority leader, John Bel Edwards. Three independent candidates joined as well.

Edwards, though the strongest Democrat, was only polling in single digits early in the race. Some party leaders encouraged him to run for attorney general instead, since that office seemed more winnable.[9] Not a single Deep South state had elected a Democrat as governor in the previous dozen years. Senator Vitter was the clear favorite, with millions already in his war chest and the support of the state's GOP establishment. But Edwards stayed in the governor's race, positioning himself as a pro-gun, pro-life moderate—a breed of Democrat now unheard of outside of Louisiana. He ran on a platform of "compassion and common sense" and sought to expand social services for the state, from education to healthcare.[10]

If Edwards's biggest hurdle was one of partisanship, Vitter's was one of prostitution (no, not a typo). He had been exposed in 2007 as a client of Deborah Jeane Palfrey, aka the "D.C. Madam," who ran a high-end escort service. Vitter had admitted to his "very serious sin" and apologized, with his wife standing faithfully next to him.[11] He was reelected to the Senate in 2010, but the issue never fully went away.

None of the nine gubernatorial candidates earned an outright majority in the general election, so Edwards (40%) and Vitter (23%) advanced to the runoff. In a move that infuriated national Republicans, fourth-place finisher Jay Dardenne, the Republican lieutenant governor, crossed party lines to endorse Edwards, citing his ability to unite the state: "I think it is fair to my supporters who are Republicans, Democrats, and

Independents, to know what I was going to do when I went into the voting booth."[12]

The runoff became intensely negative. Vitter's campaign attacked Edwards as a fake moderate who actually supported unpopular liberal politicians like Barack Obama and Hillary Clinton. And Edwards's campaign discovered that one of Vitter's calls to the D.C. Madam happened the same day that Vitter missed a Senate vote honoring twenty-eight American soldiers who'd been killed by an Iraqi missile. A brutal TV ad accused Vitter of putting "prostitutes over patriots."[13]

Edwards, though significantly outspent, ultimately prevailed with 56% of the vote in the runoff election.[14]

Primary Reform Leads to Medicaid Expansion

Medicaid was a hot-button issue because the Affordable Care Act (ACA) offered states a big incentive to expand the program's eligibility to individuals and families with annual incomes up to 138% of the federal poverty line. (In 2022, up to $38,295 for a family of four.)[15] The federal government would pay for 100% of the expansion for the first three years, and then 90% thereafter. The goal was to get more healthcare to the working poor, who were too young for Medicare and too poor to buy insurance on the ACA exchanges, but not destitute enough to meet the state's Medicaid requirements.

After the Supreme Court ruled that states couldn't be forced to accept the Medicaid expansion money, many Republican governors strenuously opposed participating in President Obama's signature domestic policy achievement. These included Louisiana's Bobby Jindal, who argued that expansion would still cost the state $1.7 billion over ten years, and would incentivize an estimated 171,000 people to give up their existing private insurance. "We should measure success by reducing the number of people on public assistance," Jindal wrote, burnishing his conservative credentials ahead of a Republican presidential primary. "Every dollar we refuse to spend on Medicaid expansion is one dollar less that we have to borrow from China."[16]

But Louisiana residents saw the issue differently in 2015. An overwhelming 72% favored expansion, including 51% of Republicans.[17] "From the very first day that I announced I was running, I championed the Medicaid expansion," Edwards told me. "That message really did resonate with the people of Louisiana. And none of the Republicans running took a contrary position to that. Some of them weren't as committed as I was, but they were certainly open to it."[18] Vitter said he was not opposed to the idea and kept the door open.[19] Republicans in the legislature even passed legislation that would help clear the way for potential expansion.[20]

On his second day in office, Edwards signed an executive order that made Louisiana the first (and, to date, only) state in the Deep South to receive the ACA's Medicaid expansion funding.[21] He acted alone and immediately because of the strong mandate he had from voters and to ensure those voters did not have to wait until the following year's enrollment period; there was no backlash in the legislature. The impact was dramatic: within the first year, 433,000 residents gained coverage through Medicaid expansion, cutting the uninsured rate among adults in half from 23% to 11%.[22] The results were quantifiable, including 139,000 more breast cancer screenings; 44,000 more people getting diagnosis and treatment for diabetes; and 193,000 getting access to outpatient mental health services.[23]

In the 2019 gubernatorial election, Edwards's two main Republican challengers could only criticize the implementation of the expansion rather than the decision (now even more popular) to accept the federal money.[24] But that critique didn't hurt Edwards; he became the first Democratic Louisiana governor to win a second term since 1975.

"If Other States Can Do It, Why Can't We?"

Good policy turned out to be good politics in Louisiana—precisely because there was no partisan primary to distort the will of the majority. When Medicaid expansion has been on the ballot in six red states, voters have adopted it every time.[25] Yet Louisiana remains the only Deep South state that has done so through an elected leader.

The contrast with Mississippi is especially illuminating. After coasting to reelection against the truck driver, Governor Bryant maintained his staunch opposition to Medicaid expansion. So has Bryant's successor, Tate Reeves, who was elected in 2019. Reeves spoke about the issue with the cockiness of a politician who only had to please his own party's primary voters: "I am opposed to Obamacare expansion in Mississippi. I am opposed to Obamacare expansion in Mississippi. I am opposed to Obamacare expansion in Mississippi. I don't know how many ways I can explain this to y'all."[26]

While Reeves casually declined $2 billion in federal funds, more than 100,000 Mississippians who would have qualified under Medicaid expansion remained without any realistic pathway to health insurance.[27] A 2023 poll found that 80% of residents, including 70% of Republicans, favored expansion. One Republican woman told a local newspaper, "I watched my son suffer because I couldn't afford medical care for him. . . . He's now 35, and I'm still watching him suffer because he's one of the working poor. There's got to be something done. If other states can do it, why can't we?"[28]

The Impact of Louisiana's Open Primary

The Louisiana election system enables greater competition between the parties, even in a politically lopsided state, by providing a pathway for candidates to appeal to a greater cross section of voters. In this case, it allowed a moderate Democrat to hold socially conservative views on guns and abortion and campaign on popular issues like Medicaid expansion. That blend of positions made all the difference. (Yes, Vitter was somewhat hurt by his personal scandal, but he likely would have defeated any Democrat more progressive than Edwards.) "The fact that we don't have party primaries allows people to run for office at the outset by trying to appeal to the broadest spectrum of the electorate," Edwards told me. "Everybody else has to run towards the middle and it helps us to govern . . . I'm not sure I would choose to run for governor in 2015 if I would have had to go through a party primary."[29]

Are the different policy outcomes between the two states simply the result of them electing governors of different parties? I think it's much more the result of the incentives created by their respective election systems. Even if Edwards had lost to Vitter in 2015, there's a decent chance the Republicans would have expanded Medicaid anyway, rather than risk angering a majority of the general electorate. The impact of Louisiana's political incentives was also evident on other issues. Edwards and the supermajority Republican legislature found common ground in passing criminal justice reform (incarcerations are down) and budget reform that included both a new sales tax and a higher earned income tax credit (helping the state plug a $700 million budget deficit).[30] Throughout his two terms, the legislature overrode only one of the governor's vetoes.

Another unique feature of Louisiana's system is that its legislature has committees that the minority party is able to chair. With the exception of Alaska, no other state legislature regularly has this feature. In addition, in 2020, the Republican House speaker was elected with a bipartisan majority over a more divisive opponent.[31] "There's an element of bipartisanship that is baked into the structure," said Edwards, who previously served as the Democratic minority leader in the state house. "There's no rule that says it has to be that way. It is that way by tradition and by custom. But if we were to go back to party primaries, I'm certain that that custom goes away the very next election."[32]

Louisiana's lieutenant governor, Billy Nungesser, is a committed Republican; he even pulls around a life-size replica of a giant elephant on a trailer when he campaigns around the state. (The elephant was originally crafted by Nungesser's father, who helped build the Republican Party in Louisiana.) Nungesser was elected in the same election as Edwards in 2015. "I committed to our governor that I wouldn't talk bad about him in office. I wouldn't run against him. We work together for the greater good of Louisiana," he told me. When some Republicans in the legislature attempted to return Louisiana to a closed primary system in 2021, Nungesser strongly opposed it. "I believe in the open primary. You've got to speak more to the greater good of your state. In a closed primary, everybody tries to out-Trump each other and say stuff they don't even believe just to win the election."[33]

The causality between electoral processes, governing incentives, and policy outcomes can be difficult if not impossible to prove, yet there are some promising data points. One study examined 180 state-level public policies between 2001 and 2010, and found Louisiana to be the fourth-most innovative state as an early adopter of new reforms.[34] Another study, of state legislators' voting patterns, found Louisiana to be the second *least* polarized state in the country over the past two decades. And one of its senators, Bill Cassidy, was ranked as the tenth most bipartisan in the U.S. Senate.[35]

Debates about electoral system design can feel irrelevant to the "real issues" people care about. However, at least when it comes to healthcare outcomes for those living in poverty in the Deep South, the ways we choose our leaders—and the difference between an election that can be hijacked by small factions and one that serves the majority of voters— can literally mean the difference between life and death.

As my Unite America colleague Richard Barton asks in a report he authored on the topic, "If Louisiana's election system can produce such measurable benefits in a state that has experienced more poverty and adversity than any other in recent decades, what can an improved electoral system without partisan primaries accomplish in other states?"[36]

A SPECTRUM OF POLICY SOLUTIONS

The Louisiana model is just one possible solution to the Primary Problem. As we consider the pros and cons of various options, none of them perfect, let me posit two key principles that any new system should uphold:

- *All* eligible voters should have the freedom to vote for *any* candidate in *every* election, regardless of party.
- A candidate must earn a *majority* of the vote in order to win an election.

A 2023 nationally representative survey of one thousand voters, conducted by Citizen Data and commissioned by Unite America, found overwhelming support for these two principles at 90% and 75%, respectively. In fact, they are so common sense that 70% of respondents wrongly assumed that our election system already guarantees them. In fact, both principles are only true for all state and federal contests in just four states: Louisiana, Washington, California, and Alaska. These states use slightly different types of election systems, but their commonality is that none of them have partisan primaries.

Abolishing partisan primaries has five main benefits:

1. *All voters' voices will be heard.* Every voter can participate in every election, regardless of their party affiliation. No longer will over 14 million independents be locked out of the primary process. No longer will members of a minority party be disenfranchised from the only election of consequence in their district and state. The right to vote will become a right to cast a vote that *truly matters.*

2. *Elections will be decided by a majority of voters, not as few as 8%.* Candidates will have to secure a majority of the vote in the general election to win, which means that election outcomes will better represent the will of the people. No longer will the majority party's primary effectively decide the election in a safe district or state. No longer will a candidate be able to win with just a plurality. The majority will rule.

3. *Elections will produce less ideologically extreme outcomes.* Candidates will immediately be incentivized to build support from across the political spectrum to attract the widest possible

coalition. The playing field will be more level for independent and third-party candidates. No longer can candidates simply rely on pandering to their base to win. No longer will narrow interest groups find it so easy to force candidates to take unpopular positions. Extremism will come with a cost, and pragmatism with a reward.

4. *Incumbents will face all voters without fear of being primaried.* Incumbent officials will need to represent and be responsive to all of their constituents in order to get reelected. No longer will they face significant risk that a more extreme primary challenger will block them from the general election. "Primary" would return to being a noun, not a verb.

5. *The positive consequences will compound.* A more representative process will lead to more leaders running for office who once thought they had no chance. More choices and competition will then lead to more voters participating in elections. Over time, a self-reinforcing cycle of division will break.

Measuring the Impact of Primary Reform

One way to measure the severity of the Primary Problem and the impact of nonpartisan primaries is to look at how many voters cast "deciding ballots" in a given election. The definition of a deciding ballot is when voters' specific preferences, rather than just the partisan composition of the electorate, determine the outcome of an election. For example, I could cast a deciding ballot by voting in a competitive general election (defined as one decided by fewer than 10 percentage points) or by voting in the dominant party's primary in a district or state without a competitive general election. However, as we've seen, many voters have no such option.

At the state house level in 2022, only 13% of eligible voters nationally cast deciding ballots—including just 3.4% in Oklahoma and

6.2% in Delaware, according to analysis by Unite America. Voters in the four states that have abolished partisan primaries for all state and federal elections cast, on average, 2.5 times as many deciding ballots as voters in states with partisan primaries. All four states were among the top ten. Louisiana was number three (25.2%) and Alaska was number one (35%).

We should care not only about the right to cast a ballot but also whether our ballots truly matter. Our votes matter when candidates are forced to reckon with what we believe and what we want them to do. Reforming partisan primaries makes our elections more competitive and therefore gives more power to all voters.

Designing the Primary Solution

There is no one-size-fits-all approach to solving the Primary Problem. Designing an election system to replace partisan primaries boils down to a few major questions:

- What role, if any, should parties play in the election process?
- Should there still be a primary election to winnow down the number of candidates?
- If there's a primary, how many candidates should continue to the general election?
- What mechanism will ensure that the ultimate winner earns majority support, not just a plurality?

Regardless of what specific form a solution may take, we must not let anyone's definition of perfect become the enemy of the good. The most important step is abolishing partisan primaries. Now that we know the goals and desired outcomes, let's dive into the three major possible paths toward the Primary Solution, and the variations among them.

PATH 1: THE NONPARTISAN PRIMARY

The most common way that states have abolished party primaries so far is by replacing them with nonpartisan primaries, often referred to as "blanket primaries" or "jungle primaries" (a derisive term that falsely implies chaos).

The rationale is straightforward: the main purpose of any election process that's run by the government and funded by taxpayers should be to determine which candidate best represents the will of the overall electorate. As a preliminary round of voting, a primary can be useful in winnowing a potentially large field of candidates down to just a few for the general election. To the extent that political parties, as private organizations, want to recruit, support, and endorse (or "nominate") candidates, they are welcome to do so through some other process that they can operate and fund. But publicly funded elections should serve the people at large rather than just the parties.

In this scenario, all voters participate in a single primary where all candidates are listed on the ballot with their self-identified party affiliation. Voters select their preferred candidates, and then the top finishers advance to the general election, where whoever earns majority support wins. The most common variations of this path are top-two, top-four, and top-five nonpartisan primaries.

Top-Two Nonpartisan Primaries

The top-two primary has been around longest and is the most widely used alternative to partisan primaries, at both the municipal and state level. California and Washington State have both used this system for more than a decade. There have been several studies of its impact in both states, so we have evidence that it achieves virtually all of the major upsides of eliminating partisan primaries.

First, voter turnout is higher. A 2020 study found that top-two primaries were responsible for a six-percentage-point increase in turnout compared to partisan primaries, after controlling for other variables that can affect turnout.[37] Voter participation in general elections in safe districts can also be more meaningful under a top-two system. In districts that skew heavily in favor of one party, it's possible that two candidates from the same party will advance to the general election. This is a feature of Top Two, as it ensures that the general election, which has much higher voter participation than primaries, determines who is elected.

Second, less extreme candidates win. A USC study of elections from 2003 to 2018 found that among new members of Congress, those elected via nonpartisan primaries are more than 18 percentage points less extreme than those elected under closed partisan primaries, based on an analysis of their voting records.[38] Once again, Top Two had its greatest impact on safe seats that would virtually always elect a Democrat or Republican, by sending two candidates from the majority party to the final round. This gives all voters the power to decide *what kind* of Democrat or Republican will represent them, incentivizing both candidates to reach beyond their partisan base.

For example, when a seat opened up in 2020 in Washington's solidly Democratic 10th Congressional District, nineteen candidates ran in the nonpartisan primary. Two Democrats, Marilyn Strickland, the former mayor of Tacoma, and Beth Doglio, a state representative, advanced to the general election. Strickland was seen as a moderate who had previously served as president of the Seattle Metropolitan Chamber of Commerce,[39] while Doglio was endorsed by nationally prominent progressives such as Bernie Sanders, Pramila Jayapal, and Jamaal Bowman.[40] In the general election, Strickland defeated Doglio, 49% to 36% (with 15% of voters writing in someone else). While Republican voters might have preferred to support a Republican in the general election, they at least got to have a voice in what type of Democrat would represent their deep blue district.

Another example occurred in 2014, a year when Tea Party–aligned candidates dominated GOP primaries. After a seat opened up in Washington's solidly Republican 4th Congressional District, twelve candidates entered the nonpartisan primary. Tea Party favorite Clint Didier, who had no political experience, received the most votes in the primary,[41] while Dan Newhouse, a moderate Republican who had previously been nominated by a Democrat to be the head of the state's Department of Agriculture, came in second.[42] It's very likely that Didier would have defeated Newhouse in a traditional Republican primary, and then coasted to Congress against any Democratic opponent. But Newhouse won the 2014 general election after receiving significant support from Democratic and independent voters.

Newhouse went on to be one of only two House Republicans (along with David Valadao of California) who voted to impeach President Trump in 2021, ran for reelection, and survived his 2022 primary. Both were from states with top-two primaries.

Third, the system produces better results. "Incumbents who know they have to worry about more than just their own party base wind up being more innovative and willing to strike legislative compromise," wrote former California governor Arnold Schwarzenegger (R) and California representative Ro Khanna (D) in a joint *Washington Post* op-ed in 2018.[43] Since Top Two passed, Californians' approval of their state government has soared twenty points.[44]

On the other hand, a top-two system has some meaningful limitations. The biggest is that even nonpartisan primaries inevitably have lower turnout than general elections, so relatively fewer voters are responsible for winnowing down a large field to just two candidates. Vote-splitting during a plurality election may also skew outcomes. For instance, imagine a scenario where two Democrats win the top two slots in a solidly red district, because a very large Republican field splits the GOP primary vote into too many slivers. This is an unlikely outcome (it happened only once in 459 legislative elections held from 2012 to 2016 in California),[45] but it might undermine confidence in the system.

The more common outcome of a top-two primary is one Democrat and one Republican. By one tally in California, this occurs about five out of every six elections, in part because the parties limit internal competition to help ensure that at least one member of their party advances to the general election.[46] Even though the surviving candidates may be less ideologically extreme than under a partisan primary system, many general elections remain Democrat-versus-Republican contests and uncompetitive in most districts. Ultimately, as political scientist Jesse Crosson concluded, "The key to the system's effectiveness lies in reformers' ability to find ways to encourage more same-party competition [in the general election]."[47]

Top-Four Nonpartisan Primaries with an Instant Runoff

The top-four primary was specifically designed to improve upon the top-two model. Sending four candidates to the general election ensures that the election with the highest turnout and most representative electorate decides the ultimate outcome. It also increases the odds that general election voters will have choices from both major parties as well as some independent or minor party candidates. That will add more diverse perspectives to the campaign trail.

Unlike a traditional runoff, where voters must come back to the polls another day if no candidate receives a majority, an instant runoff uses ranked choice voting to avoid the cost and effort of holding a second election. Voters mark their second, third, and fourth choices during the general election. The ballots are tabulated so that the candidate with the least support is eliminated, and voters who supported that candidate have their second preference counted. This process repeats until someone earns a majority of the vote.

Perhaps the biggest advantage of Top Four over Top Two: more same-party competition in the general election. Imagine a contest in a light blue district between two Democrats, a Republican, and an independent. Neither Democratic candidate would be able to win by running a scorched-earth campaign attacking the Republican, as in a typical two-way race. Both Democrats would instead have an incentive to appeal to voters who might support the Republican or the independent, but whose second choice is up for grabs.

FIGURE 12:

How an Instant Runoff Works

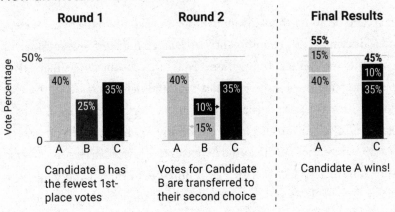

Round 1	Round 2	Final Results

Candidate B has the fewest 1st-place votes

Votes for Candidate B are transferred to their second choice

Candidate A wins!

As an added benefit of the top-four system, instant runoff elections eliminate the so-called "spoiler effect" of independent and third-party candidates. Voters can honestly vote for their most preferred candidate without worrying about "taking away" a vote from their second-preferred candidate and unintentionally helping to elect their least-preferred candidate. Both Democrats and Republicans have lost elections because of voters who supported independent, Green, or Libertarian candidates in close elections. Further, very few third-party or independent candidates win elections, or run in the first place, because voters fear "spoiling" the election between a Republican and a Democrat.

As the nonpartisan reform group FairVote noted in proposing Top Four in 2013, "By appealing to the goals of both supporters and critics of Top Two, we expect Top Four to be a serious option for future reform in some states currently using partisan primaries, as well as a simple way to improve elections in states currently using Top Two."[48] Alaska became the first state to adopt a top-four primary system in 2020 and demonstrate the true power of primary reform, as we'll see in detail in chapter 7.

Final-Five Voting

What could be better than advancing four candidates to the general election? Katherine Gehl, coauthor of *The Politics Industry* and founder of the Institute for Political Innovation, argues that the ideal number is five, in part to create more opportunities for candidates outside of the two major parties. The idea is that more competition is better, as long as it doesn't cause confusion or place a prohibitively large burden on voters. "Creating space for a fifth candidate ensures a lower barrier for diverse startup candidates," Gehl writes. "Not only might these candidates present new and exciting policy innovations, but their presence challenges the duopoly, preventing the major parties from evading accountability."[49]

Is advancing five candidates to the general election meaningfully better than four in producing the most representative outcomes and ideal incentives? Potentially at the margins. On the other hand, advancing more candidates may diminish the utility of a winnowing primary in the first place, especially in races with five or fewer total candidates—which includes over 95% of state legislative races.

Gehl branded this system as "Final-Five Voting" (FFV) and inspired reformers in Nevada to promote it as a ballot initiative in 2020. It passed with 53% support, despite a $1 million campaign by the Democratic Party machine to try to keep it off the ballot. Over 600,000 Nevadans are prohibited from voting in the state's closed partisan primaries. The initiative must pass again in 2024 in order to take effect, per Nevada's normal process for enacting amendments to their state constitution.

Though Gehl is a passionate advocate of FFV, she often reminds audiences that she is under no illusion that the result will be some kind of utopia. "Democracy is messy and hard. What we have now is messy, hard, and we have bad results to show for all that. With FFV, we'll have a democracy that is messy, hard, and with some good results to show for it," she says.[50]

PATH 2: NO PRIMARY ELECTIONS, WITH GENERAL ELECTION RUNOFFS

If replacing partisan primaries with nonpartisan primaries is one broad path for solving the primary problem, another is simply eliminating primaries altogether. That was Louisiana's pioneering idea in 1975, and we've already seen some of the positive results of its nearly half-century experiment. It's also the law for special elections to fill vacancies for certain offices in several southern states like Mississippi and Georgia.

One advantage of Louisiana's no-primary system is that it's simple and straightforward for voters. They choose their favorite candidate in the general election, from among however many have met eligibility requirements, with party affiliations next to every name. No party or independent is shut out from participating. If one candidate earns majority support, the election is over. If not, the top two candidates go head-to-head in a runoff election, about five weeks later. There's no need to rank your second-, third-, fourth-, or fifth-favorite candidates.

The obvious disadvantage of this system, however, is that runoff elections typically see much lower voter turnout. Media and social media coverage of elections usually drops off sharply after Election Day, and many voters lose interest. Research by FairVote on federal primary runoffs found that the median decline in turnout was 40%.[51] For instance, in 2016, a Democrat vs. Republican runoff for the House seat in Louisiana's 4th district experienced a 53% decline. In 2020, a Republican vs. Republican House runoff for the state's 5th district saw an even more dramatic turnout decline of nearly 75%.[52]

Exceptions include rare cases when a runoff has national implications—such as the Senate runoffs in Georgia in 2020 and 2022, which helped determine partisan control of that chamber. But even then, Georgia's impressive runoff turnout was still about 10% lower than the preceding general elections.

PATH 3: MAJORITY WINNER VOTING

Given what we know about the existing systems and their tradeoffs, if I could wave a magic wand, I'd implement what I call a Majority Winner voting system, a modest modification of several systems already in place today. It would combine the benefits of Louisiana's reduction of cost and complexity with the benefits of Alaska's improvement of competition and representation, while creating space for political parties to reclaim their own nominating processes. There is a simple way to understand this system: a single election with a backup selection.

Single Election: No Primary and New Ways of Candidate Nomination and Ballot Access

1. Under Majority Winner, like in Louisiana, there would be no government-funded primary, returning the important function of candidate nomination from the government to the political parties, by whichever means they choose. Importantly, this also reduces the length of elections and costs of both election administration and political campaigning by forgoing a multi-winner primary.

2. The Majority Winner ballot (see figure 13) would display not only the self-declared party affiliation of the candidate, but also a list of one or more qualified parties that have nominated the candidate—again, through whichever process each party prefers. This would inherently enable "fusion voting" by which one or more parties could nominate the same candidate, providing an explicit means of coalition-building, along with an on-ramp for new party formation.

3. One might fear that without a primary, general election ballots may become too cluttered and hamper a voter's ability to cast an informed vote. There is an easy solution that does not require holding an entire second election: states can leverage

ballot access requirements to screen out unserious candidates. For example, a state could reserve a limited number of slots in the general election based on the number of petition signatures, individual in-state small contributions, or some combination of both obtained by a particular deadline. (And there's no reason official signatures could not be collected online; in fact, during COVID, Massachusetts permitted secure and verified online signature gathering.)[53] In many ways, such a process is a better and fairer way to winnow down a large field than a primary election, which often is determined by name identification. While some candidates can afford to purchase name identification through expensive paid media, all candidates have the ability to organize grassroots signature drives and small donations.

Backup Selection: A General Election with a First and Second Preference

1. Under this system, the general election would ensure a majority winner by allowing voters to express more than just one preference and conducting an instant runoff. However, rather than ranking all of the candidates on their ballot like they would under traditional ranked choice voting, they'd simply be asked to indicate their preferred candidate plus one backup vote.

2. We can expect this system to produce a majority winner on the first round of tabulation most of the time, at least in districts and states that are not very competitive between both parties, without even needing to consider the backup votes. For example, across forty-three elections for governor, Senate, and House in Louisiana between 2011 and 2022, only ten went to runoffs, and half of those were ultimately won by the top finisher in the first round.

3. If no one wins an outright majority, everyone other than the top two finishers is eliminated. Then a single, second round of

tabulation counts any backup choices that went to the top two candidates, to determine the winner. (This is similar to a voting system known as the Supplementary Vote, which has been used to elect offices from the president of Sri Lanka to the mayor of London.)

4. Allowing a single backup vote to decide between the top two finishers captures the vast majority of the benefits of a fully ranked ballot, while reducing complexity in ballot design and the burden on voters. Asking less of voters is not to imply that they may be dumb or lazy, but that they are normal people whose lives do not revolve around politics and elections. It's easier to choose a favorite plus a backup than to rank four or five candidates in multiple races on one's ballot. Further, in 94% of all instant runoff races in the U.S. through 2022, the candidate who had the most first-preference votes ultimately prevailed in the election. That figure approaches 98% when considering first- and second-place finishers.[54] In other words, the chances of an election being won by a candidate that most voters would not have ranked first or second is very small, making it less necessary to capture preferences beyond a backup choice.

FIGURE 13:

Sample Ballot: Majority Winner Voting
U.S. Senate

Instructions: Select one candidate to vote for and, optionally, select a different candidate for your backup vote. If no candidate earns a majority of votes, all candidates will be eliminated except the top two finishers, and backup votes for those eliminated candidates will instead be counted.

Name	Party Nomination(s)	Your Vote (Vote for one)	Backup Vote (Vote for one different candidate)
Eliza Ho Democrat		O	O
Mariam Vaughn Democrat	Democratic Party Green Party	O	O
Jeffrey Carson Libertarian	Libertarian Party	●	O
Chelsea Nunnenkamp Republican	Republican Party	O	●
Lindsey Williams Drath Independent	Forward Party	O	O
Paul Jones Independent		O	O

Relative Advantages of Majority Winner

Overall, Majority Winner elections improve upon the existing models of primary reform in the following ways:

- Advantages over California/Washington (Top Two): Majority Winner prevents vote-splitting in a low-turnout primary from potentially producing two unrepresentative general election candidates.
- Advantages over Louisiana (general with runoff): Majority Winner eliminates the necessity of a runoff election.
- Advantages over Alaska (Top Four or Five): Majority Winner

imposes less cost and complexity on both election administrators and voters alike.

Again, no system is perfect. Majority Winner elections ask voters to give up primaries they've known their entire lives, and perhaps liked if they're enthusiastic party members. It asks them to trust a slightly new way of casting a ballot. On the whole, however, I believe Majority Winner would be the most elegant solution to the Primary Problem—balancing the necessary trade-offs between simplicity, viability, and impact while creating incentives for innovation around candidate nomination and ballot access that could further improve the election process.

Still, I am not a purist about pushing for Majority Winner. Other options we've looked at, including top-two, top-four, and top-five nonpartisan primaries, have already demonstrated an ability to win popular support and to make elections more representative of the will of the broader electorate. The differences among such options are much less important than what they share in common: abolishing partisan primaries. Having multiple policy options and some debate about them is not a weakness of a movement, but a strength. It's also up to leaders in each state to decide what works best for their state.

"It's not about getting everybody to agree. It's about having sufficient resiliency to incorporate a variety of perspectives and positions in a cohesive movement," advises John Opdycke, the founder of Open Primaries. "We need people that are totally grounded in their state, and that their interest in this issue is their state."[55]

•   •   •

Now that we've explored various options for solving the Primary Problem, let's dig deeply into one state where primary reform has become a reality over the past few years, with dramatic consequences at both the state and national levels. Alaska is where we can answer many pressing questions about the real-world impact of primary reform on improving both representation and governance.

SEVEN

ALASKA'S PROOF OF CONCEPT

laska is a unique state in just about every respect. The U.S. acquired the Last Frontier in 1867 for a mere $7.2 million (still a huge bargain at $160 million in today's dollars), and it became the forty-ninth state in 1959. Twice the size of Texas, it is by far the largest state in the country—big enough to be home to about 130 volcanoes and 3 million lakes. It's so far north that some areas of the state experience near-total sunlight or darkness for parts of the year. What Alaska lacks in population (under 1 million), it makes up for in diversity; the state is home to over two hundred federally recognized Native tribes.[1]

Alaska's politics is just as unique, as I learned firsthand when I visited for the first time in the summer of 2017, to meet Governor Bill Walker and his wife, Donna. The state capital of Juneau is home to just 31,000 people and is accessible only by plane or boat. I arrived at the governor's mansion fifteen minutes before my appointment, figuring I would need time to get through security. I walked up to the door and knocked. No one answered, so I knocked again. Governor Walker himself opened the door, with a glass of wine in hand. There wasn't a staff member in sight.

Walker was the country's only independent governor and had as-sembled a bipartisan cabinet. "We are not Democrats or Republicans, we are *Alaskans*—who are committed to doing whatever is in the best interest of Alaska," he told me.[2] At the time, Unite America's efforts were focused on electing independent candidates to office. So we spent an hour discussing how his model of governance could help inspire a move-ment across the country.

Walker is the opposite of a born politician. At age twelve, he became a janitor to help his family recover from a devastating earthquake in 1964.[3] He later became a carpenter for his family's construction business to put himself through college, eventually becoming an attorney.[4] At age twenty-seven, in 1979, he became mayor of his hometown, Valdez. He returned to politics in 2010 when he ran for governor—and the parti-san process would eventually convert him into a passionate advocate for election reform.

"There's Something Wrong with the System"

"I experienced political discrimination when I ran in a closed Republi-can primary, and it changed me," Walker later recounted in a documen-tary interview about Alaska's voting system.[5] "It just didn't feel right that so many of my supporters could not vote for me because they were not registered as a Republican. Some of them came back to my office literally in tears and said, 'We couldn't vote for you, there's something wrong with the system.'" In a candidate debate, he was asked whether he would up-hold every plank in the GOP platform if elected. Unaware of everything he'd be agreeing to, he said no and was subsequently attacked as a RINO. "I didn't even know what I didn't know. I thought a rhino was something you saw in a zoo." He lost the primary, then left the party.

In 2014, he ran again against Republican incumbent Sean Parnell—this time, as an independent. By September, it became clear that the three-way contest would reelect Parnell by splitting his Democratic and independent opposition. In a Hail Mary pass, Walker and the Democratic nominee, Byron Mallott, dropped their respective running mates and fused their campaigns as a "unity ticket." Alaska voters, a *majority* of whom were independent, loved it. Walker and Mallott won the election. Then came the hard part: governing.

As a result of falling oil prices, the state lost 80% of income from its oil and gas production tax and Walker faced a daunting $4 billion short-fall in revenue.[6] Moreover, the state's permanent fund—a giant endow-ment funded by a portion of oil revenues that pays an annual dividend to each resident—was on a path toward insolvency. Walker was prepared to grab the third rail of Alaskan politics to make necessary cuts to both the budget and dividend to keep the state afloat. "I ran to do the job, not keep the job," Walker liked to say.

He soon learned that the opposite was true of many state legislators. As Scott Kendall, Walker's chief of staff, told me: "When we were trying to forge some bipartisan compromises, there were legislators who were quite candid in saying that's the right thing to do, but nevertheless, I'm not going to do it because I won't survive my next primary."[7] Without legislative con-sensus, Walker instead used his veto to slash $1.29 billion in spending and to cut the dividend roughly in half to $1,000.[8] This was highly unpopular.

When Walker ran for reelection in 2018, he was challenged by oppo-nents from both major parties, who made his budget decisions a primary issue. Unite America supported Walker that year, along with four other independent candidates across the country: gubernatorial candidates Greg Orman (Kansas) and Terry Hayes (Maine) and U.S. Senate candi-dates Neal Simon (Maryland) and Craig O'Dear (Missouri). In the spring, we organized a nationwide tour with the group beginning at the National Press Club in Washington, D.C., and continuing to events in New York, Los Angeles, and Seattle. In August, we hosted a summit that drew over thirty other independent candidates and over one hundred leaders and activists to Denver. The independent movement—notoriously, well, *independent*—never felt more cohesive or stronger. But, by November, Walker had dropped out when it became clear he had no path to victory. On Election Day, virtually every other candidate we backed lost their campaigns, forcing us back to the drawing board to explore other strategies of improving governance.

By early 2019, reformers in Alaska, including Kendall, were exploring various ways to change Alaska's elections to better align the incentives of its leaders with the best interest of the state. They consulted with several national reform groups and decided to pursue top-four primaries and instant-runoff general elections, along with a campaign finance disclosure provision, as a ballot initiative. At the same time, Unite America pivoted away from focusing on electing independent candidates to advancing election reform by mobilizing financial resources to state-based campaigns. We sent them our very first $25,000 grant to pay for legal drafting and the first poll. Though Walker was no longer in office, our shared drive to find a way out of our national political division and dysfunction would endure and Alaska would continue to be a model for the rest of the country.

WINNING PRIMARY REFORM IN ALASKA

Alaska is no stranger to election innovation. In 1947, before it even became a state, it adopted a blanket primary, copying the one adopted by Washington State in 1935. All candidates appeared on a single ballot, and the top vote-getter from each party advanced to the general election. In the years leading up to statehood, the blanket primary became a partisan issue; Democrats opposed it because they thought it would hurt party loyalty and discipline, and Republicans supported it because they thought they could attract votes from conservative Democrats and independents. Through the legislature, the Democratic Party repealed the system in 1959, until Republicans restored it in 1966. The system remained in use, with the exception of a few election cycles, until it was ruled unconstitutional by the U.S. Supreme Court in 2000, which impacted Alaska, California, and Washington. From that point on, for the most part, Republicans in Alaska allowed independent voters—but not Democrats—to vote in their primaries, while Democrats allowed all registered voters, regardless of party, to participate in theirs.

Alaska not only experimented with reforms to its partisan primaries but also with ways to address the problem of plurality winners in the general election. In 2000, some GOP leaders helped get an initiative on the August 2002 ballot for ranked choice voting. They saw an opportunity to address vote splitting in November among independent and third-party candidates that sometimes cost them the election. For example, in 1994, Democrat Tony Knowles was elected governor with just 41% of the vote in a four-way race.[9] A similar situation would happen again in 2008, when incumbent Republican Ted Stevens, who was pro-choice, lost reelection to Democrat Mark Begich by less than 4,000 voters after a far-right candidate from the Alaskan Independence Party peeled off 13,000 votes.[10] "[RCV] eliminates the problem of our current election system, where a candidate strongly opposed by the majority can win. It assures majority rule," read an endorsement letter signed by the Republican Party and four minor parties.[11] Senator John McCain recorded an endorsement. However, the proposed system was still quite new and unknown, the campaign was underfunded, and the ballot initiative lost 36% to 64%.[12] (Given many Republicans' current opposition to RCV in Alaska, it's worth emphasizing: Republicans led the charge for RCV more than twenty years ago, for reasons that would still benefit the party today!)

From Brainstorm to Ballot Measure

When he explored pathways for election reform in 2019, Kendall became convinced of two things. First, it had to be done by ballot measure. "Legislators have proposed open primaries; it went nowhere. Legislators have proposed ranked choice voting; it went nowhere," he explained. "Most of the legislators are beholden to their parties. They're not going to change the rules when they're already winning the game."[13] Second, the measure should address three main issues plaguing the state's politics: partisan primaries, plurality winner general elections, and dark money in campaigns. Kendall noted that Washington State's nonpartisan top-two primary had been upheld by the Supreme Court and decided to pursue that model, but with four slots in the general election rather than just two. "I took that and built on it. Let's *all* go to the party—let's have a Green candidate, a Libertarian, a Democrat and a Republican. Now we're talking about all kinds of issues because everyone's trying to build that winning coalition."[14] The first poll showed initial support above 60%. Knowing that most ballot campaigns tend to bleed support by Election Day, Kendall believed the measure had enough of a buffer to be viable.

On July 3, 2019, Alaskans for Better Elections (ABE) started the process of getting on the ballot by filing their petition application and ballot language. The lieutenant governor rejected their application, noting that, according to their legal opinion, the initiative violated the state's single-subject rule for ballot initiatives.[15] ABE, represented by Kendall, turned to the courts for help. On October 28, Anchorage Superior Court judge Yvonne Lamoureux ruled in favor of ABE, concluding that the initiative fell within the single subject of "election reform."[16] (This ruling was later affirmed by the state Supreme Court.)[17] Petition booklets were made available to ABE on October 31, and just over two months later, on January 9, the campaign submitted 36,006 valid signatures.

Support and Opposition Materialize

Alaskans for Better Elections built early credibility and support from a few state legislators who were not afraid to buck their parties, including Democrat and future independent House Speaker Bryce Edgmon and future Republican House Speaker Louise Stutes. "It was almost like Stockholm syndrome. They're beholden to the parties to some degree, but they want to be let out," Kendall explained of some incumbent legislators' support. "Here's the dirty secret: Democrats and Republicans smile at each other every day. They go out for drinks. They have dinners. But in the light of day, they can't work together. They wanted to change that."[18]

Jason Grenn, a former independent state legislator, served as the executive director of ABE. "I was really pleased with the spectrum of people and groups that were supportive of the ballot measure—it was

urban groups, rural Alaskans, longtime Alaskans, new Alaskans, fisher-
men, businessmen, moms," Grenn said after the measure passed. "I think
Alaskans were ready for something like this."[19]

Yet opposition came in strong, from all directions. "We had Alaska
Right to Life against us and we had Alaska Planned Parenthood against
us. Does that make any sense? That was the dynamic we were in," Kendall said. A late texting and mail program targeted to Democratic voters
by Planned Parenthood likely took six to seven points off the campaign,
Kendall explained. "If I was a low-information voter, I may have thought
Ballot Measure 2 was just taking away choice. So there were those kinds
of tactics," he said.[20]

The Republican Party formally opposed the measure. Incumbent
governor Mike Dunleavy, a conservative Republican, urged voters to reject it.[21] In fact, one of his top aides quit his government post to launch a
group to campaign against it.[22] And while the Democratic Party did not
formally weigh in, the top Democratic leader in the state, Begich, came
out opposed. (Yes, the same Begich who won his Senate seat with less
than a majority of the vote in 2008.) He cowrote an op-ed in the *Wall
Street Journal* with former Republican governor Sean Parnell, saying the
proposed system "encourages political trickery."[23]

Begich was promptly rebuffed by his own son, a Georgetown University freshman, who responded in the *Anchorage Daily News*: "There
are very few occasions in which both Democrats and Republicans can
agree on something. Not surprisingly, their staunch opposition to [Ballot
Measure 2] transcends partisan boundaries because it poses a threat to
their control over the voting process. . . . In November, we have a chance
to show the parties that we want more control over who gets elected."[24]

"We Can Be a Great Example to the Other Forty-Nine States"

On election night, initial results showed Ballot Measure 2 significantly behind, which was not surprising, as the campaign expected
to make up ground over the following two weeks as mail ballots were

counted—especially from outlying Alaska Native communities that were notoriously independent. Results would be updated every few days. On November 13, the campaign pulled ahead, officially winning a few days later by just 1%, 174,032 to 170,251.

"I take a lot of pride in our state. I get emotional because I distinctly remember where I was when I got a text from people saying that we had crossed that threshold of winning," recalled Grenn. "I remember hugging my wife, and tucking my kids into bed talking about it. I can visualize that moment so crystal clear because I knew it would be incredibly important for Alaska's future . . . and I really do feel that we can be a great example to the other forty-nine states."[25]

Two years later, Alaska's new election system would be put to the test, including in several high-profile races with national implications. Ultimately, the system did what it was designed to do in empowering a true majority of Alaska voters to choose their leaders. The same statewide electorate ultimately voted to elect a moderate Republican senator, a moderate Democratic representative, and a conservative Republican governor—while also electing pragmatic Democrats and Republicans for the state legislature, who wound up forming a bipartisan governing coalition. Let's look at each of these outcomes.

A BIPARTISAN GOVERNING MAJORITY EMERGES

Republican state senate president Cathy Giessel was not a supporter of Ballot Measure 2 in 2020. "I was totally against it. I spoke to community groups about how this would be awful," she told me when we met for coffee in Anchorage.[26] "I was worried that conservative voices would be drowned out."[27]

At the same time, Giessel regularly worked across the aisle to make progress on issues important to Alaska. She was a strong fiscal conservative. Rather than dip into the state's savings or raise new taxes, she supported cutting back the state's permanent fund dividend (the check every Alaskan receives from the government) in order to fund basic government services. She worked with the Democratic minority leader in the senate and the independent Speaker of the state house to pass a responsible budget—bringing along a majority of Republicans, but marginalizing a far-right faction in her own party's caucus. That, of course, was a recipe for being primaried.

"I've worked in the Republican Party for decades as a precinct committee woman, a district chair, even the statewide vice chair of the party. I was Republican Woman of the Year several times. But at the district convention in 2020, I was laughed at and booed off the stage," she recalled.[28] Republican Party leaders proactively recruited challengers in several legislative districts where members were not toeing the party line, including Giessel's. "I was getting yelled at while door knocking, 'You stole my dividend and you worked with the Democrats to do that. Get off my property. I have guns.' . . . It was frightening and shocking."

In the August 2020 elections, seven GOP incumbents were primaried out of office, including Giessel. A political newcomer named Roger Holland defeated her, 64% to 36%, by claiming she had lost touch with "what her job should be as a Republican senator in a Republican state with Republican majorities in the House and Senate and a Republican governor."[29] The experience was devastating, causing her to reevaluate her position on the reform ballot measure. "I looked at it more and more. I began to realize there's too much hostility here. We're just too divided. We've got to start working together. So by the time we actually voted on that initiative, I had moved to support it."[30]

Two years later, Giessel ran again for her old seat and, under the new top-four nonpartisan primary, found it completely changed the way she campaigned. In the past, like most candidates, Giessel would purchase a voter list from a party-affiliated vendor that would tell her what doors to knock on in her district for the primary election. Using a sophisticated data analysis, the list would provide each household a rating based on their likely partisanship and likelihood to vote—saving candidates time by only talking to the voters who could vote in the primary and who were likely to support them.

This time around, since every voter could participate in the primary and vote for whichever candidate they desired, Giessel didn't even purchase a list. "I just went to every single door and it was delightful. I was knocking on doors I walked past in the past and having great conversations with incredible people of such diversity. It was just a breath of fresh air to find the common themes," she said. "It also required me to be much more authentic in how I answered a question from a voter, because I didn't know whose door I was knocking, much less what groups they belong to or what their party affiliation is."[31] Giessel was the top finisher in her three-way primary, earning 36% of the vote.

All three candidates—including the incumbent Republican who primaried her in 2020 and a Democrat—advanced to the general election. She continued to knock on every door. In the general election, voters had the option of ranking their candidates rather than choosing only one. Giessel used this to her advantage to build a broad base of support. For example, on one door, she encountered a Republican who preferred the incumbent over her. "So I'd say, 'That's fine. But you get a second choice, so I'd appreciate it if you would rank the red,'" she explained, referring to ranking all of the GOP candidates. On another door, she encountered a voter who remembered her from her prior terms. "He looks at me and he goes, 'Oh, you've knocked on the wrong door. I'm a Democrat.' And I said, 'No, sir, you're exactly the person I want to talk to.' And so we had a great conversation."[32] She explained that he could rank her second in case the Democrat doesn't win. In November, Giessel won 33.8%, the Republican incumbent 33.1%, and the Democrat 33%. In the instant runoff tabulation, the Democrat was eliminated, and Giessel prevailed with 57%. No longer could a minority of voters in one party's primary block the will of the majority of voters in her district.

By the time the new legislature gaveled into session, the Senate was no longer organized into a majority party and a minority party. Instead, in the body of twenty, nine Republicans and eight Democrats decided to form a bipartisan caucus; Giessel was named majority leader. Rather than the three far-right Republicans exercising disproportionate control over the majority party, they were ostracized into a caucus of their own. (Such legislative coalitions are not uncommon in Alaska, though it had been a decade since the last coalition in the Senate.) The bipartisan coalition put divisive social issues to the side. "We decided we're going to stay on the ideas that we can find agreement on—which is the economy, public safety, education and a balanced budget. It's just been delightful," she said.[33] For the first time in five years, the legislature passed a budget without needing to go into an extended special session.

Having to run a different kind of campaign was profoundly impactful on Giessel once in office. "I had really gotten to be more education oriented," she said. She homeschooled her three kids and her husband taught in a private school for fourteen years. "I had come from a different perspective, but there were families whose door I would knock on and I'd hear from the parents about how critical the schools are for them and their kids. It helped me see the value of just having the schools open and a safe place where kids can go and know there'll be food there."[34] The state budget included the largest increase in public education funding in the state's history.[35] "That explosive revelation going door-to-door that there were all the things in the middle gave me a lot more freedom in this last session to go, you know, I could vote for that. This is what my constituents want."[36]

FROM WRITE-IN TO RANKED-IN: THE ODYSSEY OF SENATOR LISA MURKOWSKI

"Lisa Murkowski is so liberal she voted with the Democrats in Congress against Republicans more than three hundred times.... That's why Governor Sarah Palin, Mark Levin, and the Tea Party Express support conservative Republican Joe Miller for U.S. Senate,"[37] says the narrator of a thirty-second ad produced in 2010 by the Tea Party Express, which spent over $650,000 on that primary.[38] And just like that, in a major upset, Murkowski became one of the first casualties of the Tea Party in a GOP primary decided by less than two points. First appointed to the seat by her father (then the governor) in 2002, Murkowski believed her service in Congress was over. But then hundreds of emails, phone calls, and letters started coming in from Alaskans across the state, encouraging her not to give up.

Like forty-seven other states, Alaska's "sore loser" law prevented Murkowski from putting her name on the ballot as an independent candidate after losing her primary. However, no law prevented voters from writing in her name. The proposition seemed outlandish; no statewide candidate had ever won election by write-in vote in Alaska's history, especially not one with a last name like M-u-r-k-o-w-s-k-i. And only one U.S. Senate candidate ever pulled it off in the entire country (South Carolina's Strom Thurmond in 1954). Murkowski felt torn between passionate supporters who did not like their other options and political professionals who viewed it as an impossible fight that would only further pit her against her party.[39] Two weeks after conceding, she decided she would go for it.

"This was not me waking up and saying, by God, I'm going to challenge this. It was Alaskans all over the state saying, 'I didn't have an opportunity to weigh in. I didn't have an opportunity to participate in this closed primary,'" Murkowski recalled to me.[40]

"Fill it in, Write it in: Murkowski" read a blue rubber wristband. The campaign made and distributed thousands of wristbands to remind voters not only how to spell the senator's last name but also that they needed to fill in the write-in bubble on their ballot for their vote to count. It was one of several creative tactics in a forty-six-day campaign. By the time all the votes were counted, an astounding 101,091 Alaskans wrote in Murkowski's name.

Weeks of legal challenges followed, and the ballots had to be hand counted. Kendall was working for Murkowski at the time and led her legal team. "That election told me Alaskans want a third or a fourth choice," he said. Ultimately, Murkowski prevailed, in another demonstration that the partisan primary process was not producing the kind of candidates that a majority of voters desired—not unlike the 2006 Senate

Democratic primary in Connecticut that tossed out Joe Lieberman only to see him win the general election under a third-party banner.

I hosted a dinner in Denver in 2022 for Senator Murkowski when she was seeking her fourth Senate term, twelve years after her write-in campaign. She recounted her experience for our group, then pulled up her sleeve to reveal a gold bracelet with an inscription: "Fill it in, Write it in: Murkowski." "It is the one thing that is a constant other than my wedding ring," she said.[41] It was a gift from her husband, she explained, and she wears it every day to remind herself of who she is serving in the Senate. "I was not returned to the Senate by my party. I was returned by Alaskans who wanted to have a say in who represents them in Washington. My base is made up of people from all political persuasions. So that's my daily reminder."[42] At that moment I appreciated the power of eliminating partisan primaries more than ever.

Murkowski Bucks Her Party

Murkowski remained a Republican, but especially after her 2010 re-election, she was never afraid to demonstrate her independence. For example, in December 2010, she was one of just two Senate Republicans who voted for the DREAM Act.[43] In June 2013, she became just the third sitting Republican senator to announce her support for same-sex marriage.[44] Perhaps most notably, in July 2017, Murkowski was one of three GOP senators (along with Susan Collins and John McCain) to vote against the repeal of Obamacare, ultimately killing the effort.[45]

Then came the capitol insurrection on January 6, 2021. Two days later, Murkowski was the first Republican senator to call for President Trump's resignation. Asked by a reporter if she would consider leaving her party, she replied, "I didn't have any reason to leave my party in 2010. I was a Republican who ran a write-in campaign and I was successful. But I will tell you, if the Republican Party has become nothing more than the party of Trump, I sincerely question whether this is the party for me."[46] Several weeks later, Murkowski became the only Senate

Republican up for election in 2022 who voted to convict Trump, after the House impeached him for a second time.

Murkowski Is Primaried, Again

Given her vote on impeachment, it was no surprise that Murkowski became a top target for Trump in the 2022 midterm elections. Former Trump administration official Kelly Tshibaka launched her campaign to primary Murkowski in March 2021. Not only did she earn Trump's endorsement, but the Alaska Republican Party endorsed her over the state's sitting Republican senator. Trump went to Alaska ahead of the August 2022 primary and told voters, "This is your precious chance to dump the horrific RINO Senator Lisa Murkowski, who's worse than a Democrat."[47]

In any prior election year, Murkowski probably would have been doomed. But thanks to the passage of Ballot Measure 2, there was now a single, nonpartisan primary in which all voters could participate. That meant she could attract support from independents (who comprise 58% of voters in Alaska, the highest percentage in the country) and Democrats. Her fate was no longer in the hands of a small faction of Republican base voters who, since 2010, clearly did not want her in office, even though a majority of Alaskans did.

On August 16, midterm election primaries were held in both Alaska and Wyoming, and the contrast could not have been clearer. Wyoming representative Liz Cheney—daughter of the former Republican vice president, the former chair of the Republican conference, and one of the most conservative House members—lost to her primary opponent, 66% to 29%. Her vote to impeach Trump and her subsequent cochairmanship of the January 6th Select Committee sealed her fate in the Republican primary. Hours later, when polls closed in Alaska, the outcome was much different. It was immediately clear that Murkowski was headed to the general election, along with Tshibaka, Republican Buzz Kelley, and Democrat Patricia Chesbro. In a partisan primary like Wyoming's, according to Alaska pollster Ivan Moore, Murkowski "would have had a zero percent—I mean zero percent—chance of winning."[48]

Within days, the light bulb lit up for the national political media about the significance of Alaska's new election system:

- *Cook Political Report*: "For years, advocates for ranked-choice voting and top-two (or four) primary systems have argued that these reforms will help to moderate our polarized political system. . . . Given the results of this primary season, those advocates have a stronger case than ever."[49]
- *Los Angeles Times*: "Sometimes, a reform comes along that does what backers intended. That doesn't happen often, so when it does, it's worth taking note."[50]
- *Washington Post*: "Lisa Murkowski will come back to D.C.; that is now almost certain. If her win creates national momentum for [election reform], it could light a fire that will sweep across America."[51]
- *Politico*: "At a time of rising political polarization and growing frustration with the two-party system, Trump's impeachment revenge tour has put these alternative voting systems in the national spotlight."[52]

In the November election, Murkowski won 43.4% of first-choice votes and Tshibaka 42.6%. Since neither had a majority, an instant runoff was required. The state's division of elections waited two weeks to tabulate the runoff in order to receive mail ballots by a deadline predetermined by law, causing a delay that some erroneously attributed to the new election system. After redistributing the second-choice selections of voters who had gone for Chesbro (10.4%) and Kelley (2.9%), Murkowski ended up with a 53.7% majority.

As in 2010, Murkowski was headed back to Washington, not because her party supported her but because a majority of voters did. But this time, it wasn't a fluke of the election system by write-in, it was a feature—thanks to the top-four primary.

SARAH PALIN'S LAST STAND

If the Senate race was the most consequential in Alaska in 2022, the race for its only House seat was the most dramatic, partly because it featured a nationally famous and controversial contender: former Alaska governor and Republican vice presidential nominee Sarah Palin.

At the start of the year, most pundits assumed there would be no drama at all, just another easy reelection for Don Young, who had already held the seat for forty-nine years. He was not merely an icon in Alaska politics, but the oldest and longest-serving member of the House, as well as the longest-serving Republican congressman in U.S. history. But then Young suddenly died on March 18, at age eighty-eight, on a flight to Seattle. Known for his willingness to work across the aisle, most recently by supporting President Biden's infrastructure package, Young was mourned by all Alaskans.

The U.S. Constitution requires that vacancies in the House be filled by special election. The contest to replace Young would be the state's first use of a top-four primary followed by a general election with an instant runoff. (Under the old rules, each political party's committee would have handpicked their nominee for a special election; there would be no primary.) On June 11, an astonishingly large field of forty-eight candidates ran in the special primary, even including a candidate by the legal name of Santa Claus from North Pole, Alaska. The top four finishers were Republican Sarah Palin with 27.0%, Republican Nick Begich with 19.1%, Independent Al Gross with 12.6% (he would later drop out), and Democrat Mary Peltola with 10.1%.

The most surprising among them was Peltola, a member of the Yup'ik tribe in Western Alaska. As a child, she had traveled with her father around the state as he campaigned for Don Young, which helped spark her interest in politics.[53] Peltola was a nontraditional Democrat, which would have posed a big challenge if she had been running in a traditional Democratic primary. For instance, she was a member of the NRA with a moderate stance on gun rights—more in line with her state's

electorate than with her national party. She campaigned mostly on practical issues that would help Alaskans, such as a bill to protect the state's
fisheries. She even said some nice things about Palin, describing their
friendship and bipartisan working relationship when they had served together in the state government.[54]

In the August 16 special general election, Peltola came in first with
40.2%, followed by Palin with 31.3%, and Begich with 28.5%. Because no
candidate had captured a majority, voters who had gone for third-place
finisher Begich had their votes reallocated to their second choices in the
instant runoff. The final tally was Peltola 51.5%, Palin 48.5%. Peltola
made history as the first woman and first Alaska Native to represent the
state in the House of Representatives.

Palin complained that the new system was "crazy, convoluted, confusing." She added in a late-August statement, "Ranked-choice voting
was sold as the way to make elections better reflect the will of the people.
As Alaska—and America—now sees, the exact opposite is true."[55] Other
nationally prominent conservatives echoed Palin's talking points, implying that Alaska's new system had been rigged to help Democrats. For
instance, Senator Tom Cotton tweeted: "60% of Alaska voters voted for a
Republican, but thanks to a convoluted process and ballot exhaustion—
which disenfranchises voters—a Democrat 'won.'"[56]

There are a few things wrong with this line of critique. Peltola won
a plurality of the vote, so even without RCV, the outcome would have
been the same. And a simple look at the instant runoff numbers shows
that the main reason Palin lost was that 29% of the 53,810 voters who
ranked Begich first preferred Peltola over Palin as their second choice,
while another 21% of them chose not to list any second choice.[57] An honest analysis would blame Palin for failing to appeal to enough Alaska
Republicans, rather than any alleged trickery under the new system. As
the libertarian-leaning publication *Reason* observed, "If Palin were supported by a majority of voters, then she would have won—just like the
Republicans who won in the US Senate, the governorship, and a majority
of both chambers of the state legislature."[58]

A similar contest in Washington's 3rd Congressional District in 2022 helps confirm this analysis. There, Palin-like Republican populist Joe Kent faced off in November against a Peltola-like Democrat, Marie Gluesenkamp Perez, after finishing second in a fractured primary field with just 23%.[59] Despite Kent and his fellow Republicans earning 65% of the vote in the August nonpartisan top-two primary, Perez defeated him head-to-head, just as Peltola defeated Palin.

Upon moving to Washington, D.C., to fill the remainder of Young's final term, Peltola continued her bipartisan ways. She asked Young's Republican chief of staff, Alex Ortiz, to stay in the same job through the end of the term. She also rehired Young's former scheduler, as well as a Republican communications director. She explained that she made these hires for "common sense" reasons, because those GOP staffers had in-depth knowledge of Alaska, the inner workings of the Capitol, and the federal bureaucracy.

During the next two and a half months, Peltola demonstrated how she would act in Congress, winning new allies on Capitol Hill. Then in the regular November election, she once again came in first and expanded her margin to 47.8%—followed by Palin with 25.7% and Begich with 23.3%. After the instant runoff that redistributed the second choices of Begich's voters (plus those of a Libertarian fourth candidate), the final tally was Peltola 55.0%, Palin 45.0%.

A CONSERVATIVE GOVERNOR WINS REELECTION

As we saw earlier, former governor Bill Walker learned firsthand that a pragmatic Republican could not make it through a GOP primary, nor could an independent survive the "spoiler" charge in a three-way general election. Under Alaska's top-four primary and instant-runoff general election, however, there would finally be a level playing field. "I would not be running if it was not for the new voting system," he said.[60] Walker sought a 2022 rematch against incumbent Republican governor Mike Dunleavy, a conservative who was endorsed by Trump.

Alaskans had a full range of choices in their ten-way gubernatorial primary, which ended with Dunleavy in first place with 40.4%, Democrat Les Gara in second with 23.1%, Walker in third with 22.8%, and another Republican, Charlie Pierce, taking the fourth spot with 6.6%. In the four-way general election, Dunleavy won outright with 50.3%, meaning that no redistribution of second-choice votes was necessary.

Some opponents of election reform had noted that Scott Kendall, the driving force behind Ballot Measure 2, had previously worked for both Murkowski and Walker, implying that he might have explicitly designed the new system to help those candidates. This made Dunleavy's clear victory in the governor's race especially instructive, as a demonstration of how candidates beyond self-identified moderates could still win under the new system. Because Dunleavy was able to win broad support against a broader field of competition, his reelection represented the will of the voters.

RESULTS AND IMPACT

Who won or lost various races is not the ultimate metric of success for Alaska's new voting system. Had Murkowski lost and Palin won, for example, the system would still have delivered on its promise of electing the candidate that a true majority of Alaskans wanted to represent them. There are other, more objective ways to judge the impact of the Alaska system, particularly on three key metrics of participation, competition, and representation.

Participation

This one is straightforward. Turnout was up across the board in the new top-four primary: 37% of the state's eligible population voted, which was nearly 12 points higher than in 2020 and nearly 15 points higher than in 2018, which was the most recent midterm election year and thus more directly comparable. In fact, 2022 saw the highest number of total votes cast for the U.S. Senate, U.S. House, and governor's primaries in the state's history.[61] While turnout was down slightly in the general election, that reflected national trends (2018 was an exceptionally high turnout midterm year nationwide). Even so, 2022 still had the third-highest total number of votes cast in a midterm general election in state history.

According to a post–general election poll, nearly 80% of Alaskans reported that ranking candidates in the general election was at least "somewhat simple," including 57% who said it was "very simple." These results were similar across demographics: upward of 75% to 80% of white voters, non-Native voters of color, and Alaska Native voters all found it simple, as did 76% of voters over fifty and 83% of voters under fifty.[62] I find all these numbers especially impressive because the system was brand-new. After a few more elections, even more voters will feel confident in casting their ballots.

Participation is directly related to perceptions of voter power. The same poll found that 52% of Alaskans believed that their vote "mattered more" in the November 2022 election compared to previous years.

Competition

Alaska voters got a much wider range of options across the board, compared to previous years. In the primaries, there were significantly more candidates overall. There were many more independent and third-party candidates, whose ranks grew to nearly half of all primary candidates in 2022. For the first time in the state's history, every primary for U.S. House, U.S. Senate, and governor was competitive. And not a single primary contest, from top to bottom, was left with a candidate running unopposed.[63]

The general elections, while capped at four candidates per race, also offered voters dramatically more diverse choices. On average, there were 20% more general election candidates for each race (both state and federal) in 2022 compared to 2020. While 23% of state and federal general elections were unopposed in 2020, only 11% were unopposed in 2022.[64] The 2022 election cycle also had the highest percentage of state legislative races (30%) decided by 10 percentage points or less in the last decade.[65]

The new system allowed voters to consider different flavors of candidates from the same party. Exactly half of all general elections (31 out of 62) featured multiple Republicans or multiple Democrats. In general, intraparty competition in general elections incentivizes members of a dominant party to appeal to independent voters and members of the minority party. This often requires avoiding any extreme positions those candidates might otherwise be rewarded to embrace, even in a district or state with a strong partisan lean.

Representation

In 2022, Alaska's candidate pool and ultimate winners looked more like the Alaskan population, in terms of both demographics and partisan identification, than ever before.

Let's start with demographics. Statewide elections featured the largest percentage of women running (31.1%) in at least a decade.[66] Alaska had never previously had a state legislator who was openly LGBTQ, but four such candidates ran in 2022, and three of them won their races.[67] In terms of partisan identification, a think tank that studies the Pacific Northwest observed, "The [statewide] primary candidate pool came closer than ever to reflecting the independence of Alaska voters. . . . The share of independent candidates came closer than any recent election to mirroring the Alaska electorate's majority-independent composition."[68] As a result of this broader range of choices, 10% of the state legislative seats up for election were won by candidates not registered with either major party—more than in any recent election.

A poll taken after the general election found that 47% of all voters thought the overall quality of candidates in 2022 was "better" than in past years, and only 24% found it to be worse.[69]

THE BATTLE FOR REFORM IS FAR FROM OVER

Do all these positive outcomes in Alaska mean that election reformers like Scott Kendall and Jason Grenn can declare victory and move on? Not even remotely. Politicos who had mastered the old system but struggled in 2022—led by losing candidates Kelly Tshibaka and Sarah Palin—have mobilized to repeal Alaska's top-four primary system.

A conspiracy-minded group, Alaskans for Honest Elections (AHE), has been advancing a 2024 ballot initiative that would revert the state to partisan primaries and plurality-winner elections. The group's founder, Dr. Art Mathias, was blunt about his hatred for the new system: "Alaska is the epicenter for this. If we kill it in Alaska, we kill it in America."[70] The group claims to have more than 5,000 volunteers statewide who will help collect the nearly 27,000 valid signatures required to place the repeal initiative on the 2024 ballot. Notably, according to campaign finance complaints, Mathias created a fake church to funnel money to AHE while generating tax deductions for contributors and shielding them from disclosure.[71]

Beyond the efforts among grassroots activists, Republican lawmakers are also attempting to undo many of the changes enacted by Ballot Measure 2 through the legislature, though legislative repeal will be harder, since many newly elected and reelected leaders—like Giessel—prefer the new system.[72] In 2023, there were several public hearings on a repeal bill. Citizens from across the state called into the committee to testify, overwhelming the phone lines. Here are some excerpts:

- "I feel liberated because I am no longer forced to deal with this closed primary where the whole list of choices that I have are controlled by either the Republican Party or the Democratic Party." —Catherine M.
- "I am a 30 year resident and nonpartisan registered voter. I always felt like my voting rights were violated when I had to choose a

primary ballot—particularly when my favorite candidate for one seat might be a Republican, and for another seat, a Democrat or independent." —Kim N.

- "Even though my first choice candidate might not have won, all my preferences were counted. Furthermore, in none of the races did I feel like I needed to vote *against* somebody. All my votes were *for* a candidate. I did not have to game the system to vote for whom I thought was the most electable. I just voted for whom I thought was best." —Mark D.

- "I think it will help get rid of some of this partisan rancor that most of us are getting more and more concerned about. Congress can't do anything anymore. There's no agreement. There's nothing. I don't want that to come to Alaska." —Margaret M.

Reflecting on Alaska's pioneering election system and the controversy around it, Murkowski told me: "This is not some scheme by Democrats to get more Democrats elected or an alternative scheme by Republicans to get Republicans elected. It is designed to get more people engaged in elections in general. . . . I think it makes us better candidates, and I also think it gives greater satisfaction to the electorate, who feels like they actually have a say in the election outcomes."[73]

Despite efforts to repeal election reform, Kendall remains confident—and such testimony from real voters was a big reason why. "I'm very optimistic that we will defeat a repeal because, as the misinformation has fallen away, it's become more understood and more popular. The reform worked the way we promised, and people like when promises are kept." But as Alaska's own history shows, reforms can be implemented, repealed, restored, struck down, reinvented, and passed again. "Even if it did somehow get narrowly repealed, I don't think that would be the end of the story, now that people have tried it," says Kendall.[74]

The story continues not only in Alaska but across America, where reformers have been inspired to pursue similar efforts. I asked Kendall

if Alaska's unique demographics and tendency toward quirky independence make the state an unreliable test case to predict future successes.
He replied that he gets dozens of emails every week from politicians and
activists alike across the country, all hoping to replicate or adapt Alaska's
groundbreaking reform. When it comes to political innovation, the Last
Frontier may be anything but last.

EIGHT

A BETTER WAY TO PICK A PRESIDENT

A March 2023 NBC survey found that half of Democrats did not want President Biden to run for office again, and one-third of Republicans said the same of former President Trump—yet both are (as I write this) the clear frontrunners for their respective parties' nominations.[1] It is shaping up to be a déjà vu of 2016, when voters registered historic levels of discontent with their options. In that election, the final Gallup favorability poll taken found:

Hillary Clinton: 47% favorable, 52% unfavorable, –5% net
Donald Trump: 36% favorable, 61% unfavorable, –25% net[2]

Trump set a record in 2016 for the highest unfavorability in the history of Gallup's final preelection poll, which had been conducted since 1956. But Clinton had no reason to gloat, since her 52% unfavorable was the second-worst ever.

A CNN headline that October dubbed 2016 "the ultimate 'lesser of two evils' election."[3] While many voters held their nose to select the "lesser evil" in November, many abstained altogether. If "did not vote" was a candidate, that candidate would have earned over 100 million votes and won forty-four states.[4]

So how did these two unpopular candidates capture their respective nominations? The short version is that Clinton's money, influence, and name recognition cleared the field of many would-be contenders for the nomination. And within a relatively small field, she jumped out to a modest but insurmountable lead in Democratic delegates against her surprisingly popular main competitor within the party, Bernie Sanders. Trump, meanwhile, won nearly 60% of the delegates at the GOP convention, despite winning only 45% of the popular vote in the primaries and caucuses. He had faced a crowded, splintered field that began with seventeen major contenders. By the end of primary season, Trump had received just over 14 million Republican primary and caucus votes,[5] while Clinton had received just under 17 million Democratic votes.[6] This meant that only about 31 million primary voters—just 12.4% of all eligible voters—had selected the options everyone else in the country had to choose between in November.

Moreover, in the general election, there was no viable alternative to Clinton and Trump—despite their being widely viewed as unacceptable by a sizable number of voters. Of course, there still were several other candidates on the ballot who attracted what amounted to a protest vote. Libertarian Gary Johnson, Green Party candidate Jill Stein, and independent Evan McMullin won a combined 6.7 million votes (4.9%). Johnson was on the ballot in all fifty states, Stein in forty-four, and McMullin in just eleven, in part because of his late start.

Lest we want to keep repeating this painful exercise, it's time to find a better way to pick our president.

WHY DO 260 MILLION VOTERS GET ONLY TWO VIABLE CHOICES?

Republican Doug Bailey and Democrat Gerald Rafshoon were on opposite sides of the Ford vs. Carter presidential election in 1976; each ran general election advertising for their respective candidate. They became lifelong friends at a time when such friendship was not as unusual as it seems today. The rise of partisan polarization hastened their exit from electoral politics, yet also was the reason they decided to come out of retirement in 2006 with an idea to disrupt a dysfunctional system. Dubbed Unity08, their initiative sought to organize an online convention to nominate a bipartisan presidential ticket in 2008. A ruling by the Federal Election Commission (FEC), which is controlled by both major parties, hampered the group's fundraising and the effort failed to get any traction.

But from my perspective, as a high school junior and volunteer for Unity08 at the time, their passion and imagination introduced me to the political reform movement. In 2010, I took a year off from college to help Bailey launch Americans Elect, the successor organization to Unity08, for the 2012 presidential election. It was resurrected by financier Peter Ackerman, who led a successful lawsuit against the FEC to level the fundraising playing field, and CEO Kahlil Byrd. We raised over $35 million,[7] recruited E-Trade's former CTO to build the technology for a secure online convention, and collected millions of signatures from ordinary citizens to establish a line on the ballot in forty-one states for our eventual ticket. I was in charge of our college program, and organized chapters of volunteers on over 150 campuses.

Throughout 2011, Bailey briefed sitting senators, former defense secretaries, ex-governors, and other prominent Americans on the unique opportunity to get to the general election ballot without needing to contort themselves in either party's primary. The problem? None of these potential candidates saw a realistic pathway of first getting on the presidential debate stage, whose criteria for admission was an unrealistic polling threshold designed to keep out anyone beyond the two major parties—yet another way the duopoly exerts its control. As a result, no credible candidate stepped forward to seek the nomination, and the effort disbanded.

My takeaway from Americans Elect was that even in this age of small-dollar online fundraising, it would likely take a self-funder to get the ball rolling in any kind of serious independent presidential campaign. Winning is not as simple as earning a plurality in a national three-way race; instead, it's fifty state contests in a race to win an outright *majority* in the Electoral College. (If no candidate secures an Electoral College majority, the election is decided by Congress.)

Michael Bloomberg, the billionaire former mayor of New York City, gave the possibility of an independent run serious consideration in 2016. But after rigorous polling and analysis, Bloomberg opted against even trying, which underscores just how high the barriers are.

In 2020, former Starbucks CEO Howard Schultz took an independent exploratory campaign several steps further than Bloomberg had. He was particularly concerned about the prospect of an election between Trump and Sanders. I attended his first public appearance at a book signing in New York City, where he was literally shouted down by an activist: "Don't help elect Trump! You egotistical billionaire asshole!"[8] Soon after, I was invited to Seattle to meet with Schultz and his team, to impart some insights. He was earnest about his intentions and inquisitive about the growing political reform movement. His early operation included well over a hundred people and was already investing millions of dollars in a sophisticated data infrastructure.

I advised his campaign team that Schultz's number one objective should be to make clear he was running to win but that he would not continue his campaign if it became apparent he would "spoil" the election.[9] Such a statement would help create a permission structure for both Democratic and Republican voters to support him. His campaign instead largely avoided the topic and could not overcome the deafening media narrative that a Schultz campaign would guarantee a Trump reelection. He dropped out before even formally announcing a run. By all accounts, the ruthless attacks he came under for daring to offer Americans another option were devastating for him and his family— quickly sending one of America's most successful entrepreneurs back into the private sector.

As of this writing in late-2023, the possibility of a bipartisan, third-party presidential ticket is being pursued by a group called No Labels, which is running a similar playbook as Americans Elect. They have faced a torrent of criticism from those who, once again, fear that any independent ticket would spoil the election by taking more votes away from Biden and helping reelect Trump. Can No Labels overcome the obstacles that stymied similar previous efforts? It is highly unlikely. What's more likely is that millions of Americans will again head to the polls in November 2024 and vote *against* the candidate they most dislike.

MAJOR PROBLEMS WITH THE WAY WE PICK OUR PRESIDENT

As we have seen throughout the book, the combination of partisan primaries, which produce unrepresentative outcomes, and plurality-winner general elections, which thwart alternatives to both major parties, conspire to give voters only two viable choices that they often do not like. Presidential elections are no exception. In fact, we feel this problem most acutely at the presidential level because, compared to a state legislative or even congressional district, the stakes of the election are exponentially greater.

During the primary phase, both parties' nomination processes are not necessarily representative of their voters, let alone the public at large. On the Republican side, a candidate can win all (or most) of a particular state's delegates by simply winning a plurality of the vote. In a crowded field and over multiple states, such a system can produce a nominee who is not supported by a majority of voters. For instance, in 2016 Donald Trump won all of the delegates in several states where he earned less than a majority of support, such as Florida (where Trump only got 46%), Arizona (46%), and South Carolina (33%).

On the Democratic side, delegates are awarded proportionally; however, any votes for candidates who do not earn at least 15% of the vote are essentially discarded, totaling nearly 1 million ballots in 2020 across all fifty states.[10] For instance, Bernie Sanders won 50.7% of the popular vote in his home state of Vermont in 2020, while 27% of the vote went to candidates who were all under the 15% threshold. As a result, Sanders was awarded a disproportionate share of the state's pledged delegates (11 out of 16, or 69%).

Further, in 2020, both parties locked out about 30 million independents nationally from voting in the twenty-four states (and D.C.) with closed presidential primaries.

The second major problem is that, in the general election, there is no realistic pathway for a candidate outside of the two major parties. As I described earlier, there are several significant obstacles facing any independent candidate. It begins with simply getting on the ballot: since there is no "public" or nonpartisan primary they can run in to get to the general election, any independent candidate must instead collect close to 2 million signatures state by state and defend against inevitable legal challenges—an expense that can easily total tens of millions of dollars. Raising that money is never easy; while a major-party candidate is eligible for public funds for both the primary and general, an independent is only eligible for the latter.[11]

Then, regardless of whether they're on the ballot in all fifty states, an independent can only qualify for the presidential debates by polling at least at 15% nationally. This threshold is set by the Commission on Presidential Debates, a private entity that is in effect controlled by both major parties. One analysis showed it would cost nearly $270 million to achieve the national name recognition necessary to meet this arbitrarily high threshold.[12] Finally, an independent would need to win enough states to earn a majority of the Electoral College vote. That is a tall order when many voters believe a vote for a third candidate would uninten-tionally help elect their least-preferred candidate, thanks to the spoiler effect of plurality elections.

If we want to break the "lesser of two evils" trap of presidential elec-tions and include more Americans in the process of choosing our na-tion's leader, there are at least five powerful, practical, and nonpartisan reforms we should pursue: instant runoffs in the primary and general elections; proportional electoral vote allocation; eliminating caucuses; opening all primaries to independent voters; and rotating early states in the run-up to a single national primary day.

INSTANT RUNOFFS FOR PRESIDENT

The most practical and powerful way to improve how we pick our presi-dent is to implement instant runoffs in both presidential primary and general elections, using ranked choice voting.

In the primaries, RCV would ensure that a presidential candidate earns majority voter support in order to win a party's nomination, not a mere plurality. This would help consensus-type candidates—those who build broader coalitions within their party and would be more competi-tive in the general election. Further, RCV would also solve the problem of wasted votes when candidates drop out too close to an election to re-move their name from the ballot. Over 3 million voters cast wasted bal-lots in the competitive Democratic primary in 2020, for example.[13] With RCV, those voters would have their ballots automatically transferred to their second or third choice.

During the 2020 Democratic presidential primaries, five states used RCV: Alaska, Hawaii, Kansas, Wyoming, and Nevada. All five saw dra-matically higher turnouts—in the range of double or triple their 2016 turnouts—and none of those votes were wasted on already-withdrawn candidates.[14] Voters seemed to find it simple to rank several candidates in order, and the last-place candidates were easily eliminated until the remaining candidates had all reached the 15% threshold necessary for delegation allocation.* Several Republican primaries will use RCV in presidential primaries for the first time in 2024.

In general elections, an instant runoff would mitigate the unintended consequences of any candidates beyond the two major parties spoiling the election. With RCV, voters could safely rank their most preferred candidate first, knowing that if their candidate fails to earn sufficient support, their second ranking would instead count. For example, RCV would have helped avoid the controversy in Florida in 2000, when 97,421 voters supported Green Party nominee Ralph Nader over Al Gore (their likely second preference), ultimately handing George W. Bush the state by 537 votes. (The same could happen in reverse in the future, with a strong Libertarian candidate potentially spoiling an election for the Republican nominee.) Further, RCV might be the reason independent candidates who don't see an easy pathway to the presidency actually run—and potentially win.

Maine was the first state to use RCV in a presidential election in 2020. Unlike other states, Maine (like Nebraska) awards one electoral vote to the winner of the popular vote in each of its two congressional districts, and two electoral votes to the winner of the popular vote statewide. Under this system, Trump won one electoral vote and Biden won three. Alaska will join Maine in using RCV for president in 2024. In a bipartisan vote, the Oregon legislature referred a RCV proposal to the ballot for voters to decide in 2024; if it passes, Oregon will use RCV for president beginning in 2028.

We have evidence of how different electoral processes produce more representative presidential outcomes in other countries. In 2017, France elected an independent candidate, Emmanuel Macron, over a far-right,

---

*Nevada did not implement RCV in the same way as the other four states. Rather, the state's Democratic Party used RCV as a form of early caucus participation, allowing voters to select their top choice and backup choices. Because Nevada did not eliminate candidates until all remaining candidates had at least 15% of the vote, its delegate allocation was less proportional than the allocation in other states.

Trump-like populist, Marine Le Pen, and did so again in 2022—through a voting system that is functionally similar to a RCV general election but occurs over two different rounds of voting. All candidates are listed on the same ballot in a single election, but if no candidate receives an outright majority, a runoff election is held. More than eighty countries worldwide elect their heads of state through a similar two-round method.[15]

If France had the same presidential election system as we do, it is unlikely that Macron would have either been able to win the nomination of either the major left or right party or be competitive as an independent candidate. Voters would have had to settle for their own version of the lesser of two evils, and Le Pen, who has repeatedly echoed talking points from Putin's Russia and does not reflect the views or values of a true majority of French voters, would likely now be in her second term.

A COMPROMISE SOLUTION ON THE ELECTORAL COLLEGE

Even with RCV, candidates running outside of the two major parties will still face the enormous challenge of the Electoral College, because electoral votes are awarded on a winner-take-all basis, state by state. That's why, in 1992, Ross Perot won 19% of the vote nationwide but did not win a single electoral vote.

Whether you love or hate the Electoral College, one thing is undeniable: it is not serving its original purpose as designed by the Founders, who envisioned a body of educated, well-respected citizens who would use their own discretion to pick the president. The Electoral College was seen as the main way presidential candidates would be nominated, if not elected, president—independent of any political parties or popular vote. Many Founders assumed the body would not be able to achieve a majority vote for a single candidate and Congress would wind up casting the deciding ballots for president. In George Mason's estimation, this would likely happen "nineteen times out of twenty." The reality today is much different: electors are bound to each state's popular vote, with merely a ceremonial role. Rather than keep using a system that is clearly no longer functioning as intended, we should be open to considering some kinds of modernizing reforms.

Some advocate a national popular vote to avoid scenarios where a popular vote winner winds up losing the election (as in 1876, 1888, 2000, and 2016) or where Congress must decide the election in the absence of an Electoral College majority (as in 1800 and 1824). To get around the heavy lift of a constitutional amendment, proponents have instead advanced an interstate compact that would effectively implement a national popular vote if adopted by a sufficient number of states. However, this proposal raises doubts about enforceability in a contested election and could wind up precipitating a constitutional crisis. Further, in nationalizing our presidential election, a close contest could trigger a nationwide recount, simultaneously in all fifty states, for which there are no protocols and in which single points of failure could create new election security risks that carry severe national ramifications.

An alternative proposal is to have states proportionally allocate their electoral votes among the top two finishers according to the popular vote. For example, if a state has twenty electoral votes and the top two finishers each won 50% of the popular vote, each would be awarded ten electoral votes. Proportional allocation of Electoral College votes could be an achievable compromise between both parties. As Republicans desire, it maintains the Electoral College as an institution that ensures national elections are still state-based and ensures that smaller states can still wield influence by continuing to award at least three electoral votes per state, regardless of population. As Democrats desire, it gives greater influence to the voices of individual voters, making the ballots of Republicans in California and Democrats in Texas actually matter in presidential elections. "Party officials outside of swing states would likely support a change that can bring presidential campaigns to their states to help with down-ballot races," writes Kevin Johnson, executive director of the Election Reformers Network, a proponent of the proposal.[16]

This reform would integrate well with instant runoffs and, as third-party or independent advocates desire, would further level the political playing field. In a hypothetical rerun of the 2016 election, imagine that in Pennsylvania, among first-choice votes, Clinton wins 29%, Bloomberg 32%, and Trump 39%. Through an instant runoff, Clinton is eliminated and her votes are redistributed such that Bloomberg ends up with 55% and Trump with 45%. The state's twenty electoral votes would be proportionally allocated: eleven to the independent and nine to the Republican. Applied across all fifty states, this process would have left voters much more satisfied with their options, and America could have very well elected its first president from outside both major parties in well over 150 years.

This proposal is not theoretical. In 1950, Senator Henry Cabot Lodge Jr. (R-Massachusetts) and Representative Ed Gossett (D-Texas) proposed a constitutional amendment for a proportional allocation system, and it passed the Senate, 64–27, before failing in the House.[17]

ELIMINATE CAUCUSES

The idea of banning caucuses is hard to argue against, except perhaps by those who feel beholden to the traditions of Iowa and a few other states. It has been well-documented that states that hold presidential caucuses see significantly lower turnout than those that hold primaries. In 2016, for instance, average caucus turnout for both parties was only 9.9% of eligible voters, compared to 32.4% turnout in states that held primaries.[18]

As former presidential candidate John Delaney put it in our conversation: "It seems to me if we were figuring out a way for people *not* to vote—and we all went into a room with a whiteboard and didn't know anything—we'd come up with a caucus system."[19]

This is mainly due to the much greater time and energy required to participate in an in-person caucus at a large public space, like a local high school gym. Participants usually "vote with their feet" by standing in certain areas with other voters who support the same candidate. Every attendee can see who everyone else is favoring, which discourages those who don't feel comfortable being open about their preferences. As less-popular candidates are eliminated for not meeting minimum thresholds,

their supporters have to walk to another corner to declare a new allegiance. Multiple speeches are often given by advocates for the candidates
during each round, which can increase the time commitment for a caucus
night to several hours.

Another big strike against caucuses, in this age of rampant conspiracy theories and allegations of voter fraud, is that they rarely leave
a full paper trail. Clumps of voters simply walk around a high school
gym, with officials quickly conducting and recording literal headcounts.
There's often no mechanism to make sure that the numbers jotted down
and reported to state party officials match the bodies on the gym floor.
The lack of a paper trail and transparency can lead to suspicions of in-
competence or foul play, as happened in Iowa in 2020, when the report-
ing process broke down and it took several days to find out the winner of
the Democratic caucuses.

REQUIRE ALL PRESIDENTIAL PRIMARIES TO BE OPEN TO ALL VOTERS

All independent voters should be able to participate in either major presidential primary. The logic here is almost as hard to argue with as eliminating caucuses. All registered voters, regardless of their party affiliation,
should have a say in choosing the final candidates for president.

Currently, twenty-four states plus DC have closed presidential primaries, meaning that independent and minor party voters do not have
a guaranteed right to participate in presidential primaries. As a result,
about 30 million independents in those states are locked out of both primaries. (In seven of these states, the Democratic Party allows independent voters to participate, while the GOP doesn't.) Another eight states
have "semi-open" presidential primaries, meaning that independents can
choose which primary they want to participate in, but registered party
members can't cross over. The remaining eighteen states have fully open
presidential primaries: all voters can choose whichever party's primary
they would like to vote in.[20]

A MORE SENSIBLE PRIMARY CALENDAR LEADING TO A NATIONAL PRIMARY DAY

One fact about American politics that baffles people from other countries is how long our presidential election cycle takes. For instance, the primary season in 2020 ran from February 3 to August 11—longer than an NFL football season.

This long schedule means that early states have the most active competitors and therefore draw the most media attention. They also offer underdog candidates the biggest opportunities to make a splash and attract new voters and donors nationwide. While the current schedule can help level the playing field for an upstart candidate, it can also be problematic, because the early states that enjoy this outsized influence (especially Iowa and New Hampshire) tend to be small and unrepresentative of the nation's demographics. In contrast, large and diverse states like California and Texas often go so late, after numerous contenders have dropped out, that their results have little impact on the ultimate nomination.

If both parties held their presidential primaries on the same day nationwide, primary turnout would increase significantly. Primary day would become a big deal nationwide, with every media outlet and social media activist urging people to vote. No one would have to look up when their state's primary was being held, and then hope to remember it. There would be countless visible reminders at every turn.

A national primary day would also equalize the impact of primary voters in all fifty states. The current unfair advantages of the early states would vanish, and no state's primary would become anticlimactic. There would also be far fewer wasted votes, because no one would be voting after some contenders had already dropped out.

There are, however, downsides to a national primary day. The current months-long process allows voters to evaluate candidates over time. If a little-known candidate surges during the beginning of the primary voting season, the current system provides plenty of time for voters to learn about them—including any past scandals or transgressions.

204 THE PRIMARY SOLUTION

Eliminating this vetting period could result in a party being stuck with a previously unknown nominee who peaks in popularity just before primary day, wins the contest, and then becomes embroiled in a scandal that hamstrings their candidacy.

Ideally, the presidential primary system would combine the best of both of these worlds: a long vetting period and a national primary day with higher turnout. FairVote founder Rob Richie has proposed such a system that would maintain state primaries but over a tighter three-month period. To ensure that smaller states are not ignored, Richie proposes letting them vote first but rotating the exact order. These initial primaries would narrow large fields of contenders—like the 2016 GOP and 2020 Democratic fields—down to a handful of finalists who earn at least 20% of the delegates. These finalists would then compete in a nationwide, single-day primary in June, with every voter in every state and territory casting an equally valuable vote in the primary of their choice, regardless of whether they voted in the first round or not.

This system ensures that the nominee is always decided on a national primary day in a fair contest that no one could realistically argue is open to manipulation. Unlike the convoluted process we see today, the simple principle of "majority rules" would determine the outcome. Richie noted that had such a system been in place in 2016, "Clinton and Sanders would have known all along they were heading toward a single final primary—something that would have removed all the sourness associated with the race being effectively over early on and giving the party a chance to confirm who it wanted as the nominee. The entire tenor of the Republican campaign would have changed as well. Trump would have needed a true majority, likely still facing his party's strongest candidates."[21]

PRESIDENTIAL ELECTORAL REFORM IS AN AMERICAN TRADITION

A major overhaul of our presidential election process may seem like a long shot. But as with the rest of our election system, it's worth noting how much presidential elections have *already changed* since 1789, especially in the wake of electoral outcomes that were viewed as problematic by large swaths of the country.

The chaos and controversies of the elections of 1796 and 1800, for example, precipitated a constitutional amendment that led to a separate Electoral College vote for the vice president, rather than the office going to the runner-up for president. At first, party caucuses in Congress nominated presidential candidates, until reforms in the 1820s and 1830s dethroned "King Caucus" and led to party conventions taking on this role. By 1912, direct primaries, where actual voters got a say, started to influence convention delegates. And by 1976, both major parties had established binding primaries or caucuses, open to all party members, in all fifty states.

If anything, we are overdue for the next evolution of how we pick our president and should be ready for the next window of opportunity. For example, we may be one election away from a credible third-party contender throwing presidential selection to Congress for the first time since 1824, which would be widely seen as unacceptably outdated and undemocratic.

With the possible exception of my proposed Electoral College reform, each of the other changes laid out in this chapter can be enacted at the state level or by the national political parties—without requiring an act of Congress, let alone a constitutional amendment. The final part of this book will explore how we can make such reforms a reality.

PART IV

THE PATH TOWARD NATIONWIDE REFORM

O n December 13, 2022, President Biden signed a bill that even just two decades earlier seemed like a far-off dream for its advocates. The Respect for Marriage Act requires the federal government and all state governments to recognize all same-sex and interracial marriages. While the Supreme Court had already ruled in 2015 that same-sex marriage is a constitutional right, this new law meant that the rights it granted in *Obergefell v. Hodges* were now solidified under federal law, and much harder to revoke, in the event the case was overturned.

Even more surprising to political pundits: the vote was bipartisan in both chambers. It passed the Senate, 61–36, with twelve Republicans voting yes—enough to prevent a filibuster by the bill's opponents. Then it passed the House, 258–169, with thirty-nine Republicans voting yes, along with every Democrat. "My fellow Americans, the road to this moment has been long, but those who believe in equality and justice, you never gave up. We got it done," Biden said in a speech on the White House lawn, where a celebration included performances by the city's Gay Men's Chorus and pop singers Sam Smith and Cyndi Lauper.[1]

Adding to the emotional impact, the law repealed the 1996 Defense of Marriage Act (DOMA), which had barred the federal government from recognizing same-sex marriages that took place under state law, thus restricting benefits such as Social Security survivorship and the ability to file joint tax returns. DOMA had been signed by a Democratic president, Bill Clinton, and had sailed through the Senate with yes votes from every Republican and thirty-two Democrats—including Delaware senator Joe Biden.

The new law also felt surreal to me, as a gay man who didn't come out until after college in 2012, and even then only to friends and family. When I ran for Congress in 2014 in a conservative rural district in Pennsylvania, I chose not to disclose this part of my identity, mostly because I did not feel ready and comfortable to do so. At the same time, I cautiously rehearsed what I would say if I was asked, as I promised myself I would never lie about it. The question never came directly, but I still vividly recall the times when I was asked if I supported marriage equality—usually by a voter who would not take kindly to my affirmative answer. My heart would race, and I would stumble through my words. That was the radically different world of just ten years ago and a reminder to me of how much things can change in a relatively short period of time.

Political activists of any stripe have to be prepared to be dismissed as overly idealistic and naive about what changes are possible at any given moment in time. We also have to keep the faith during setbacks, as I've learned during my decade of advocating for election reform. That's why I'm inspired by the relatively rapid success of the marriage equality movement, which pulled off a stunning triumph against seemingly insurmountable odds.

As I now shift from asking what a better election system might look like to how we can make one a reality, it's worth first examining how the marriage equality movement navigated the long, twisty road from DOMA to the Respect for Marriage Act.

CLIMBING A STEEP MOUNTAIN, ONE STEP AT A TIME

In the 1990s and well into the 2000s, supporting same-sex marriage was considered to be a position outside of the political mainstream. Moderate and even liberal Democrats usually tried to avoid the topic, while many Republicans saw it as a wedge issue they could use to their advantage.

While activists for marriage equality had been making their case for years, the debate didn't dominate headlines until November 2003, when the highest court in Massachusetts ruled that the state constitution required equal marriage rights for everyone. The following year, with President Bush fighting for a second term, Republicans saw an opportunity to drive turnout among conservatives and win over swing voters. In eleven states, the GOP sponsored successful ballot initiatives that banned same-sex marriage, even though none of those states were anywhere close to passing it in the first place. Most observers said the issue helped Bush and many 2004 Republican congressional candidates.[2]

The next few years were tough for the movement, because Massachusetts remained the only state with same-sex marriage until October 2008, when a ruling by the Connecticut Supreme Court raised the total to two. By then several states had passed various kinds of civil union laws, but full marriage equality was still opposed by both major-party platforms, by every major-party presidential candidate, and by a majority of Americans, according to polls.

Marc Solomon ran the state campaign in Massachusetts, trying to prevent the legislature from passing a constitutional amendment that would overrule the court. "I was just dying for state number two. Then we wouldn't have the bull's-eye on our backs every day. There were three or four lawsuits decided against us by one vote. It was really frustrating," Solomon, author of *Winning Marriage: The Inside Story of How Same-Sex Couples Took on the Politicians and Pundits—and Won*, told me.[3]

As a U.S. senator running for president in 2008, Barack Obama said, "I believe that marriage is the union between a man and a woman. Now, for me as a Christian . . . it is also a sacred union. God's in the mix."[4] His biggest rival for the Democratic nomination, Hillary Clinton, essentially agreed during a primary: "How we get to full equality is the debate we're having, and I am absolutely in favor of civil unions with full equality of benefits, rights, and privileges."[5] On Election Day 2008, even liberal California passed the Prop 8 ballot initiative, which amended the state constitution to ban same-sex marriage.

But Solomon and his fellow activists didn't give up; they kept working state by state, legislature by legislature, court by court. And they kept the faith that eventually, when a sufficient number of state laws were changed—as well as a sufficient number of people's attitudes nationally— the Supreme Court or Congress would give them a national victory.

Their progress was gradual, but unmistakable. In May 2012, many were shocked when Vice President Biden disagreed with his boss during an interview on *Meet the Press*. Asked what he thought about same-sex marriage, Biden went off script: "I am absolutely comfortable with the fact that men marrying men, women marrying women, and heterosexual men and women marrying another are entitled to the same exact rights, all the civil rights, all the civil liberties."[6] Obama, risking his re-election that fall, used the opportunity raised by his VP's controversial comments to modify his position and endorse same-sex marriage. Other well-known politicians began to do the same. In early 2013, Senator Rob Portman became the most prominent Republican to back same-sex marriage—two years after his son came out.[7]

By the time of the *Obergefell* decision in 2015, polls indicated that about 60% of the public were okay with same-sex marriage, up over 20 points since a decade earlier.[8] Not everyone, of course, but the movement didn't need everyone. They needed, and won, enough supporters in both parties to move the idea from unthinkable to mainstream.

As Solomon notes, "Our theory of change was that we needed to win in a bunch of states before Congress or the Supreme Court would act. That was based on other civil rights fights, like the fight to get rid of bans on interracial marriage. The federal government never starts things.

You need to prove your concept in the states. Once same-sex couples started marrying, people saw that our opponents' arguments were just not viable—the institution of marriage was not going to fall apart or be degraded."

TAKEAWAY LESSONS FOR PRIMARY REFORM

The marriage equality movement offers seven principles that those of us pursuing election reform would do well to heed.

Craft a Diversified, Long-Term Strategy

Leaders from several activist groups collaborated on a 2005 strategy document called "Winning Marriage: What We Need to Do" with a fifteen-year time horizon. It included benchmarks that they called "the 10-10-10-20 plan." In fifteen years, by 2020, "We could win marriage in ten states. . . . We could win civil union or 'all but marriage' status in another ten, secure limited protections in another ten, and grow support in the final twenty."[9] By diversifying the goals, the document helped unify many stakeholders in the movement—especially those who did not always see eye to eye on specific policy objectives—and focused everyone on staying the course for the long haul.[10]

Defend Early Wins Vigorously

Each early victory is a critical beachhead that must be defended. After that surprising 2004 court victory in Massachusetts, opponents made multiple attempts to pass a state constitutional amendment banning marriage equality, first via the legislature and then via a ballot initiative. It took the movement years of legal work, lobbying, and fundraising for supportive candidates just to keep that one state in the marriage equality column. Putting all those eggs in the Massachusetts basket was very risky, but ultimately successful. The state became a role model for the rest of the country and an inspiration to keep building national momentum.

Identify and Reach Out to Persuadable Opponents

It's easy to see everyone who disagrees with your movement as the enemy. But some of them, maybe a lot of them, will be open to persuasion. As Solomon notes, "The thing we've all lost is the ability to listen carefully to what opponents are saying and be able to answer questions. In fights about LGBT issues, I think progressives are [sometimes] too quick to call somebody a bigot, a hater. It's too much name-calling and not enough listening carefully to deeply engage and persuade. All social movements could use a lot more of that these days."

Marriage equality activists set up meetings with opposing state legislators—some of whom, intentionally or not, had said offensive things about the LGBTQ community. They mobilized supporters in their target districts, and brought gay couples who lived in those districts to meet with their representatives. Those constituents were able to humanize the issue, describing the problems they faced in their daily lives by being denied the right to marry. Such face-to-face encounters won over a good number of moderate or even conservative opponents.

Embrace Unexpected Allies

Any national movement needs strong leaders, as we saw in the history of election reform going back to people like La Follette in Wisconsin and Norris in Nebraska. One key reason the Massachusetts breakthrough endured was the strong support of Governor Deval Patrick. Similarly, Governor Andrew Cuomo played a key role in passing a marriage equality bill in New York in 2011, after it had previously failed.

But unexpected advocates or allies can be even more impactful in terms of increasing public support to a level sufficient to sway Congress or the Supreme Court. As early as August 2004, marriage equality found a surprising ally in Vice President Dick Cheney. During a campaign Q&A in Iowa, the conservative Republican revealed his disagreement with President Bush's support for a constitutional amendment to ban same-sex marriage. "Lynne and I have a gay daughter, so it's an issue our family is very familiar with. With respect to the question of relationships, my general view is, *freedom means freedom for everyone. . . .* People ought to be free to enter into any kind of relationship they want to."[11]

Recalls Solomon, "We wanted to have strong public support in every region of the country, including a sufficient amount of public support from Republicans. And we wanted to personify that support not just with polling but with individuals from different walks of life who could speak up for the freedom to marry. So we worked extraordinarily hard to get a diversity of voices, especially Republican voices, to stand up with us." He joked, "As much as I hated quoting Dick Cheney over and over, we did."

Pivot Your Message When Necessary

Early on, marriage equality activists stressed the rights and obligations of marriage as their main talking points. Why should gay couples be denied all the legal and financial benefits of marriage that straight couples take for granted? This logical question drew a logical response from many opponents: civil unions or domestic partnerships could convey benefits like joint tax returns and hospital visitation, without changing the definition of marriage.

To go further, the movement had to talk less about material benefits and more about the emotional impact of marriage—the deeply human desire to join in lifelong union with a partner. They began to replace their talk of rights and obligations with an emphasis on love and commitment. By focusing on this emotional appeal to equal dignity, activists had much more success in winning over skeptics to support full equality.

"We needed to demonstrate that our relationships exhibited deep love and commitment and were permanent," says Solomon. "That was the only way we were able to get straight people to see what we had in common with them. I think on almost every issue, it's crucial to figure out how to emotionally connect with people. The more your opponents use fear to separate and divide, the more you need to deeply connect."

Learn from Setbacks and Choose Your Battles Accordingly

For the marriage equality movement, the 2000s were a decade full of many setbacks along with many gains. As many as thirty-five states passed bans on same-sex marriage (whether in statute, their state constitutions, or both) prior to the Supreme Court's ruling.[12] Proposition 8 in California in 2008 was especially discouraging, as was the success of a referendum that undid the state government's passage of same-sex marriage in Maine in 2009.

The activists studied each of those setbacks and decided where to apply their limited resources. Rather than fight unwinnable battles in states like Mississippi, Alabama, and Texas, they focused on lower-hanging fruit. They challenged Prop 8 in court, and won. They kept lobbying in Maine, and voters approved a ballot initiative to legalize same-sex marriage in 2012. Every contested state was chosen as a component of the overall national strategy.

While setbacks are always discouraging, Solomon reminds us, "Any time you try to accomplish something big, there are going to be opponents who will try to stand in your way. Setbacks are part of any important fight. If you didn't have any setbacks, it would mean that perhaps you're not taking on a big enough fight."

Prepare to Hit a Tipping Point

A common trend in social movements is that, as hard as it can be to score early wins, there's often a tipping point when the floodgates open, creating a critical mass of diverse support. The precise inflection point is hard to predict, but it's a key sign of victory ahead. Recalls Solomon, "We went pretty quickly from Obama and Hillary being opposed to marriage in 2008 to—less than a decade later—having a lot of folks on board. I was surprised that it took so long to get state number two and state number three. Then I was surprised that so many states happened so quickly, in 2011, 2012, 2013."

Change tends to happen the way Ernest Hemingway described a character going bankrupt: "gradually and then suddenly."

LOOKING AHEAD

Marriage equality is part of a long tradition of successful movements, such as those to give women the right to vote, limit child labor, and end Jim Crow segregation. At first, such campaigns seemed extremely idealistic, if not impossible. But over time, they all overcame steep obstacles with a blend of strategies—legislative, legal, and cultural—usually state by state over numerous years. They centered their cause on *people*, not just process; they focused on changing hearts, not just minds. Our movement for primary reform must follow their example to succeed.

Chapter 9 will lay out the tenets of a strategy to win, aiming to apply many of these principles. Then chapter 10 will offer responses to the most common objections raised against reform.

NINE

WINNING: ONE STATE AT A TIME

Abel Maldonado first got into politics after his hometown of Santa Maria, California, denied him a building permit for his family's strawberry farm. The son of Mexican immigrants, he was elected to the city council at age twenty-six in 1994 and then elected mayor two years later. Maldonado is a Republican, but he enjoyed the nonpartisan nature of local politics. "When we repaved the streets, we didn't care where Democrats live or Republicans lived," he told me.[1] But when he tossed his hat into the ring for state assembly in 1998, he was quickly introduced to a new kind of politics—which he would spend the next decade working to fix.

"This is not a race that you want to get into," he was warned by a local party leader. A GOP county chair was next in line, and Maldonado was told to wait his turn. He did not. "The new primary system allowed me to thumb my nose at them and say I'm running, no matter what."[2] That was California's first year with a blanket primary: voters could vote for any candidate, regardless of party, and the top Democrat and the top

Republican would advance to the general election as their parties' nominees. He won with support from Republicans, as well as many independents and Democrats who had gotten to know him as mayor.

Maldonado often broke with his party and became known as an independent voice in Sacramento. But then, in 2000, the Supreme Court ruled California's blanket primary system unconstitutional, and primaries reverted to being open to only party members. "Within ten minutes of the decision, a member comes over to my desk on the floor," Maldonado recalled. "He says, 'You'—pointing his finger at me—'You better change your voting because you are going to lose your next election.'"[3] It was at that moment that Maldonado committed to restoring an open primary in California.

The first bills he crafted were shut down. "They made it very clear to me, this is not going to happen. It came from the Republican leader and the Democratic leader—both. This was the only issue that united these guys."[4]

Meanwhile, after serving for twenty years in the state house and state senate, Steve Peace began meeting with former colleagues about a strategy to reform California's dysfunctional politics. "Frankly, we were lamenting what a poor job we had all done," he told me.[5] With the encouragement of his former chief of staff, Dan Howle, Peace chose primary reform as the best way to make the state government more responsive to the electorate. "The problem with the partisan primaries isn't about who gets elected; it's about the behavior of the people after they get elected," he said.[6]

And around the same time that Maldonado and Peace embraced primary reform, the issue caught the interest of Charles Munger Jr.—the son of Warren Buffett's business partner, a physicist by profession, and a major Republican donor. Munger had noticed how gerrymandered districts and partisan primaries "created this rush of highly unrepresentative, highly polarized and invulnerable politicians on both sides of the aisle." He told me, "My state was broken. Partisan primaries were killing off the very people whom the general electorate would choose, if they only could. And every single Republican and Democrat who went to the state legislature and Congress was in a fortress; they couldn't lose no matter what happened."[7] Munger was prepared to invest millions to change the system.

Then came an opportunity for Maldonado, Peace, and Munger to coordinate their separate proposals and strategies to reform California's primaries. Facing a $41 billion budget deficit in the wake of the 2008 financial crisis, the Democratic majorities in the state assembly and senate needed to pass a budget that included unpopular spending cuts and tax increases.[8] At the time, passing a budget required a two-thirds vote, and Democrats were one vote short. Maldonado recalled: "I was called to an office and told, 'Abel, we need your help on this budget. What is it that you want?'" He replied, "I want an open primary. I am not going to budge from this. I'm here till the cows come home. My heels are into the ground and I'm not moving."[9]

That same day, February 19, 2009, Munger and Peace met for lunch to discuss joining forces. Both assumed any primary reform would need to be put on the ballot through a signature drive. But then Peace's cell phone rang twice—first the Senate pro tem, then the chief of staff to Governor Arnold Schwarzenegger.[10] Both took Maldonado's ultimatum seriously and wanted to review the constitutional amendment Peace had already spent months preparing with lawyers. His proposal was modeled on Washington's top-two nonpartisan primary, which the Supreme Court had upheld in 2008.* Ultimately, the Democratic leaders and the Republican governor agreed to refer the proposal to the ballot for voters to decide. After years of advocacy, Maldonado's resolve, Peace's proposal, and Munger's war chest converged on a single day to change the course of California's history.

While the ballot initiative earned the enthusiastic support of

---

*The system solved for the blanket primary's legal challenges by advancing the top two finishers to the general election ballot, regardless of party, thus not designating official party nominees.

Governor Schwarzenegger, who had successfully championed other reforms including independent redistricting, both major parties united in opposition. In the legislature, Assembly Speaker Karen Bass moved to put it on the June 2010 ballot, rather than in November, hoping to tank the proposal among a more partisan electorate. Opponents also used a legal proceeding to attempt to change the title and summary of the initiative in a way that would make it less appealing to voters. Both efforts failed, if not backfired entirely. Schwarzenegger publicly campaigned for it. Munger invested $3 million to fund a voter turnout effort led by the Independent Voter Project targeting unaffiliated voters. And voters adopted Proposition 14 by a decisive 54% to 46% margin. Over 2.8 million voters took power into their own hands and chose to abolish partisan primaries.

It would not have happened without key strategy decisions, a strong cross-partisan coalition, and courageous leadership—critical ingredients to any successful reform effort. I asked each of the three leading reformers to reflect on their experience.

"I knew it wasn't going to be a silver bullet, but I did know that every member who was going to run for office after we got the top-two primary was going to have to talk to more and more Californians, not just their own party," Maldonado said.[11]

"I am about as Republican and Steve about as much a Democrat as can be found," Munger said. "We saw primary reform as the right tool to bring the parties back to their duty, and each of us was as pleased to pull the other party back as we were to pull our own."[12]

And Peace invoked Victor Hugo's novel *Les Misérables*, specifically the scene when activists built barricades in the narrow streets of Paris to protest the monarchy and demand political reform. While the protest was quickly put down, it planted the seeds for the more successful Revolution of 1848 and the Second French Republic. "I always told my students to watch the movie and look at the two main characters standing behind the barricades," said Peace. "Those are two bourgeois guys, okay? It always takes somebody who is a beneficiary of the moment to help fund or drive the revolution."[13]

A NATIONAL ROAD MAP

As this California story demonstrates, there's arguably no more difficult task in politics than changing the rules under which leaders are elected, because many politicians who thrive under the status quo—and their deep-pocketed donors—will fight to preserve it. That's the bad news. But the good news is that, by and large, the *people* want reform. A national poll commissioned by Unite America in July 2022 found that 65% of voters support replacing partisan primaries with nonpartisan primaries and majority winner general elections, including majorities of Democrats (71%), Republicans (56%), and independents (68%). Only 13% of voters were outright opposed; another 22% were undecided.[14] Translating existing public support into public policy over the knee-jerk opposition of the political establishment is the essential task of our movement.

There are five critical steps to winning the Primary Solution nationwide:

1. Set a North Star goal and interim milestones.
2. Craft a state-by-state strategy to advance complementary policies.
3. Build strong and sophisticated legislative and ballot campaigns.
4. Create victory conditions nationally to accelerate the state work.
5. Lay the groundwork for an ultimate victory at the federal level.

All will require maintaining dogged persistence in the face of inevitable losses and setbacks. But all are achievable.

STEP 1: SET A NORTH STAR GOAL AND INTERIM MILESTONES

Every reform movement needs both a clear and compelling goal (often called a North Star), plus interim milestones along the way to track progress and keep people motivated with momentum-building victories. Women's suffrage? The goal was giving every woman in the country the right to vote, and the milestones were changes to voting laws state by state leading to federal change. Desegregation? The goal was overturning "separate but equal" nationwide, and the milestones were every successful integration of a lunch counter, public school, bus system, or workplace. You get the idea.

One challenge for the election reform movement is that we don't have a universally agreed upon goal. Much like the Progressive Era a century ago, there are disparate coalitions pushing for different reform policies. That's not necessarily a bad thing; those Progressive Era reformers accomplished quite a lot. But our movement would accelerate if we had a North Star that could fit on a sign, or ideally even a bumper sticker.

I believe that the North Star of election reform should be to abolish partisan primaries—so every voter has the freedom to vote for any candidate in every taxpayer-funded election, regardless of party. That's clearer than a more abstract ambition to create a more functional and representative democracy (which is the outcome we desire!) or getting into the weeds about top-four vs. top-two primaries. As a Unite America board member, Neal Simon, once advised me: "Clarity drives velocity." Let's align around and articulate a single, simple goal: solving the Primary Problem in American politics.

An Interim Milestone

Realistically, abolishing partisan primaries in most or all fifty states may take fifteen to twenty years. The power of primary reform, however, is that we don't need to win everywhere to make a transformative impact nationally. A reachable interim milestone that would significantly improve Congress and unlock progress on many national challenges: winning primary reform in six more states by 2026, the year of America's two hundred fiftieth birthday.

Why six states? Because persuading six more to abolish partisan primaries, while defending the current systems in Louisiana, Washington, California, and Alaska, will bring the total to ten states. The twenty senators and dozens of House members from those states, roughly divided by party, would be liberated from the Primary Problem and no longer under the threat of being primaried by the fringes. It would not be necessary to replace these elected leaders to see an improvement in governance, since changing their incentives will likely change their behavior.

Of course, this doesn't mean that the Senate would gain twenty moderates overnight; that's not our goal. We simply want our legislators to represent a majority of their voters. If they do so, these leaders will be more likely to form coalitions to get results on issues of significant national importance.

There's already a model for this approach, even in today's hyperpolarized politics. In the 2021–22 session of Congress, the Bipartisan Policy Center identified sixty senators (equally divided by party) who helped spearhead eighteen different pieces of bipartisan legislation. To make the list, a senator had to be a cosponsor of the bill, a member of committee leadership that guided the bill, or part of a "gang" that drove a final compromise.[15] A dozen of those pieces of bipartisan legislation ultimately became law, some prominent (e.g., gun violence prevention) and others not (e.g., postal reform).[16]

Not only did all eight senators from the four states without partisan primaries make this list, but half of them—Senators Cassidy (R-Louisiana), Murkowski (R-Alaska), Cantwell (D-Washington), and Murray (D-Washington)—were among the top influencers in the entire Senate, shepherding three or more pieces of bipartisan legislation. "While there's no longer a reliable group of 20–30 members who consistently support moderate positions, creating bipartisan coalitions on specific issues among differing groups of partisan members remains possible," wrote Jason Grumet, founder of the Bipartisan Policy Center.[17]

We have seen such groups work their magic in Congress before. Most of the time, the Senate leads and the House follows. A Gang of 10 in 2008 crafted a framework around renewable energy and conservation; it didn't pass, but helped inform future action. A Gang of 20 in 2018 catalyzed criminal justice reform, with the passage of the First Step Act. A Gang of 10 in 2020 broke an impasse on COVID relief, which led to a $900 billion relief package. With more members of Congress freed from their party bases, the body would have more flexibility to create other bipartisan efforts.

STEP 2: CRAFT A STATE-BY-STATE STRATEGY TO ADVANCE COMPLEMENTARY POLICIES

Article I, Section 4, Clause 1 of the Constitution holds the key to our strategy: "The Times, Places and Manner of holding Elections for Senators and Representatives, shall be prescribed in each State by the Legislature thereof; but the Congress may at any time by Law make or alter such Regulations, except as to the Places of chusing Senators." In other words, each state can decide how to hold its own elections, but Congress has the right to get involved and, for federal elections, supersede the states. Election reform can therefore be won state by state, and if enough states embrace it, the federal government may be pressured to require it for everyone.

As we saw, this state-by-state approach is how we got direct primaries to begin with during the Progressive Era, along with other reforms like the secret ballot. It's also how virtually all other social movements have been won, from women's suffrage to marriage equality. In the 1990s, voters or legislatures in twenty-three states passed congressional term limits (before the Supreme Court struck them down as unconstitutional in 1995).[18] Today, we are seeing state-by-state campaigns for marijuana legalization and a higher minimum wage. In many cases, state momentum builds up to a federal victory, whether in Congress, the Supreme Court, or both.

There are two ways to change election policy at the state level: by passing a bill through the legislature, or by going around the legislature directly to the voters via a ballot initiative. An important caveat is that only about half the states have a ballot initiative process, and in some places such initiatives are under attack by legislators who would rather take back that power for themselves.

There are trade-offs for both the legislative approach and the ballot initiative approach. Legislative campaigns tend to be less expensive and easier to sustain once passed, which makes them appealing. But because state legislators tend to resist dramatic changes, the bills they produce are usually more incremental in terms of policy and can require many years of advocacy to pass. Ballot campaigns are the exact opposite: more expensive and harder to sustain once passed (since legislatures can try to repeal them), but they can often be more aggressive in terms of policy changes and more immediate in impact.

These approaches are not mutually exclusive. They can happen in parallel (such as when a legislature refers a measure to the ballot) or in sequence, when a movement gets as far as it can in the legislature before going directly to the voters.

Incremental Policy Advancement

As part of a long-term strategy, our movement must carefully consider which policies to pursue, in which states, in which sequence. I'm not just referring to what should replace partisan primaries, but also what *other* policies can mitigate the Primary Problem if abolishing partisan primaries isn't feasible yet. We'll need the equivalent of the civil union laws that the marriage equality movement recognized as useful stepping stones in some states.

The advocacy and adoption of at least three complementary policy solutions can advance the ultimate goal of abolishing partisan parties—by drawing attention to the Primary Problem, shaping a national narrative, and building power and momentum at the state level. These solutions are opening primaries to all voters, ending partisan gerrymandering, and implementing instant runoffs.

Open Primaries to All Voters

Taxpayer-funded elections should be open to all eligible voters, as a matter of principle. "Something to remember about party primaries is that they are, essentially, state welfare for political parties in most states, in that the state government pays for a party's private election," writes Danielle Allen, a Harvard political theorist and political reformer.[19] Yet as we've seen, fifteen states do not guarantee the right to vote in primaries to all voters, disenfranchising about 14 million independent voters in state and congressional elections alone.* We can lobby those fifteen states to allow independents to vote in either party's primary (a "semi-open" primary), or to give this option to all voters regardless of their affiliation (a fully "open" primary). On average, over the last four midterm elections, states with open primaries saw more than double the turnout (21%) of states with more restrictive rules (9%).[20]

End Partisan Gerrymandering

The anti-gerrymandering movement has a simple mantra: voters should pick their politicians, not the other way around. In twenty-six states, self-interested state legislators hold all the power to draw congressional district lines. Most of them use that power to protect incumbents from competition and maximize their party's political power, thus depriving voters of meaningful choices in the general election. (Other states

*For a list of states, please see figure 9.

require input from a nonpartisan commission or outsource the process entirely to independent commissions.)*

There are several models for improving this system. Colorado has the gold standard: an independent citizen redistricting commission, with full authority to draft and implement district maps without interference by the legislature. Interested citizens from any party or no party can apply (as long as they're not current or recent politicians). Their applications are subject to review by a panel of judges. The panel then randomly selects four Democrats, four Republicans, and four independents to make up the twelve-member commission. To approve a map, eight of the twelve must vote in favor, and at least two of the eight must be independents. Commissioners are assisted by nonpartisan staff, and all proposed maps are subject to public hearings.[21]

Independent redistricting commissions virtually eliminate partisan gerrymandering, leading to increased competition in elections. A 2023 study found that districts drawn by independent commissions are more than twice as likely to have competitive elections (i.e., a winning margin of 10% or less) than those drawn by state legislatures.[22]

While rooting out partisan gerrymandering won't solve every problem in our politics, as most "safe" districts reflect our own geographic self-sorting, it's a good step toward more representative democracy and an organizing opportunity for our movement.

Implement Instant Runoffs

Even my seven-year-old nephew, Aston, and four-year-old niece, Arabella, have learned to say, "Majority rules!" when we're deciding on what activity to do together. It's not only common sense, but also a bedrock

---

*In another seven states, legislatures control the congressional redistricting process, but must either first consider maps drawn by a separate commission, or, if the legislature reaches an impasse, they lose their power to a commission.

principle of American democracy. But as we've seen, it's not how most elections actually work.

To replace plurality elections, we can lobby to give voters the option to rank their candidates, or at least select a backup option, through an instant-runoff election system. As of this writing, two states and fifty-one municipalities use instant runoffs, which also save time and money relative to traditional runoff elections.

Instant runoffs in partisan primaries can ensure more broadly representative nominees, and in general elections can level the playing field for candidates who want to run outside of the major parties without being dismissed as spoilers. Further, normalizing a ranked ballot can help pave the pathway for eventual top-four primaries, which rely on using instant runoffs in subsequent general elections to ensure majority winners.

STEP 3: BUILD STRONG AND SOPHISTICATED LEGISLATIVE AND BALLOT CAMPAIGNS

Since 2010, there have been twenty-two statewide ballot initiatives for open or nonpartisan primaries, redistricting reform, and instant runoffs. These initiatives, on average, won 54.7% of the vote and seventeen were successful. And since 2018, there have also been a handful of legislative advancements. Maine adopted semi-open primaries. New Mexico passed an advisory commission for redistricting. Colorado, Utah, and Virginia established municipal-level pilot projects for instant runoffs. These and other successful campaigns suggest three best practices that we can replicate elsewhere: carefully consider strategy decisions, build authentic bipartisan support, and don't be afraid to play political hardball.

Strategy Reigns Supreme

The German military historian Carl von Clausewitz said, "In strategy everything is very simple, but not on that account very easy."[23] Kent

Thiry keeps that quote handy as he advises state campaigns around the country on campaign strategy. Thiry, the cochair of Unite America and a former Fortune 200 healthcare CEO, first got involved in election reform in 2006, when he helped spearhead California's state legislative independent redistricting commission. Since then, he's funded and led eight successful statewide ballot initiatives for election reform, mostly in Colorado. Three critical strategic decisions led to his first victory in Colorado in 2016.

First, Thiry decided to take on the issue of closed primaries before partisan gerrymandering. He knew closed primaries were an affront to voters and the issue would be easier to frame in messaging. As he recalls: "It was our assessment that we would've failed in gerrymandering. That issue wasn't ripe enough at that point. Our electorate wasn't ready."[24] He also decided to pursue semi-open primaries—that is, opening primaries to independent voters so they can choose either party's ballot—rather than nonpartisan primaries, based on viability polling.

Second, while working on the open primaries initiative, Thiry drafted a second, more popular initiative that would replace Colorado's presidential caucus system with a primary open to all voters. It was submitted immediately before the semi-open primary initiative, so that they would be numbered Propositions 107 and 108, with the more popular measure appearing first on ballots. The campaign, Let Colorado Vote, crafted advertisements that urged voters to support both initiatives. "In a bike race, you can improve your time and exert less energy by drafting off the fastest biker," Thiry explained.

Finally, the reformers did not rely on their own motivations (making politics function better, reducing partisan extremism, and improving governing outcomes) when crafting campaign messages. "It was hard to put aside what resonated with us, but we were committed to following the data," Thiry told me. Surveys showed that only one message would break through with enough voters: fairness. Coloradans wanted their election system to be fair to all voters, including independents, who pay for elections they, at the time, could not participate in.

Open Primaries president John Opdycke underscored the importance of this messaging decision: "The way you pitch primary reform is
based on fairness, not on outcomes. This is about a level playing field for
all voters and all candidates. When you start saying we're going to elect
better politicians, this and that, you're starting to put a value judgment
on who's a good politician and who's a bad politician, which should be
the voters' decision, not ours."[25]

This combination of strategic choices, before a single ad or speech
was made to promote the campaign, worked. "Fairness" resonated with
voters, Prop 108 drafted off Prop 107, and both reforms passed with 52%
and 64% of the vote, respectively. Over 280,000 Colorado voters who
were previously disenfranchised cast ballots in the next primary election.[26] Two years later, building on the momentum from open primaries, Thiry led a successful campaign to end partisan gerrymandering in
Colorado, and the state gained one more competitive district. Together,
the ballot campaigns for primary and redistricting reform cost $11.2
million—an impactful investment in the future of a healthy democracy
in the Centennial State.[27]

Building Bipartisan Support

Roughly one in three voters in Maine (some 361,000 as of 2022) are unaffiliated with either major party. For decades, bills to open up the state's
closed primaries to independent voters would be introduced, only to fail.
In 2019, a new group called Open Primaries Maine brought political talent and sophistication to the cause. A reintroduced bill made it through
the house and, for the first time, to the state senate. But it stalled there,
despite polls showing support from a whopping 80% of Maine voters.
"We learned a ton from that first session," said Kaitlin LaCasse, campaign manager of Open Primaries Maine. "I'm a big believer in figuring
out what worked, what didn't, and how to shift moving forward."[28]

One of the biggest lessons was the critical need to build authentic
support from within both major parties—not just from independent

voters and the handful of independent legislators. A breakthrough finally came in 2021, when Open Primaries Maine endorsed a bill introduced by Democratic senator Chloe Maxmin and cosponsored by Republican senator Matthew Pouliot. Maxmin represented a district where Democrats, Republicans, and independents each composed about one-third of registered voters.

As Maxmin told me, "Half of millennials are registering as independents, and half of veterans are registering as independents. Whether we have open primaries or not, there is an exodus from the party infrastructure. I believe open primaries will create candidates who are more representative of the communities that they're coming from and who can better understand the vast variety of perspectives."[29]

Open Primaries Maine helped the pair secure additional bipartisan cosponsors, and helped recruit former Republican senator Olympia Snowe and incumbent Democratic representative Jared Golden to the cause. "In every press release, if we quoted a Democrat, then we quoted a Republican. When we released a list of about forty former lawmakers who supported the bill, we had an equal number of Republicans and Democrats," LaCasse explained. This bipartisan approach was driven by both principle and strategy. Validation from members of both parties, she added, "made it so people can focus on the policy and worry less about whether it would help or hurt their opponent."

The most common argument against opening primaries to all voters was the concern of party raiding, which I'll address in more detail in the next chapter. "Any of us involved in political campaigns know how challenging it is to get people to vote for who you want them to; that there would be some conspiracy that anybody would be able to organize in any meaningful way to get folks to vote for the *opposite* person just seems foolish," LaCasse said. Nevertheless, this concern was addressed directly in the new version of the bill, which prohibited voters from unenrolling from either major party within fifteen days of the election. This addition helped quell partisan opposition.

Open Primaries Maine worked with the Democratic Party, which controlled both legislative chambers and the governorship, to get to a neutral position on the bill. And by pushing the implementation date out to 2024 to allow more time for planning, the group also persuaded the secretary of state not to oppose it.

On June 8, 2021, the open-primaries bill won in the state senate with a bipartisan 27–7 majority. The following day, it also won in the state house, 92–52.[30] The campaign's decision not to go negative against opponents paid off; some thirty-six legislators who had previously voted against the very similar 2019 bill ultimately backed the new version.

"I remember sitting up in the House gallery watching the vote and just being completely stunned at how much we won by," Maxmin recalls. "The same thing happened in the Senate. It was really exciting because it was deeply bipartisan. I feel proud of that because it's going to expand the number of people who can engage with our democracy. And I think that's what we need now more than ever."

The reformers spent $150,000 over three years to pay for professional staff, seasoned lobbyists, and tools for grassroots education and mobilization. Relative to a multimillion-dollar ballot initiative, the legislative campaign demonstrated great bang for the buck. The most valuable part of the campaign? Its bipartisanship.

Playing Hardball to Support Pro-Reform Candidates

Supporting pro-reform legislators, in both major parties, is another critical strategy to complement both ballot and legislative campaigns. And that may require playing political hardball.

In 2019, Unite Virginia (a former state affiliate of Unite America) was part of the coalition to end partisan gerrymandering ahead of the next round of redistricting, by requiring an independent redistricting commission. The obstacles were daunting: to amend the state's constitution, an initiative would need to be passed by voters, but first it would have to pass in both chambers of the state legislature in two consecutive sessions.

In the House of Delegates, Democrats were mostly in favor (since they were out of power and risked bearing the brunt of gerrymandering), and Republicans were mostly opposed (since they expected to be the ones drawing the new districts). The Senate, however, was significantly more open to redistricting reform across party lines, as many members had been a part of the frustrating 2011 redistricting process, during which the governor vetoed state legislative maps passed by the legislature.[31] As a compromise to win the required support, the reformers agreed that the new commission could include both citizens and legislators. After the House of Delegates and Senate initially failed to agree, a conference committee led to a bill that ultimately passed with widespread bipartisan support in both the House (83–15) and in the Senate (40–0).

Knowing that the bill needed to pass again the following year, Unite Virginia spent nearly $165,000 to assist pro-reform legislators in both parties who faced competitive primaries.[32] These included Democratic newcomer Suhas Subramanyam and incumbent Republican state senator Emmett Hanger; both prevailed in their primaries and the general election. Meanwhile, Democrats recaptured control of both chambers, which instantly turned the tables on redistricting reform: most Republicans now supported it, while many Democrats—under intense pressure from their party to retain the power to gerrymander—cooled on the reform bill.

Subramanyam and Hanger, with the support of Unite Virginia, founded the bipartisan Commonwealth Caucus—a group of seventeen legislators who met periodically to discuss election reform and find common ground on a range of other policy issues. When redistricting reform came up for a final vote in 2020, the caucus was instrumental in holding a bipartisan coalition together, especially in the state house. Nine Democrats, including Subramanyam, bucked their party leadership to support sending the amendment to the ballot. Later that year, it passed with 66% of the vote.

In addition to using the carrot of support for pro-reform candidates, Unite Virginia also took up the stick of directly opposing anti-reform candidates. As part of that 2021 election cycle, the group targeted one Democratic legislator, Ibraheem Samirah, who had flip-flopped on his support of the redistricting measure and voted against it once his party demanded so. Unite Virginia's support helped elect a pro-reform challenger to replace Samirah.

This kind of electoral engagement proved that election reform, which legislators might normally see as a minor issue, actually had influential stakeholders who were paying attention to how they voted. Further, it created a positive feedback loop to reinforce critical relationships with legislators who were brave enough to use their political capital to do what was best for voters, even if their party was opposed.

STEP 4: CREATE VICTORY CONDITIONS NATIONALLY TO ACCELERATE THE STATE WORK

While our movement wages state-by-state campaigns such as the one in Virginia, it also needs to do as much as possible to foster national conditions that will make success more likely for those campaigns. Three of the most critical conditions are strategic alignment among advocacy organizations, broad-based support among grassroots activists, and the financial resources to compete in key states.

Aligning Various Advocacy Organizations

This one is less obvious than it sounds. Having spent the last decade in the election reform movement, I've seen how easy it is for well-intentioned reformers to get in our own way, pitting our ideas and proposals against each other, rather than investing our collective resources in high-impact strategies. When multiple groups care about the same issue, the result can be "1 + 1 = 3" or, if they aren't careful, "1 + 1 = 0."

The best (worst?) recent example is a ballot campaign in Seattle in 2022 that asked voters to choose between two possible reforms: approval voting (in which voters can cast votes for all candidates they support) or ranked choice voting. This forced both camps to waste political and financial capital attacking each other. While RCV prevailed, both proposals came within 2% of losing on the first half of the two-part ballot question, which asked whether voters wanted to change the current system at all.[33,*] On the other hand, Scott Kendall's advocacy in Alaska is a brilliant example of how different groups of reformers teamed up to combine their proposals into a single ballot initiative: nonpartisan primaries, ranked choice voting, and campaign finance reform. One approach was zero-sum, the other positive-sum.

"The difference in winning movements is that leaders manage to put their egos and organizational identities to the side (if only temporarily) so disparate factions can come together around a common agenda," writes Leslie Crutchfield, author of *How Change Happens*.[34]

Winning Broad-Based Support for Reform

To build a robust national constituency for primary reform, we need to go beyond technocratic, process-driven arguments and focus on the moral argument that every voter should have the freedom to vote for any candidate in every taxpayer-funded election, regardless of party. And we need to identify and engage communities of voters who are most impacted and therefore most likely to become passionate advocates for change.

We can see the power of emotionally driven grassroots organizing on both sides of the debate over firearms, for example. The political power of the NRA is often misunderstood to be a function of its political contributions; while those are important, the NRA's money is far less influential than its network of 5 million highly engaged members.

---

*Voters in Seattle were asked two separate questions. First, if they wanted some form of election reform, and, second, if they preferred RCV or approval voting. The first question needed to pass for the second to have any meaning, but if it did, whichever system received more votes in the second question would be implemented. The first question narrowly passed, and RCV won 76% of the vote on the second question.

Everyone in Congress knows that NRA members write letters and emails, join protests, and vote.[35] On the other side, Moms Demand Action was formed one day after the shooting at Sandy Hook Elementary School in 2012, and grew to 4 million members by 2017.[36] Modeled after Mothers Against Drunk Driving, it has used emotional appeals to drive state-by-state policy changes, while lobbying for national reform.

How can we nurture a passionate constituency for primary reform? Certainly, we should start with the 14 million Americans who are unaffiliated with both parties, live in closed primary states, and are disenfranchised in primaries. That number grows to 30 million when adding in Democrats and Republicans who are locked out of the primary of consequence in their particular congressional district. Many of these voters are military veterans. The group Veterans for All Voters, for example, was started in 2021 to engage and mobilize veterans to support election reform nationally. With state-based task forces, their members have lobbied elected officials, organized events, and even appeared in campaign ads. Another model for grassroots organizing is the group RepresentUs, which was launched in 2011 to build cross-partisan opposition to political corruption. To date, they have mobilized thousands of volunteers to help win 171 reform victories, large and small, in cities and states across the country.[37]

Amassing Financial Resources

Few reformers actually enjoy fundraising, but it's absolutely essential if we want to have the resources to compete against the extremely well-financed opposition that benefits from the status quo. During the 2022 midterm cycle, nearly $17 *billion* was spent on partisan politics[38]—mostly on ads telling one half of the country why the other side is evil. In contrast, one analysis estimates that about $150 million went to non-partisan democracy organizations working to reduce polarization that year, of which election reform was a subset.[39] We are at such a financial disadvantage that every dollar matters.

On ballot campaigns, for example, we need significant budgets in order to reach, persuade, and turn out voters. Having more money won't guarantee success, as we saw in the unsuccessful campaigns for nonpartisan primaries in Oregon in 2014 and ranked choice voting in Massachusetts in 2020; each raised and spent nearly $10 million. But not having enough resources will guarantee failure. Ballot campaigns are like criminal trials where the "Yes" side must prove their case to a jury beyond a reasonable doubt. All the "No" side has to do is poke holes, which is why most voters default to "No." It takes real resources to persuade them otherwise.

We relaunched Unite America as a philanthropic venture fund in 2019 to help solve this challenge, and I'm thrilled by the progress we've made in building a cross-partisan community of philanthropists. Our first fund mobilized $50 million for election reform. As I write this we're working to raise our second fund, with a $100 million target.

Philanthropists Laura and John Arnold have been the earliest and largest donors in the movement. The couple has described their attraction to election reform philanthropy as a high-impact way to promote an important, solvable, yet neglected issue—especially one that can unlock progress on other issues they care about. At our biannual Invest in Democracy Summit, I asked them how they remain undaunted by the risks of campaigns and the uncertain timeline of impact. Laura replied: "What we do know is that the current system is failing. It's failing all of us. That conviction is also an important part of the equation."[40]

Charles Munger Jr., who has invested over $27 million to win and defend election reform and other good governance initiatives in California, agrees about the importance of funding this work. "You do not get a tax deduction for work in politics, but from my point of view, it is philanthropy. For that amount of money, I could have endowed large numbers of chairs at the University of California. I could have my name on a building in academia. Heck, I could probably have given a research wing to a hospital. All of that would have earned me a number of celebratory dinners, a number of speeches, and the polite applause of 100% of the people of California."[41]

Instead, Munger says he got a lot of grief for getting into politics—yet he also got the positive impact, at scale, that he was seeking. "The California budget is $300 billion. If a structural reform that costs $10 million to pass will keep even a tenth of 1% from being wasted, or worse, that reform will pay for itself thirty times over in the first year; and a reform works in perpetuity. The leverage—good achieved for sweat and dollars invested—is enormous. I don't know another charitable or philanthropic endeavor where it is that big." He hastened to add: "Some people enjoy politics. I don't. I considered this my patriotic chore."[42]

David Crane, the founder of Govern for California, popularized the phrase "political philanthropy" to describe making financial contributions that aim to have a positive impact on a wide range of issues by improving the political process in a nonpartisan way. Unlike traditional, tax-deductible charitable contributions, they are not exclusively made to 501(c)(3) organizations, but rather to campaigns (like ballot initiatives) that aim to elevate the public interest over narrow party or special interests.

"If we want to make progress on solving any problem we care about, the share of resources being invested in improving our democracy through nonpartisan reform must dramatically increase," wrote Unite America cochairs Marc Merrill and Kathryn Murdoch in *Fortune*.[43]

STEP 5: LAY THE GROUNDWORK FOR AN ULTIMATE VICTORY AT THE FEDERAL LEVEL

At this point, it may seem unimaginable that Congress would pass national legislation to abolish partisan primaries. Yet advocates for other movements thought the same, years or decades before they eventually succeeded. So while we cannot rely on federal action as a core strategy in the short term, we should contemplate and prepare for what such action could look like down the road.

There is certainly precedent for Congress to be involved on such matters. For example, Congress has previously used its constitutional authority to standardize aspects of elections across states, grounded in its right to determine the time, place, and manner of congressional elections. The Help America Vote Act (2002) set standards for voting machines, and the National Voter Registration Act (1993) mandated that citizens should be able to register to vote when they apply for or renew their driver's licenses. Congress also passed the Voting Rights Act (1965) and renewed it five times since to root out racial discrimination in election administration.

The Open Our Democracy Act

Maryland Democrat John Delaney saw a great chance to make a first run for Congress in 2012, after the 2010 redistricting cycle. When the state's advisory commission released a draft set of maps, it looked like his home would be in a new district with an open seat, an extremely rare opportunity. But after word got out about his plans and the next draft of the redistricting map was released, he noticed something peculiar. "My little neighborhood was notched out of the district," he recalled. "Google Maps said I was twenty-eight seconds from the district line. Literally, it was half a block away."[44]

It soon became obvious that the district was being hand-drawn to maximize support for Rob Garagiola, the majority leader of the Maryland state senate, who was endorsed by the state's entire Democratic establishment, from the governor to both senators to several members of Congress.[45] Delaney ran anyway, which was legal, since the Constitution does not require a representative to live within their district. He played up the obvious gerrymander as a campaign issue, knowing voters on both sides were upset about it, and won the seat.

"I pledged when I was running that this would be an issue I would tackle because I saw it firsthand," he told me.[46] In his first term in Congress, Delaney followed through on that pledge by introducing the Open Our Democracy Act. "Let's make the House of Representatives actually representative," he wrote in the *Washington Post*.[47] The bill offered three reforms: top-two nonpartisan primaries, independent redistricting commissions, and making Election Day a federal holiday. The bill was introduced in 2013, 2015, and 2017, but never even got a vote on the House floor.

Delaney didn't take those defeats as a permanent failure. "It was an interesting piece of legislation in that it was overwhelmingly supported by constituents, but it didn't get nearly as much traction as it should have in the Congress."[48] He suggested that if a similar future bill were to have any chance at passage, it would require strong presidential leadership to get attention and support from the public. Otherwise, entrenched insiders from both parties would continue to use the flawed argument that Congress has no role messing with how individual states hold their elections.

Moving Forward Federally by Giving the States More Freedom

As tempting as it may be to lobby for federal laws that we think would create the best possible election system, we'll get farther faster by being *less* prescriptive. Any bill is more likely to pass if it focuses on key principles, rather than dictating to the states the details of implementing those principles. Those principles, as you can probably recite with me at this point:

1. *All* eligible voters should have the freedom to vote for *any* candidate in *every* election, regardless of party.
2. A candidate must earn a *majority* of the vote in order to win an election.

Congress can write laws that give states the flexibility to comply with these requirements as they see fit, such as via nonpartisan top-two or top-four primaries, and with old-fashioned or instant runoffs.

As election law scholar Edward Foley writes, on the latter point, "This freedom would enable states collectively to conduct a natural experiment among the various acceptable alternatives. The experiment would then determine which of these various majority-winner systems might prove most successful and durable, or whether perhaps a variety of different majority-winner systems ought to remain long-term, as their different features may suit different states in a federalist system."[49] This approach would have solid precedents, Foley points out. Congress passed a law in 1866 that required majority winners for Senate elections, which were at the time decided by state legislatures; this law became obsolete with the passage of the Seventeenth Amendment and the direct election of senators.

Another federal proposal that might be more viable in the near-term would be for Congress to establish a national primary day, or at least give states a financial incentive to join one. Currently, states hold primary elections on nineteen separate days between March and September. Consolidating all those primaries would surely increase national awareness and voter participation, making them more appealing to loosely affiliated or unaffiliated voters, rather than merely the most passionate and extreme partisans.

"This variability may prove a barrier to voter participation, because it makes it less likely that voters will know when to show up at the polls," according to a report by the Bipartisan Policy Center. "We found that when states in the same region hold their primary on the same day, participation rises."[50]

In 2013, a bipartisan Commission on Political Reform, whose co-chairs included former Senate majority leaders Tom Daschle (D) and Trent Lott (R), recommended a single national primary day to be held in June.[51] This, too, would have a precedent. For more than a half century under the Constitution, states held their general elections at different times. For instance, elections to choose representatives to the 19th Congress were held between July 7, 1824, and August 30, 1825.[52] It wasn't until 1845 that Congress passed a law establishing a national Election Day, to be held "the Tuesday next after the 1st Monday in November, in every even numbered year."[53]

A Pathway to the Supreme Court

Finally, it's not out of the question that the Supreme Court may find that publicly funded partisan primaries violate a constitutional right, probably equal protection, since they deny millions of voters the right to determine their representatives based on their party affiliation. Getting to such a decision could require many years of painstaking and strategic lawsuits, similar to those pursued by the marriage equality movement. We would need to find good cases that have a shot at getting through the lower courts and appeals courts, before finally reaching the Supreme Court.

The group Open Primaries is pursuing a litigation approach to challenge the system of partisan control of elections. Part of their goal is to establish legal standing—proving that potential plaintiffs are actually harmed by a state's current system. For example, New York prohibits independent voters from serving as primary poll workers, and Arizona does the same for election inspectors; both are arguably discriminatory. "By challenging discrete, and constitutionally suspect, aspects of partisan election administration—such as partisan election boards, poll workers, poll watchers, election judges, etc.—we expect to begin a process for reforming election administration in the U.S., create valuable precedents, and advance the public conversation."[54]

There have already been several cases related to primaries before the Supreme Court, beyond the cases that upheld the constitutionality of the nonpartisan blanket primary. In *United States v. Classic* (1941), the Supreme Court protected a party member's right to vote in primaries after three election commissions in Louisiana were charged with violating the civil rights of voters in a Democratic primary. "This right of participation is protected . . . where the primary is by law made an integral part of the election machinery."[55] Since partisan primaries "impose serious restrictions upon the choice of candidates" that voters have in general elections, the court determined that primaries were subject to federal laws and constitutional protections. Using this foundation, the court then ruled in *Smith v. Allwright* (1944) that "white primaries" (which prohibited African Americans from participating) were unconstitutional.

While the court established the government's interest in regulating primaries, it has also consistently protected the interests of political parties. In *Tashjian v. Republican Party of Connecticut* (1986), the court upheld the right of political parties in states with closed primaries to decide whether or not to open them up to unaffiliated voters. In contrast, the court has never recognized the right of unaffiliated voters to participate in partisan primaries regardless of the parties' preferences. At least, not yet.

GEARING UP FOR THE LONG RUN

To be successful, the reform movement requires a balance of idealism and pragmatism. Activists need to combine a motivating vision of a better future with the grit to face down tactical setbacks and fierce opposition.

The general strategy I've laid out, drawing on the lessons from previously successful reform movements and from victories within our own, should pay off in the long run. It's impossible to predict just how long it will take to have an election system that truly represents the voters. But we can shorten the process by following these five steps. And, as you'll see in the next chapter, by addressing our opponents' objections.

TEN

OVERCOMING OBJECTIONS TO PRIMARY REFORM

A couple of years ago I was invited onto a major cable network to offer my views on the news of the day, which included Marjorie Taylor Greene claiming that a single elementary school received $1.6 billion to fund critical race theory (yes, she said "billion" with a *b*), and Matt Gaetz demanding the Pledge of Allegiance be recited before every committee hearing. I used my airtime to note that these were both great illustrations of the Primary Problem, and that if we reform our election system we'll get more serious legislators, who will be incentivized to focus on the country's real problems.

Soon after the show ended, I got an angry call from the anchor, saying that my kind of answer was unacceptable if I wanted to be invited back. They were looking for fresh voices and new perspectives, but they didn't want me going on and on about election reform. The implication: it's boring and viewers don't care. They want guests who choose a side in our polarized political culture and contribute to the never-ending war between left and right. Conflict drives ratings; problem-solving doesn't.

That incident was a stark reminder that even great ideas offered by a reform movement will face an uphill battle against the inertia of the status quo. Primary reform has flown below the radar relative to other election reforms, not only because it has lacked attention from the media but also because it has lacked a constituency among public-opinion shapers, such as party leaders and political scientists.

To the extent party leaders even talk about reform options, they push ideas they think are most likely to benefit them, either directly by tilting the playing field or indirectly by pandering to their base voters. For instance, Democrats usually support automatic voter registration, while Republicans support stricter voter ID rules (even though their assumptions about the perceived partisan advantages of these measures are faulty). Likewise, Democrats support stricter campaign finance rules and Republicans support term limits; both poll well among their bases, though both are highly unlikely to pass.

In addition, many political scientists are skeptical about primary reform because they believe that political parties have an important role to play in our democracy, and they see this issue as driven by anti-party activists. Instead, many political scientists focus on potential solutions that may be theoretically beneficial but are far more unrealistic, such as expanding the size of the House. (You can make a logical case that the 1929 limit of 435 representatives is a century out of date, and we ought to have 1,000 or 1,200 representatives to rebalance district sizes. But voters have little interest in paying for more jobs for politicians; only 28% recently supported that idea.)[1]

If primary reform is going to succeed, advocates will need to refute the objections raised by these and other skeptical groups. Winning over a threshold number of die-hard partisans in both parties, working with political scientists to design and evaluate election reforms, and telling a compelling story for the media to cover are all mission critical.

In this chapter, as a sort of field guide for advocates, I'll address the seven most common objections to primary reform. In my experience, they are:

1. Primary reform advantages one party over the other.
2. Centrism or moderation isn't the answer to our political problems.
3. Parties should get to pick their own candidates.
4. Ranked choice voting is confusing, partisan, and flawed.
5. Election reform would hurt communities of color.
6. Primary reform has not proven to reduce polarization.
7. Primary reform is too incremental.

OBJECTION #1: PRIMARY REFORM ADVANTAGES ONE PARTY OVER THE OTHER

"This initiative can largely be seen as a plan by progressives to take control of Alaska's political system."

—Ann Brown, vice chair of the Alaska Republican Party, 2019[2]

Given record-high levels of political polarization, the most potent charge an opponent can make against primary reform is that it is just a Trojan horse to help candidates of the other party. As soon as an election reform proposal becomes polarized between the parties, many voters and legislators will take their cues from party leaders and decide their positions accordingly. We saw this in chapter 7, when angry Republicans in Alaska immediately claimed that the new system that elected Democrat Mary Peltola to the House in a special election must have been rigged. By that fall, when Nevada held a 2022 ballot initiative on a similar reform, its support among Republicans had collapsed from 50% in mid-August to 30% at the end of September.[3] The false claim about Alaska's new system had already become an article of faith for many GOP voters, who paid attention to all those angry tweets and videos.

The truth is that primary reform does not advantage either major party; instead, it levels the playing field for *all* candidates in two ways. First, every candidate, regardless of party affiliation, competes on the exact same ballot. Second, a majority-winner requirement in the general election eliminates the so-called "spoiler effect" of candidates that might otherwise tilt the outcome one way or another. The system treats every candidate fairly and, just as important, treats every voter fairly.

Alaska proves this to anyone willing to look objectively at the results. As we saw, the same statewide electorate chose a conservative, Trump-endorsed Republican governor, a moderate Republican senator who had voted to convict Trump, and a moderate Democratic House member. The new system did exactly what it was designed to do; it empowered voters to make nuanced decisions among multiple candidates—including different types of candidates from within the same party.

Primary reform allows both major parties to advance more competitive candidates in general elections and ensure that each winner has majority support. It is a separate question whether the parties will leverage reform to their advantage, both in advocating for it and adapting to it. If only one party in a state with closed primaries allows independent voters to participate, for example, they may have an advantage in the general election. Or if only one party in a state with nonpartisan primaries recruits and supports more mainstream candidates, they may also have an advantage. Both scenarios reflect how nimble and strategic the parties are, not any inherent bias within the system.

Montana is a great example of how both major parties would benefit from a more level playing field. According to two local political scientists, "In the 2012 U.S. Senate race in Montana, Democratic aligned groups bought ads to prop up Libertarian candidate Dan Cox, presumably in an attempt to damage the Republican candidate. Meanwhile, in 2020, the Montana Republican Party spent a considerable amount of money to help qualify the Green Party for the 2020 ballot, presumably to hurt the prospects of Democratic candidates."[4] In 2023, top-two nonpartisan primaries were endorsed by the state Republican Party and passed by the state senate—presumably to eliminate the possibility of a spoiler candidate in the 2024 U.S. Senate election. A bill filed by Senator Greg Hertz read, in part, "The Legislature desires that winners of Montana's U.S. Senate contests garner a majority of voters to ensure our federal elected officials have broad support in the absence of term limits and due to the longer terms in office."[5] Hertz noted that three of ten elections since 1992 produced senators without a majority of the vote, including in 2018 when Democrat Jon Tester won with 48.6%.[6]

There will inevitably be specific states and districts where a more level playing field will play to the short-term advantage of one party. For instance, if a party has gerrymandered its way into power, it follows that adopting independent redistricting commissions to undo that gerrymander may reduce its power. But that's not a sign of bias in the new system; it's a sign of unfairness in the old system. So when politicians claim that primary reform will only benefit the other side, what they really mean is that they don't want to face more competition or accountability that threatens their own power.

OBJECTION #2: CENTRISM OR MODERATION ISN'T THE ANSWER TO OUR POLITICAL PROBLEMS

"Moderate is not a stance. It's just an attitude towards life of, like, 'meh.'"

—*Representative Alexandria Ocasio-Cortez, 2019*[7]

I agree with AOC: centrism or moderation *is not* always the answer to solving a particular problem. And it's not the central objective of primary reform. What is? Representation and results.

By representation, I mean electing leaders who reflect the values of a true majority of their constituents and legislatures that reflect the full diversity of their population. In a representative system, deep blue districts will elect progressives, and deep red districts will elect conservatives, but all of them will have an incentive to reach out beyond their respective bases of primary voters. And legislatures will be composed of a mosaic of representatives from across the ideological spectrum, rather than relatively narrow factions of the two major parties.

And by results, I mean elected leaders who work with others to get things done. Leaders who represent a majority of voters are more likely to do what most of those voters want. It turns out that a majority of Democrats, Republicans, and independents can actually agree on a fair amount of what defines a well-functioning government. On many issues, making progress is not about splitting the difference between two polar viewpoints, but liberating our leaders to put the public interest ahead of partisan interests—regardless of where the solutions come from.

When I think about leaders from states without partisan primaries who are both representative of their constituents and results-oriented, I don't just think about true moderates like Senator Lisa Murkowski and Representative Mary Peltola, who (as we saw) both represent independent-minded Alaska, despite their different party labels. I also think about Representative Ro Khanna of California, a progressive Democrat who represents a deep blue district, and Senator Bill Cassidy of Louisiana, a conservative Republican from a deep red state.

Khanna is a product of California's top-two nonpartisan primary. He ran against a senior Democratic incumbent and lost narrowly in 2014, but tried again and won in 2016. "It gives a lot more opportunity to take on someone in your own party," he told me, explaining that a larger electorate reduces the advantage otherwise enjoyed by incumbents within their own party. "It allows for new voices to emerge."[8]

Khanna is not a centrist; he's a member of the Congressional Progressive Caucus. He has thrown his vocal support behind the Green New Deal,[9] Medicare for All,[10] abolishing the filibuster to pass voting rights legislation,[11] and Bernie Sanders' College for All Act, which would make public college tuition-free.[12] Nevertheless, Khanna often tries to find common ground with others and get things done.

In 2022, he visited Indiana to talk about enhancing domestic manufacturing, telling a local group: "Look, you people in this room will disagree on where I stand on abortion, on gay marriage. But why can't we find the place where we do agree? . . . I just think we've got to wake up as a country across the political divide and come together on how we build the next generation of manufacturing in America."[13] Khanna is even a regular on Fox News, telling *Roll Call*: "The more we can do that . . . the less people will see us as monsters, as the other, as foreign. You have to communicate with people to understand where they're coming from. And that's the whole nature of a democracy."[14]

Khanna sees himself as a reformer, not a soldier for his party, whose leadership he is willing to challenge. He is among the five members of Congress who do not accept contributions from PACs. In 2017, he coauthored an op-ed with Representative Mike Gallagher (R-Wisconsin) to make a bipartisan case for ending gerrymandering and banning former members of Congress from lobbying their ex-colleagues for five years.[15]

Cassidy is in many ways Khanna's mirror image on the other side of the aisle. He, too, isn't a centrist; he has a lifetime conservative score of 64% from Heritage Action,[16] 69% from FreedomWorks,[17] and 70% from Club for Growth.[18] He supported Trump's tax cuts[19] and the Supreme Court's decision to overturn *Roe v. Wade*,[20] and opposes bans on any types of firearms, including assault rifles.[21]

At the same time, Cassidy has been part of several bipartisan Senate initiatives. According to the Bipartisan Policy Center, he was a key influencer on several successful pieces of bipartisan legislation including the Infrastructure Investment and Jobs Act, the CHIPS Act (Creating Helpful Incentives to Produce Semiconductors), and the reauthorization of the Violence Against Women Act. In 2023, he began working with Senator Angus King (I-Maine) to address the long-term solvency of Social Security—an issue that both parties are reluctant to touch. "Both Joe Biden and former President Trump have the same plan, which is to do nothing on Social Security and to allow a 24 percent cut to benefits when the fund goes insolvent in about eight or nine years," Cassidy said on *Meet the Press*.[22]

Through all of his bipartisan efforts, Cassidy eschewed the

"moderate" label, telling *Axios*: "People assume that if you're moderate in tone and you wish to connect with others for a common goal of improving our country in some way, you don't have true colors. If I can work with other people and make our country better, then I'm a conservative who's got his job done."[23]

Centrism is sometimes the right policy path, but it doesn't work as the default answer to every problem. Progressives and conservatives working together to represent their constituents and solve problems—*that* should be the default answer.

OBJECTION #3: PARTIES SHOULD GET TO PICK THEIR OWN CANDIDATES

> "I think [primary reform] goes against the First Amendment, of the right of association. I believe Republicans, who desire to have a primary of their own, should have that right to have a primary of their own."
>
> —*Glenn Clary, chair of the Alaska Republican Party, 2019*[24]

Here again, I agree with the premise of this objection. Yes, parties have a right to nominate their own candidates. But no, it's not fair to have an exclusionary party-nominating process organized and run by the government and subsidized by all taxpayers. If the parties want to pick their own candidates, they are free to organize and pay for some other process. Justice Clarence Thomas agreed with this distinction in 2008, writing for a 7–2 majority that upheld nonpartisan primaries when they were challenged on claims that they infringed on the parties' right to free association.

When attempts were made to close Louisiana's primaries, Republican congressman Garret Graves responded: "You're asking me if I think it makes sense to limit the candidates that somebody can vote for? That sounds entirely un-American to me. I think people should be able to vote for anyone in the world they want to vote for."[25] He was right.

The Real Kind of "Party Raiding"

Some partisans fear that giving all voters the option to cast a ballot for any candidate in either party's primary, or in a nonpartisan primary, may lead some to attempt to sabotage the opposing party by casting ballots for its least-competitive candidate. The reality is that such attempts at "party raiding" have been exceedingly rare and highly ineffectual, even when well-organized and promoted.

For instance, during the 2008 presidential primary season, conservative radio host Rush Limbaugh encouraged his millions of listeners to "wreak havoc with the Democratic primary system" by voting in Democratic primaries, including by switching their registration if necessary. He called this plan "Operation Chaos."[26] As Barack Obama emerged as the favorite, Limbaugh told his fans to vote for Hillary Clinton to drag out the process and weaken the eventual nominee. If party raiding was ever going to work, it would be this attempt, led by someone with massive reach and credibility with his base, during a highly consequential election.

But a statistical analysis of voter registration data and election return data found that even Limbaugh was unable to sway the Democratic primaries. The researchers found "no evidence of a Limbaugh-motivated switch in political party registration or of a large or statistically significant Limbaugh-motivated increase in voting for Sen. Clinton. . . . The absence of a Limbaugh effect suggests that states or parties holding open primaries have little to fear about their elections being mischievously influenced by activists from the opposing party."[27]

In the fifteen states that have fully open partisan primaries (where any voter can participate in either primary), voters overwhelmingly pick the primary of the party they are most closely aligned with. There is no evidence of widespread party raiding; one study found that fewer than 2% of voters may cast strategic ballots in the opposing party's primary. There was also no significant difference in the extent of raiding between open and closed primaries, since those who wish to cross over in a closed primary simply have to change their party registration to do so.[28]

To the extent that outside actors are successfully manipulating the candidate nomination processes of their opponents, it's not voters casting ballots for candidates in an opposing party's primary; it's partisan political groups that deploy large campaign expenditures in these elections. As we saw in chapter 4, Democrats spent over $50 million to boost far-right candidates in Republican primaries in 2022 to give themselves a competitive advantage in the general election. This malicious strategy was effective: six such candidates were nominated, and all six then lost in the general election.[29]

John Pudner, head of the right-leaning group Take Back Our Republic, makes this case to his fellow Republicans: "Opposing [nonpartisan primaries] in essence condones the tactics used in all these elections to get the Republican who could win off the ballot to let the Democrat cruise to victory."[30] There is only one way Republicans can end this primary tampering: not by closing their primaries, but by opening them up and advancing multiple candidates to the general election. The same is true for Democrats, as Republicans will inevitably begin mirroring their tactics.

OBJECTION #4: RANKED CHOICE VOTING IS CONFUSING, PARTISAN, AND FLAWED

Several models of nonpartisan primaries—such as Alaska's successful top-four model—include instant runoffs with ranked choice voting for the general election. Thus, it is important to address several objections that specifically focus on RCV, which often gets the lion's share of the attention due to its novelty.

But first let me underscore: abolishing partisan primaries does not *require* the adoption of RCV. An instant runoff, for example, can also be achieved by giving voters the option of selecting a single backup candidate, rather than asking them to fully rank their ballot and potentially conducting multiple rounds of tabulation, as I highlighted in my proposal in chapter 6. Further, a Washington-style top-two nonpartisan primary system, or a Louisiana-style no primary system, does not include any instant-runoff component.

Here are rebuttals to the three most common attacks on RCV.

RCV Is Confusing

"This proposal would make voting more complicated and difficult at a time when we should be encouraging everyone to participate in our democracy."

—*Senator Catherine Cortez Masto (D-Nevada)*

Casting a ranked ballot is not complicated, in part because everyone is still free to vote only for their first choice and leave the rest blank. If they do choose to rank their preferred candidates, it's as easy as, well, 1-2-3. Exit poll after exit poll shows that the vast majority of voters find using RCV "simple"—including 78% of voters who tried it for the first time in New York City in 2021,[31] 81% in several cities in Utah in 2021,[32] and 79% in Alaska in 2022.[33] In fact, during Alaska's first year with RCV, 99.9% of ballots were cast without a problem, while 99.7% of voters cast valid ballots in New York City's rollout in 2021. These numbers only improve over time as voters gain familiarity. In a 2013 survey of voters in four RCV cities that had been using the system for a few years, 90% of respondents viewed their ballot as easy to comprehend.[34]

RCV Is a Democratic Trojan Horse

"Ranked-choice voting is a scam to rig elections."

—*Senator Tom Cotton (R-Arkansas)*[35]

RCV was first used in U.S. federal elections in Maine in 2018. In the state's competitive 2nd Congressional District, which had been represented by Democrats for twenty years before it flipped in 2014, independent voters would play a decisive role. But in a four-way race against a Democrat and two independents, incumbent Republican representative Bruce Poliquin campaigned *against* the new RCV system, rather than using it to his advantage.

"He basically executed a checklist of 'things you shouldn't do in a RCV campaign' that included mocking the independent candidates who together won nearly 10% of the vote," said FairVote's Rob Richie.[36] No candidate received a majority, and when the second choices of voters who backed the independent candidates were redistributed, the Democrat won. Poliquin's loss in 2018 kick-started the idea that RCV somehow favors Democrats.

Poliquin challenged the result in court and claimed the system was stacked against his voters. Judge Lance Walker, a conservative appointed to the federal bench by President Trump, rejected his claims: "[Plaintiffs] have not demonstrated disparate treatment, let alone a discriminatory intent. The RCV Act, after all, is party-blind."[37] That "party-blind" feature was evident just two years later in Maine, when Senator Susan Collins won reelection under the system, and Donald Trump won an electoral vote from the state's 2nd Congressional District in a RCV election* (they both earned an outright majority of the vote). Poliquin himself greatly toned down his anti-RCV rhetoric when trying to win back his seat in 2022, commenting, "Ranked-choice voting, we now know what it is. We didn't know what it was when it was first used in 2018. We know what it is now, and it's really easy."[38]

Republicans have found value in RCV in other states beyond Maine. In Utah, the GOP legislature approved a pilot of RCV at the municipal level to save money in administering costly runoff elections. Six Republican states, including Senator Cotton's Arkansas, use RCV for overseas and military voters, who would otherwise be unable to vote by

---

*In presidential elections, Maine and Nebraska award the statewide winner two electoral votes, and the winner of each congressional district a single vote.

mail in quick turnaround runoff elections. The Virginia GOP has used RCV to nominate candidates in select contests every year from 2020 to 2023, including to nominate now-governor Glenn Youngkin out of a seventeen-candidate field in 2021. "Using ranked-choice voting in party-run nomination contests in Virginia has dramatically improved the precision and quality of Republican campaigns," Rich Anderson, who chairs the state GOP, told *Governing* magazine.[39]

Further, a study by the Center for Campaign Innovation compared two Virginia congressional primaries in 2022—one that used RCV (the 10th district) and one that did not (the 7th District). The Center found that RCV did not change the outcome of the 10th District race but directly contributed to producing a nominee with a net favorability rating 27 percentage points higher. "The positive primary campaigns that RCV delivers are a nice goal on their own, but most importantly, they help our candidates win. After a positive campaign, the party is united and ready to hit the ground running for November," wrote the Center's executive director, Eric Wilson.[40]

The GOP would be wise to consider its expansion. Between 1998 and 2016, Republicans lost ten Senate races in which the Democratic candidate won less than a majority of the vote and a right-leaning spoiler won more than the margin of difference. In 2016, for example, New Hampshire Democrat Maggie Hassan defeated Republican Kelly Ayotte by just 1,017 votes; there were also 30,339 votes cast for independent and Libertarian candidates. "Had runoff elections or ranked choice voting been employed in these elections, Republican candidates likely would have been favored to win in most of them," noted FairVote.[41]

RCV Is Flawed

> "If nobody receives a majority of first place rankings, election officials eliminate the candidate with the least votes . . . until they create a faux majority for one of the remaining candidates."
> —*Jennifer C. Braceras, director, Independent Women's Law Center*[42]

Critics point out that winners under RCV can actually be decided by less than a majority. Imagine a race with ten candidates that requires multiple rounds of tabulation to decide. By the end, an individual voter's ballot can become "exhausted" and not count toward selecting the final winner, if they did not rank a sufficient number of candidates. Thus the winner of the final tabulation might not have earned a majority *of total votes cast in the entire election.*

While this hypothetical scenario is technically possible, all voters would still be better off than under an old-fashioned, first-past-the-post election, in which the winner of that ten-candidate field might have a very small plurality. In the latter case, every vote other than one for the winner is instantly "exhausted"—meaning irrelevant—under a traditional system.

In a slightly different scenario where the top two vote-getters return for a traditional runoff a few weeks later, we know that significantly fewer voters participate in second-round elections. (Those are truly exhausted voters.) RCV is the best way to make sure that the most voices contribute to the final result.

A related critique is that RCV can "squeeze out" centrist candidates, including those who might win in head-to-head matchups against all other candidates. Consider a hypothetical three-way race between a far-left, far-right, and centrist candidate in a narrowly divided district. Many Democrats would rank the far-left candidate first and the centrist second. Many Republicans would rank the far-right candidate first and the centrist second. With the fewest first-place votes, the centrist would be the first eliminated under an instant runoff, *even though* in a two-way race in the same district, the centrist would likely beat both the far-left and far-right candidates.

It's true that this scenario is theoretically possible, but it immediately prompts three questions: How often does it happen? If and when it does, is that an objectively bad or unrepresentative outcome? And is there any superior voting system that's viable to both pass and sustain? The answers, respectively: very rarely, it depends, and highly doubtful. Still, other alternatives to plurality voting exist, ranging from Approval Voting to Total Runoff (also known as Head-to-Head)—with each bringing a set of pros and cons. For example, a system that could produce a technically more representative outcome could also be so complicated that it is less politically feasible to adopt. Similarly, a system that could be easier for voters to use could also introduce ways for other voters to game it.

Reformers can (and do!) spend a lot of time debating the merits of various election methods; ultimately, however, *there is no perfect voting system*. As far back as 1951, Nobel Prize–winning economist Ken Arrow established what became known as the "impossibility theorem": no voting system can simultaneously satisfy all the criteria of what would ideally describe a maximally fair voting system. As Arrow put it, "Most systems are not going to work badly all of the time. All I proved is that all can work badly at times."[43]

We should aim for the least imperfect voting system that we can implement, rather than chasing a nonexistent perfect alternative. One thing is abundantly clear: RCV is far superior to today's plurality voting system.

OBJECTION #5: ELECTION REFORM WOULD HURT COMMUNITIES OF COLOR

> "It has become clear we cannot support a change to our state constitution that would likely further silence the minority communities or candidates within these districts."
>
> —*Patricia Brigham, president, League of Women Voters of Florida*[44]

Unlike critics on the right, who claim that reform will rig elections in favor of Democrats, critics on the left often claim that reform will hurt communities of color, both as voters and candidates. This line of attack is unsubstantiated by any credible research, but it is effective in influencing some audiences, especially white progressives who are highly sensitive to any such claims.[45]

During a ballot initiative for nonpartisan top-two primaries in

Florida in 2020, a group led by former Democratic politician Sean Shaw claimed that the reform would lead to "a flood of white GOP voters in safe Democratic districts [who] will 'bleach' seats and seriously erode the voting power of African-Americans and Hispanics."[46] Despite a two-year deliberative process and detailed study that led to their initial support for the reform, the League of Women Voters of Florida reversed course overnight, under pressure from the state Democratic Party.

"It breaks my heart that we would lose another bipartisan organiza-tion, because we don't have many," said Brenda Carr, who resigned from the board of a local league chapter after the reversal, to continue her own advocacy for the ballot initiative. Carr recalled to me canvassing in her neighborhood and asking a voter if she would support the initiative. "She got the newspaper out and said, 'Here. The league says don't vote for this. I'm not voting for that.'"[47] The initiative earned 57% of the vote, short of the 60% required to change the state's constitution. "Thanks in part to the League's political miscalculation," editorialized the *Orlando Sentinel*, "Flor-ida remains one of nine states with a closed primary system—one that ex-cludes nearly 4 million voters, including 1.2 million minority voters."[48]

Election results indicate that nonpartisan primaries and other elec-tion reforms could actually lead to greater representation for communi-ties of color. In the elections following California's adoption of top-two nonpartisan primaries, the state's legislative Black Caucus increased by 50% and the Hispanic Caucus grew by 25%.[49] More research is still needed to determine causation with greater confidence. On the other hand, nonpartisan primaries unambiguously empower voters of color. About 37% of Latinos and 30% of African Americans are not registered with any party.[50] They are thus barred from participating in primaries in closed-primary states, including Florida. In this respect, the old prohibi-tions that kept African Americans from voting in primary elections in southern states endure, though in a more subtle way that only impacts independent voters. A switch to nonpartisan primaries would immedi-ately increase their collective power and voice.

After studying the consequences of nonpartisan primaries and RCV for communities of color, two political scientists note that several surveys have found "no difference in ease of understanding between white and non-white voters in RCV cities."[51] For instance, following the first use of RCV in New York City's Democratic mayoral primary in 2021, exit polls found similarly high rates of white, Black, Hispanic, and Asian voters finding their ballot "simple" to complete, while all four demographic groups said they understood the RCV process well.[52]

The researchers also noted that more open primary systems "foster higher turnout in both the primary and in the general election, more so for people of color than for whites."[53] This is largely due to the fact that Hispanic and Asian Americans, in particular, choose not to register with any party at higher rates than white voters. In other words, maintaining closed primaries has an outsize impact on disenfranchising certain communities of color. The scholars concluded: "We see no systematic evidence that adjacent reforms such as the top-two primary or RCV elections advantage white constituents or candidates in terms of participation, representation, or policy provision."[54]

OBJECTION #6: PRIMARY REFORM HAS NOT PROVEN TO REDUCE POLARIZATION

Early assessments from political scientists who examined the impact of primary reforms suggested that they don't hold much promise for decreasing polarization. These assessments were often repeated by media outlets and shaped a pessimistic view of reform among influential people who follow such things closely. However, updated research and alternative methodologies offer a much more optimistic view on the impact of primary reform.

Impact Takes Time

When Unite America analyzed every academic study done on nonpartisan primaries as of 2021, we found that the most recent data being used to drive conclusions came from 2014 at the latest, and often earlier. Most of the studies examined California's top-two system in the years immediately following its 2012 implementation, finding no change in levels of polarization in the state legislature or among the state's congressional delegation. There are a couple of limitations to this early research.

It takes time for any election reform to fully take effect. While reform can immediately shift incentives for incumbents, it has an even greater impact as it shifts who decides to run and who wins—but those results often have to wait until an incumbent decides to retire. And while reform immediately changes how voters cast their ballots, it has an even greater impact as candidates (and the politicos who advise them) change how they campaign and how broadly they reach out to voters. Evaluating the impact of election reform after only one or two election cycles is like changing your diet and getting on the scale only one or two weeks later. You can't let modest early progress discourage you.

Further, as you may have noticed, American politics has changed dramatically since 2014. For example, those who assumed political trends would hold likely missed predicting Trump's election. Similarly, there is good reason to suspect that the difference between partisan and nonpartisan primaries matters much more post-2016 given the rise of Trump and Sanders and their respective political movements. And it's quite likely we still haven't reached the apex of polarization.

More recent research paints a different picture. In 2020, Christian Grose, a political scientist at USC, published an article that replicated earlier research by using the same methods, but with more data. Whereas earlier work found that nonpartisan primaries had no impact after just one or two election cycles, Grose found that Top Two significantly reduced polarization.[55] In a Unite America report on top-two nonpartisan primaries, Richard Barton, a political scientist at Syracuse University, replicates earlier studies using even more recent data, and finds that Top Two moderates state legislators and members of Congress. A number of other recent studies reinforce these new findings.[56]

Data on Polarization Is Imperfect

Virtually all analysis of the impact of primary reform is built upon a score of ideology called DW-Nominate, which ranks legislators from –1 to +1 on a left-right spectrum, based on voting patterns. For example, a legislator who sometimes votes with the opposing party might generate a score of 0.7, which suggests they are more moderate than another who scores 0.95. However, there are several significant limitations to DW-Nominate.

First, these scores tend to be less a measure of ideology—what legislators believe—and more a measure of mere partisanship—how often they vote with their party. In 2018, Senators Ted Cruz and Jeff Flake had roughly equivalent DW-Nominate scores, as they generally voted with the GOP at a similar frequency.[57] But they are actually nothing alike; for starters, one helped encourage the January 6 insurrection and the other denounced it.

Second, party leaders increasingly control what issues get voted on in the first place. Imagine a state where, prior to reform, the majority party enacted polarizing legislation to appeal to their base, via party-line votes in the state legislature. Now imagine that, after reform, the majority party in that same state can no longer pass such polarizing bills, because they now have to appeal to a broader electorate. If party-line voting remains roughly the same before and after, a DW-Nominate analysis will suggest that nothing has changed, when in fact the nature of the legislation may have changed dramatically.

Finally, DW-Nominate (and similar measures for state legislatures, known as Shor-McCarty scores) doesn't capture how individual incumbents evolve. Scores are relative measures between one legislator and another in any given session, but they don't capture individual behavioral shifts across years in office. As my colleague Richard Barton said, "If the failure to account for the prospect of incumbent legislators changing their behavior, in response to primary reforms, sounds like a hugely problematic limitation in a study about the effects of primary reform, that is because it is."[58]

Data Can Miss the Story

Some academics underestimate the impact of primary reform by asserting that primary voters and general election voters from the same party actually aren't all that different. *Sure, there are fewer of them, but they generally tend to hold the same views and values,* they say of primary voters. Several studies even suggest that independent voters who participate in open primaries are not much different in terms of ideology from their partisan counterparts.[59] If these factors are true, skeptics suggest, primary reform won't have much of an impact on polarization.

But even if we assume these tendencies are accurate, the conclusion drawn is entirely wrong. We know that low-turnout primaries are more easily manipulated by narrowly partisan and special interest groups in partisan primaries. Solely looking at voters' ideology may miss who they are being influenced by during each election cycle and which candidates are benefiting from interest group donations and support. In elections where all the candidates share the same party affiliation, name identification alone (how familiar a candidate's name is to the voter) plays a large role in shaping outcomes. And when ideological activists and donors are most likely to help campaigns drive name identification by knocking on doors and paying for mailers, candidates have an incentive to cater to their issues.

Moreover, the depolarizing impact of primary reform is not a function of primary election voters being much different from their same-party counterparts in the general election. It's a function of having an election in which all voters are able to vote for any candidate they desire, regardless of party, in both the primary and the general. While elections with partisan primaries tend to produce candidates who represent the median voter of the majority party, elections without partisan primaries tend to produce candidates who represent the median voter of the entire electorate.

There Are Other Methods of Study

Fortunately, some political scientists have recognized the inherent limitation of relying on quantitative data alone to draw conclusions about the impact of partisan primaries and primary reform.

"Today's dominant methodological approaches in political science prioritize top-down research designs that are centered on falsifiable hypotheses and thus are concerned exclusively with testing them empirically, using quantitative analysis," write political scientists Elaine Kamarck and James Wallner.[60] They took a different approach, going beyond quantitative measures of roll-call voting to actually speak to dozens of members of Congress, and concluded: "While the links between primaries and polarization cannot be established using big data, the interviews with members of Congress presented herein illustrate that their attention to advocacy groups, which play in the primary arena, is a major source of today's polarization."[61] Similarly, we can't measure who chooses not to run in the first place because of partisan primaries.

The hardest part of demonstrating the impact of primary reform is that it's exceedingly difficult to identify hypothetical bad outcomes that didn't happen, rather than pointing to actual results, positive or negative. If you start exercising and then *don't* have a heart attack, how can you prove causality for preventing a bad outcome?

I asked Steve Peace, the former state senator who helped craft California's top-two primary, about the assertion that the reform hasn't made much difference because California still isn't a shining example of effective governance. He replied: "Only a person who has never been in the legislature could have that view. . . . For those who lament the terrible conditions in Sacramento, I can only say—it would be that much more terrible but for these changes."[62]

OBJECTION #7: PRIMARY REFORM IS TOO INCREMENTAL

With the range of threats facing our democracy today, some dismiss primary reform as too slow to make a big-enough difference fast enough. These skeptics usually fall into one of two camps: defaulting to a strategy focused on defeating anti-democratic or extremist candidates, or advocating for even more aggressive structural changes. There is nothing wrong with the alternative approaches, but they are each limiting and risky in their own right. The former risks battling a perpetually growing fire with a garden hose; the latter risks the fire truck never showing up.

Fortunately, election reform is not a zero-sum game. There are and ought to be many advocates and organizations pursuing many different ideas and strategies. Ultimately, we cannot be confident in what will work until we try. And if the states truly are laboratories of democracy, it's better to run different experiments with different approaches than to put all of our reform eggs into one basket. However, primary reform is worth *prioritizing* because it is the most powerful reform currently viable and, importantly, because its success can both complement other reforms and change what else may be viable in the future.

For example, some reformers advocate for fusion voting, which allows multiple parties to nominate the same candidate. A general election ballot would then list the candidate with each party supporting him or her. It was a common practice in the nineteenth century by minor parties in order to gain influence and power, which is precisely why the major political parties outlawed it in all but a handful of states. Proponents of re-legalizing fusion voting argue that it would dampen polarization by allowing more fluid coalitions within the two major parties and new parties. They may be right. Fortunately, this approach is compatible with primary reform. A general election ballot featuring the top four candidates from a nonpartisan primary could easily list multiple party endorsements for any particular candidate.

Other reformers advocate for proportional representation. Under this system, congressional districts would elect multiple members at large through ranked choice voting, such that a candidate may only need to win 20% of the vote in order to win one of the five seats from that district. For example, Massachusetts might send at least one Republican to Congress and Oklahoma at least one Democrat—rather than zero each. Since proportional representation would require an act of Congress, it is a much harder reform to achieve. However, primary reform can advance reform-minded leaders, who may be more likely to support ambitious changes in Congress. For example, the Fair Representation Act (which would implement proportional representation) is cosponsored by Representative Ro Khanna, who was elected under California's top-two system.

As the old saying goes: the best time to plant a tree was thirty years ago; the second-best time is now. If we want transformation in our political system, we have to embrace some elements of incrementalism to get there. The spectrum of policies that are viable at any given time can shift. And those shifts can be engineered as the public sees real change happen and benefits from those changes. Primary reform may not be every reformer's ultimate objective, but chances are, it could be a smart component of both a near-term and long-term strategy.

BUILDING CONVICTION IN PRIMARY REFORM

There's a lot we still do not know about primary reform, and a lot we cannot know until we actually see how it works in more states. The uncertainties, alternatives, and trade-offs can be paralyzing. That is, until we remind ourselves of the system we *already* have today, in which 8% of Americans elect 83% of Congress via partisan primaries that fuel gridlock and anti-democratic extremism. Our current reality should be an unacceptable option.

So let's review what we do know about primary reform, contrary to some critics' assertions: It empowers all voters equally, regardless of party. It produces the most representative outcomes, whether left, right, or center. It preserves a role for political parties to recruit, endorse, and support their own candidates. Where it has been used, voters like it and historically marginalized communities benefit from it. It reduces polarization and improves the incentives for our leaders to actually govern. And it very well may help to unlock other ambitious, long-term reforms.

To be sure, we can make a strong case for primary reform with facts and reason, but that will not be enough. The greatest forces that oppose progress on this issue are not interested in having an intellectual argument, though they may make such claims. They are focused on one thing and one thing only: power. And in the battle for power, as we will see in the conclusion, we must summon two forces that can overcome the status quo: moral clarity and courageous leadership.

CONCLUSION

Colors of Democracy

In lands divided, our dreams inspire,
To douse the flames of partisan ire,
Abolishing primaries, we conspire,
To rise above the fray, and lift us higher.

No longer blue nor red confined,
A spectrum of voices, now aligned,
Where principles lead, and truths unwind,
A tapestry of colors, no longer maligned.

A common ground, where hope sustains,
Breaking chains, where fairness reigns,
The spirit of democracy, its vibrant dance,
Brings nonpartisan primaries, a bold advance.

That poem was not written by me . . . or any human. It was written by
ChatGPT, an artificial intelligence chat bot released by the company
OpenAI while I was working on this book. Pretty good, eh? Artificial
intelligence like ChatGPT is already doing things that would have been

considered science fiction not so long ago, from powering self-driving cars to reading X-rays. The implications for our privacy, security, economy, and quality of life are daunting, to put it mildly.

Given this reality, do you believe our leaders in Washington or in any state capital are up for the task of developing public policy to harness the benefits and regulate the liabilities of this cutting-edge technology?

Many of our leaders are too preoccupied with wedge issues to score points, get attention, and raise money to prevail in their next partisan primary. Others have no conception or understanding of the kind of world in which apps write poetry, because their insulation from any kind of political competition has given them something approaching lifelong tenure in office. The average age of a member of Congress is now nearly sixty, and nearly a quarter of Congress is over seventy.[1] In a 2022 congressional hearing on TikTok, three different representatives called the social media app "Tic Tac," as in the breath mint.[2] Lest you think they were just confused by the name, another questioned the CEO whether the app had the ability to access his home Wi-Fi network.[3]

As I wrote in the introduction: primaries matter because elections do, and elections matter because that's how we decide who will shape the policy that governs our future. While we are making stunning advances in medicine, education, and technology, for example, the same cannot be said about democracy. "Governance may be the only realm of modern life in which we are becoming steadily less capable," says Charlie Wheelan, the founder of Unite America.[4] The 2024 presidential election is likely to be a vivid illustration of this decline, which ails our body politic at every level. Surely we can do much better. We owe it to future generations to upgrade our democracy.

Partisan primaries may have been a necessary invention of the early twentieth century, but reforming them is now the preeminent political task of our time.

Cultivate the Karass

I dedicated this book to Doug Bailey, my late mentor who founded Unity08 (the online presidential nominating convention I described in chapter 8), and Jake Brewer, another mentor who was only thirty-four (my current age) when he was killed during a charity bike ride in 2015. Jake was working in President Obama's Office of Science and Technology Policy at the time, after a stint at Change.org, where he hired me to help create a mobile app that made it easier for voters to research their ballot ahead of Election Day. Both were visionary reformers, from different parties and generations.

When Jake's mom, Lori Brewer Collins, went to clear out his office in the Eisenhower Executive Office Building, she found a Post-it note on his computer monitor that read: *Cultivate the Karass.* She discovered the meaning of the word "karass," coined by the novelist Kurt Vonnegut, and adapted it to: "a group of individuals who are unwittingly linked, in cosmically significant ways, all committed to doing work for the common good." Jake was committed to breaking down barriers and bringing people together to work on big problems, across disciplines and identities. His sticky note was a daily reminder to himself about how big change happens: when we advance it *together*.

So whether you are a Democrat, Republican, or independent, political junkie or newbie, activist or philanthropist—I hope you will join me in a growing karass to reform our elections and renovate our democracy.

Moral Clarity and Courageous Leadership

In 2020, alongside the Institute for Citizens & Scholars, Lori and I helped start a fellowship in Jake's honor, bringing together two dozen leaders within the democracy reform movement to supercharge our collective efforts. We met several times over the next two years. At one meeting, in early 2022, we gathered to discuss Russia's historic invasion of Ukraine. Most experts had predicted the country would fall within days. Why had that prediction been so off target? What could we learn from it?

The discussion prompted me to write down two phrases in my notebook: *moral clarity* and *courageous leadership*. President Volodymyr Zelenskyy channeled both to rally his people and the entire Western world to Ukraine's defense. He called out the invasion as crossing an intolerable line in violating another nation's sovereignty. And when he was offered rescue out of the country, he famously quipped: "I need ammunition, not a ride."

I believe we can draw upon these same principles when strategizing how to rescue our democracy from the fringes today—recognizing that America's greatest enemy is not a foreign dictator but our own political division. Ours is a time of choosing: Will we choose to love our democracy more than we choose to hate roughly half of those with whom we share it? If so, we cannot tolerate partisan primaries that disenfranchise voters, fuel division, and disincentivize problem-solving. It's that simple. Primary reform is a *moral issue* because the health and survival of our democracy is—for America and the world.

Fortunately, unlike in Ukraine—and unlike in past American crises going back to the Revolution—no one is being asked to lay down their lives to defend our democracy. Instead, we need activists to run reform campaigns, donors to invest in them, legislators to vote with us, and voters to support all of the above. We cannot and will not win without sufficient social, financial, and political capital to overcome the inertia of our broken system and political opponents who will stop at nothing to preserve their own power. This work will not be easy. It will require courageous leaders among us and acts of courageous leadership from all of us.

The Status Quo Is Unacceptable and Unsustainable

The economist Herb Stein once expressed what became known as Stein's Law of economic trends: "If something cannot go on forever, it will stop." The same is true in politics.

Nearly half of Americans no longer affiliate with either major party, and more than 60% believe that both are doing such a poor job that a new one is needed.[5] "Ironically, both the Democratic Party and the Republican Party have become victims of their own success in building barriers around themselves. They've remained static while the world has changed," said Steve Peace, the former state legislator and political reformer from California.[6] Rather than fear the uncertainty of a new election process, both parties should realize that a failure to adapt and evolve will almost certainly lead to their long-term demise.

Nor can our dangerous polarization continue indefinitely. In 2017, a gunman showed up to a congressional baseball practice in Alexandria, Virginia, and asked a player leaving the field early, "Can you tell me who's practicing? Are these Republicans or Democrats?" He was told it was the Republican team; he then fired seventy rounds from his assault rifle and semiautomatic handgun—injuring six people including the then U.S. House majority whip, Steve Scalise.[7] The Virginia attorney general described the event as "an act of terrorism . . . fueled by rage against Republican legislators."[8] Years later, an attacker showed up to Speaker Pelosi's home in San Francisco and asked "Where is Nancy?" before bludgeoning her husband with a hammer. He later told police he was angry that the Democrats "were finally able to steal an election" in 2020.[9] The risk of these seemingly one-off events leading to large-scale political violence may not seem significant until you consider that roughly 3% to 10% of Americans say they're open to violent actions if their party loses the next election. At the lowest estimate, that's millions of Americans.[10]

Even if you don't believe that America is at the precipice of democratic collapse or civil war, we are certainly not headed in the right direction. "We should not take democracy for granted. There is nothing intrinsic in American culture that immunizes us against its breakdown. Even our brilliantly designed Constitution cannot, by itself, guarantee democracy's survival," Levitsky and Ziblatt, authors of *How Democracies Die*, remind us.[11]

A democracy that is controlled by its fringes at the expense of the majority, offering division over solutions, simply cannot endure over the long haul. The self-reinforcing cycle of hyper-partisanship cannot break itself. Therefore we must not judge proposals to change our current course against definitions of "perfect"—but against the status quo. Make no mistake: if abolishing partisan primaries is the *only* thing we do, it will not be enough. There is no panacea to solve our political polarization. But if there is *one* thing we could and should prioritize doing, this is it.

Our Democracy Gives Us the Tools

I have full confidence and optimism in our ability to solve the Primary Problem because I have had the fortune to meet and work alongside some incredible leaders who are already *winning* crucial victories from coast to coast.

"The name of the game right now, if you care about this country and your community, is the state of democracy. The question I asked myself was, is there something that I could help get done that would move things back to where they were and where they ought to be?" reflected David Thornburgh, the Pennsylvania reformer working to open primaries. "I jumped in with both feet."[12]

"We've stared into the abyss over the past several years and people are looking for something that keeps the republic safe and gets us back to working together," said Scott Kendall, the reformer from Alaska who led the successful nonpartisan primary initiative. "At first, I didn't think election reform was anything more than an interesting research project. Now, my two children joke it's my third child, and maybe my favorite child, because I spend so much time with it."[13]

As I learned when I was campaigning for Congress as a twenty-five-year-old independent candidate a decade ago, there is nothing so wrong with our democracy today that our same democracy does not give us the tools to fix. The only question is whether we—including *you*—will use them while we still have the time.

ACKNOWLEDGMENTS

I first pitched writing a book about fixing American politics to Keith Urbahn in 2014. I had just finished my congressional campaign, and he had just opened a new literary agency, Javelin. Keith was kind to get back to me and candid in saying I wasn't ready—but to stay in touch. So I did. Nine eventful years later, he told me the time was right and helped make it happen.

I am grateful to Bob Bender at Simon & Schuster for seeing the promise of the idea and using his decades-long career to guide a new author through the publishing process. Thanks also to Bob's colleague Johanna Li and the entire team at S&S.

I am deeply indebted to my research assistant, Carlo Macomber, and my collaborator, Will Weisser, for helping bring this idea to life. Will's skillful editorial support was indispensable, as were Carlo's deep research and dry wit, which regularly brought joy to a painstaking process. Amy Cesal brought sharp design to spreadsheets of data in creating the graphics.

Unite America founder Charlie Wheelan, FairVote founder Rob Richie, and Open Primaries president John Opdycke provided excellent feedback to early drafts. Moreover, they have long been leaders who inspired my reform activism—because of their integrity as much as their ideas. One of Charlie's books, *The Centrist Manifesto*, informed my thinking about politics; his latest, *Write for Your Life*, informed my writing about it.

My grandma Maryann Jagger, parents, Louis and Denise Troiano, and sister, Tiffany Bard, have been with me on this journey every single step of the way with unconditional love and support. My nephew, Aston, and niece, Arabella, brought me new purpose in this work. My boyfriend, Chris Fallon, kept me centered, and my pup, Rocky, kept me company through a few intense months of writing.

My colleagues at Unite America, past and present, have passionately dedicated themselves to the mission of reforming our political system. In the process, they have helped inform the ideas in this book, while helping organizations and campaigns around the country actually win them. They also were gracious in giving me the time and space I needed to put pen to paper.

Thank you to Alana Persson, Alex Teixeira, Amber Hatch, Amos Rothstein, Anastasia Marchese, Andrew Crutchfield, Andrew Short, Ann Lewandowski, Ashley Brundage, Chris Ashby, Beth Hladick ("10/83 for life"), Blake Wright (an indispensable partner since our work at Americans Elect in 2011), Branden Shafer, Brett Maney, Carlo Macomber, Chelsea Nunnenkamp, Chris Deaton, Dan Krassner, Danielle LeGrand, Eli Nunes, Emily Baller, Gillian Muller, Jeffrey Carson, Julia Anastos, Holly Collier, Hunter Wallace, Jared Garson, Karen Moldovan, Kelsie Hower, Kyle Butts, Laysa Shreves, Lindsey Williams-Drath, Luis Acosta-Herrera, Luke Cohler, MacKenzie Beckel, Matt Scoble, Melissa Browne, Meghan Dulsky, Michael Wade, Monika Andony, Nicole Carlson, Patrick Cole, Pete Walker, Owen Medina Loftus, Rebecca Fitzmaurice, Dr. Richard Barton, Robby O'Neill, Ron Fournier, Ross Sherman, Sarah Jane Higginbotham, Seth London, Terrance Carroll, Tyler Fisher (who helped build Unite America from the ground up as its second team member), Victoria Fosdal, and Walker Donaldson.

Unite America's cochairs—Marc Merrill, Kathryn Murdoch, and Kent Thiry—have generously provided their leadership to the movement and their support to me. I'm also grateful to members of their teams for their dedication and partnership, including Brooke Russell, Chip Smith, Devin Wagman, and Jason Bertolacci.

Marc and his wife, Ashley, made the first big bet on me and Unite America with long-term vision, patriotic conviction, and total selflessness. At our first event together in 2017, Marc pointed to a graph of the rise of political independents and observed that any industry with a duopoly that has alienated over half its potential customers is ripe for disruption. History will prove him right.

Kathryn's landscape analysis of the pro-democracy movement in 2019 was a catalyst for our joining forces and pivoting Unite America to focus on election reform and mobilizing a growing cross-partisan philanthropic community behind the cause. Unite America would not be what it is today, or where it is, without her strategic guidance. From the starting gate, Kathryn's significant and sustained investment of both time and treasure has been transformational for our organization and the movement as a whole. Her willingness to break new ground, forge diverse alliances, and take big risks in a public way during a time of political upheaval is an example of citizenship in its highest form.

Kent was leading efforts against gerrymandering before most knew what the term meant, even as a full-time CEO of a public company. With a tireless focus on winning, he has demonstrated in spades how the skills of business leaders—strategy, management, relentless execution—can be put to use for the good of our democracy.

I've drawn inspiration from our entire board (and their books), past and present: Ben Goldhirsh, Bill Obenshain, Bill King, Carlos Curbelo, Carolyn Bordeaux, Chad Sweet, Derek McDowell, Charlie Wheelan, Christian Hendricks, Cory Gilchrist, Greg Orman (*A Declaration of Independents*), Gregg Sherrill, Jason Altmire (*Dead Center*), Jeff Binder, Lenny Gail, Jim Jonas, Linda Killian, Lindsey Young, Lisa Rice, Neal Simon (*Contract to Unite America*), Randy Peeler (whose generosity and encouragement made writing this book possible), Ron Christie, Ron Shaich, Sam Mar (a true mentor), Shawn Riegsecker, Sophia Nelson, Tom Curren, and Trey Grayson. And I'm thankful to Pam Peak and Christie St. Clair, who helped get the original Centrist Project ball rolling.

I am lucky to learn from so many leaders in the movement who run extraordinary organizations and state campaigns—a list that is too long (a good sign!) to fully include here. However, the movement for primary reform would not be where it is today without Katherine Gehl and her advocacy for Final-Five Voting. As the founder of the Institute for Political Innovation and coauthor of *The Politics Industry*, she not only helped lay the intellectual foundation for primary reform but also got involved with her time, talent, and treasure to support reform campaigns from Alaska to Nevada and beyond, motivating many other business leaders to do the same.

Last but not least, many teachers guided my path from elementary school through college, including a few whose belief in me challenged me to dream big and dare greatly—Jeffry Burnam, Tom Burns, Susan Curtin, John Crounse, Ann Finnerty, Leslie Clementoni Lordi, Mark Robbins, and Marc Valentine.

APPENDIX

HOW TO GET INVOLVED

Please reach out to Unite America if you're interested in investing in election reform: invest@uniteamerica.org. Or if you'd like to host a virtual or in-person event tied to this book: book@uniteamerica.org.

If you are looking to get more involved in helping to advance election reform, there are many other nonpartisan, national organizations that are worthy of your support. The following list isn't intended to be comprehensive, but it will point you toward excellent organizations that Unite America has been proud to partner with.

ORGANIZATION	WEBSITE	DESCRIPTION
RepresentUs	represent.us	RepresentUs brings together conservatives, progressives, and everyone in between to pass powerful state and local laws that fix our broken elections and stop political bribery. Their strategy is central to dismantling the root causes of inequities in our democracy, and ending political corruption, extremism, and gridlock. RepresentUs can also connect you with any local or state election reform campaigns where you live.
Open Primaries	openprimaries.org	Open Primaries is a movement of diverse Americans who believe in a simple, yet radical idea: no American should be required to join a political party to exercise their right to vote. The mission of Open Primaries is to advocate for open and nonpartisan primary systems, counter efforts to impose closed primaries, educate voters and policymakers, advance litigation, train spokespeople, conduct and support research, and participate in the building of local, state, and national open primaries coalitions.
FairVote	fairvote.org	FairVote is a nonpartisan organization seeking better elections for all. Their team researches and advances voting reforms that make democracy more functional and representative for every American.
Veterans for All Voters	veteransforall voters.org	Veterans for All Voters mobilizes veterans and supporters to advocate for election innovations to make our political system less toxic and more competitive.
Rank the Vote	rankthevote.us	Rank the Vote helps everyday people build robust movements for ranked choice voting in their own states.
Issue One	issueone.org	Issue One is the leading crosspartisan political reform group in Washington, D.C. Issue One unites Republicans, Democrats, and independents in the movement to fix our broken political system and build a democracy that works for everyone.

ORGANIZATION	WEBSITE	DESCRIPTION
Millennial Action Project	millennialaction.org	The Millennial Action Project has an audacious mission: activate young leaders to bridge the partisan divide and transform American politics.
RepresentWomen	representwomen.org	RepresentWomen's mission is to strengthen our democracy by advancing reforms that break down barriers to ensure more women can run, win, serve, and lead.
Protect Democracy	protectdemocracy.org	Protect Democracy is a nonpartisan nonprofit dedicated to preventing American democracy from declining into a more authoritarian form of government.
Campaign Legal Center	campaignlegal.org	The Campaign Legal Center seeks to protect and strengthen the U.S. democratic process across all levels of government through litigation, policy analysis, and public education.

NOTES

INTRODUCTION

1. "Public Trust in Government: 1958–2022," Pew Research Center, June 6, 2022, https://www.pewresearch.org/politics/2022/06/06/public-trust-in-govern ment-1958-2022/.

2. "A Majority of Americans Think US Democracy Is Broken. Here Are 12 Ideas for Repairing It," CNN, October 14, 2022, https://www.cnn.com/2022/10/14 /opinions/american-democracy-broken-solutions-roundup/index.html.

3. Carlo Macomber, "Poll: Voters Overwhelmingly Support Eliminating Partisan Primaries, Requiring Majority Winners," Unite America, August 7, 2023, https://www.uniteamerica.org/news-article/poll-voters-overwhelmingly-sup port-eliminating-partisan-primaries-requiring-majority-winners.

4. "Apportionment Population and Number of Representatives by State: 2020 Census," U.S. Census Bureau, accessed May 2023, https://www2.census.gov /programs-surveys/decennial/2020/data/apportionment/apportionment-2020 -table01.pdf.

5. Joshua Ferrer and Michael Thorning, "2022 Primary Turnout: Trends and Lessons for Boosting Participation," Bipartisan Policy Center, March 2023, https:// bipartisanpolicy.org/download/?file=/wp-content/uploads/2023/03/Primary -Turnout-Report_R03.pdf.

6. NPR Staff, "Romney Adviser's 'Etch A Sketch' Comment Draws Flak From Rivals," NPR, March 21, 2012, https://www.npr.org/sections/itsallpoli tics/2012/03/21/149085301/romney-advisers-etch-a-sketch-comment-shakes -up-criticism-from-rivals.

7. David R. Mayhew, *Congress: The Electoral Connection* (New Haven, CT: Yale University Press, 1974).

8. Steven Kerr, "On the Folly of Rewarding A, While Hoping for B," *Academy of Management Journal* 18, no. 4 (December 1975).

9. Louis Jacobson, "McConnell reverses position on Conrad-Gregg budget commission," PolitiFact, February 1, 2010, https://www.politifact.com/

factchecks/2010/feb/02/mitch-mcconnell/mcconnell-reverses-position-con
rad-gregg-budget-co/.

10. Christopher Ingraham, "How Pennsylvania Republicans Pulled Off Their
    Aggressive Gerrymander," *Washington Post*, February 6, 2018, https://www
    .washingtonpost.com/news/wonk/wp/2018/02/06/how-pennsylvania-republi
    cans-pulled-off-their-aggressive-gerrymander/.

11. "Primary Results: Pennsylvania," *New York Times*, accessed May 2023, https://
    www.nytimes.com/elections/2010/results/primaries/pennsylvania.html.

PART I: ORIGINS OF THE PRIMARY PROBLEM

 1. Jordan Levy, "Pa.'s Senate Race Was the Most Expensive in History. What Else
    Could You Get for $375 Million?" Billy Penn, November 18, 2022, https://bil
    lypenn.com/2022/11/18/senate-race-pennsylvania-375-million-bryce-harper
    -uzi-vert/.

 2. Julia Terruso and Sean Collins Walsh, "John Fetterman Sees Striking Lack of
    Democratic Endorsements in Pa. Senate Race," *Philadelphia Inquirer*, May 12,
    2022,   https://www.inquirer.com/politics/election/john-fetterman-pa-senate
    -race-endorsements-20220511.html.

 3. *Philadelphia Inquirer* Editorial Board, "Conor Lamb Is the Best Choice Dems
    Have to Flip a Senate Seat," *Philadelphia Inquirer*, May 8, 2022, https://www.in
    quirer.com/opinion/editorials/conor-lamb-us-senate-pennsylvania-2022-elec
    tion-endorsement-20220508.html.

 4. Caroline Vakil, "Oz Says He Was 'Exhausted' When He Made Video of Cru-
    dité Shopping Trip," *The Hill*, August 18, 2022, https://thehill.com/homenews
    /campaign/3606307-oz-says-he-was-exhausted-when-he-made-video-of-cru
    dite-shopping-trip/.

 5. David McCormick, *Superpower in Peril: A Battle Plan to Renew America* (New
    York: Center Street, 2023), 2.

 6. Michael Smerconish, interview with author, March 31, 2023.

 7. Jeff Bartos, interview with author, April 17, 2023.

 8. Ibid.

 9. Ibid.

10. Ibid.

11. Ibid.

12. "Polls Conducted by Research Co. in the United States—November 7, 2022,"
    Research Co., November 7, 2022, https://researchco.ca/wp-content/up
    loads/2022/11/Tables_StateRaces_USA_07Nov2022.pdf#page=10.

13. David Thornburgh, interview with author, March 31, 2023.

14. Ibid.

15. "Pennsylvania Election Code Act of Jun. 3, 1937, P.L. 1333, No. 320," https://
    www.legis.state.pa.us/WU01/LI/LI/US/PDF/1937/0/0320.PDF.

ONE: THE INVENTION OF PARTY PRIMARIES

1. "Washington's Farewell Address to the People of the United States," United States Senate, 1796, accessed May 2023, https://www.senate.gov/artandhistory /history/resources/pdf/Washingtons_Farewell_Address.pdf.

2. "From John Adams to Jonathan Jackson, 2 October 1780," Founders Online, accessed May 2023, https://founders.archives.gov/documents/Adams/06-10 -02-0113.

3. Aric Gooch, "Candidate Emergence in the First Party Era, 1788–1816," PhD diss., University of Missouri–Columbia, 2022.

4. Alan Ware, *The American Direct Primary: Party Institutionalization and Transformation in the North* (Cambridge, UK: Cambridge University Press, 2002), 57.

5. John F. Reynolds, *The Origins of the Direct Primary* (New York: Routledge, 2018), 45.

6. Ibid.

7. Frederick W. Whitridge, *Caucus System* (New York: Messrs. Rand, McNally and Co., 1883), 21.

8. Chapman Rackaway and Joseph Romance, *Primary Elections and American Politics: The Unintended Consequences of Progressive Era Reform* (Albany: State University of New York Press, 2022), 28.

9. Susan Welch, John Gruhl, Sue Thomas, MaryAnne Borrelli, *Understanding American Government* (Boston: Cengage Learning, 2003), 224.

10. Mark Hirsch, "More Light on Boss Tweed," *Political Science Quarterly* 60, no. 2 (June 1945): 268.

11. Braxton Fralick, "The Legacy of Boss Tweed on Tammany Hall," Belmont University, 2015, 2, https://www.semanticscholar.org/paper/The-Legacy -of-Boss-Tweed-on-Tammany-Hall-Fralick/fa916fc34108a395500abef511ff 3fa2c63ff573.

12. Ware, *The American Direct Primary*, 26.

13. Paul H. Giddens, "The Origin of the Direct Primary: The Crawford County System," *Western Pennsylvania History* 60 (April 1977): 145–58.

14. Kaori Shoji, "When Do Party Leaders Democratize? Analyzing Three Reforms of Voter Registration and Candidate Selection," Academic Commons, Columbia University Libraries, 2013.

15. Ibid., 283.

16. Giddens, "The Origin of the Direct Primary," 152.

17. Shoji, "When Do Party Leaders Democratize?," 283.

18. Ibid., 287.

19. Quoted from the *Crawford Democrat*, August 16, 1842, in Giddens, "The Origin of the Direct Primary," 151.

20. Allen Fraser Lovejoy, *La Follette and the Establishment of the Direct Primary in Wisconsin, 1890–1904* (New Haven, CT: Yale University Press, 1941), 22.

21. Ibid., 25.

22. Ibid., 28.

23. Ibid., 34–46.
24. Robert M. La Follette, *Autobiography* (Garden City, NJ: Country Life Press, 1912), https://history.hanover.edu/courses/excerpts/260lafol.html.
25. Lovejoy, *La Follette and the Establishment of the Direct Primary in Wisconsin*, 61.
26. Ibid., 82–88.
27. "Election Years in Which the Direct Primary Has Been Specifically Authorized," Green Papers, last modified May 19, 2021, https://www.thegreenpapers.com/Hx/DirectPrimaryElectionYears.phtml.
28. Ware, *The American Direct Primary*, 220.
29. Ibid., 100.
30. Ibid., 119–24.
31. Sid Milkis and Carah Ong, "Transforming American Democracy: TR and the Bull Moose Campaign of 1912," Miller Center, https://millercenter.org/transforming-american-democracy-tr-and-bull-moose-campaign-1912.

TWO: THE WEAPONIZATION OF PARTY PRIMARIES

1. Lee Drutman, "The Case for Fusion Voting and a Multiparty Democracy in America, New America, September 2022, https://centerforballotfreedom.org/wp-content/uploads/sites/199/The_Case_for_Fusion_Voting_and_a_Multiparty_Democracy_in_America_2022.pdf.
2. Ibid.
3. Karlyn Bowman, "The Decline of the Major Networks," *Forbes*, July 27, 2009, https://www.forbes.com/2009/07/25/media-network-news-audience-opinions-columnists-walter-cronkite.html?sh=5d363b6747a5.
4. Megan Brenan, "Americans' Trust in Media Remains Near Record Low," Gallup, October 18, 2022, https://news.gallup.com/poll/403166/americans-trust-media-remains-near-record-low.aspx.
5. Robert Boatright, data given to the author, 2023. Robert G. Boatright, "What Do the 2020 Congressional Primaries Tell Us about the Direction of the Democratic and Republican Parties?," prepared for the 2021 State of the Parties Conference, Ray C. Bliss Center, University of Akron, November 4–5, 2021, https://uakron.edu/bliss/docs/State-of-the-Parties-2021/boatright-sop21.pdf.
6. Elaine Kamarck, "Lessons from the 2022 Primaries—What Do They Tell Us about America's Political Parties and the Midterm Elections?" Brookings Institution, September 7, 2022, https://www.brookings.edu/blog/fixgov/2022/09/07/lessons-from-the-2022-primaries-what-do-they-tell-us-about-americas-political-parties-and-the-midterm-elections-part-i-who-runs/.
7. Joe Lieberman, interview with author, May 3, 2023.
8. Robert G. Boatright, *Getting Primaried: The Changing Politics of Congressional Primary Challenges* (Ann Arbor: University of Michigan Press, 2014), 136.
9. Joe Lieberman, interview with author, May 3, 2023.
10. Ibid.

11. Associated Press, "Rep. Schwarz Defeated in Michigan Primary," NBC News, August 9, 2006, https://www.nbcnews.com/id/wbna14263102.

12. Boatright, *Getting Primaried*, 201.

13. Ron Elving, "ANALYSIS: Castle's Loss Is Victory for Partisanship," NPR, September 15, 2010, https://www.npr.org/sections/itsallpolitics/2010/09/15/129877484/castle.

14. "October Verified Voter Omnibus—National Political Update," Echelon Insights, October 2022, https://echeloninsights.com/in-the-news/2022-omnibus-october/.

15. Meredith Conroy and Nathaniel Rakich, "Progressives Took a Step Back in the 2022 Primaries—But They're Playing the Long Game," *FiveThirtyEight*, September 27, 2022, https://fivethirtyeight.com/features/progressives-democrats-2022/.

16. Ibid.

17. Drew Desilver, "The Polarization in Today's Congress Has Roots That Go Back Decades," Pew Research Center, March 10, 2022, https://www.pewresearch.org/fact-tank/2022/03/10/the-polarization-in-todays-congress-has-roots-that-go-back-decades/.

18. Ibid.

19. Norm Ornstein, "Yes, Polarization is Asymmetric—and Conservatives are Worse," *The Atlantic*, June 19, 2014, https://www.theatlantic.com/politics/archive/2014/06/yes-polarization-is-asymmetric-and-conservatives-are-worse/373044/.

20. Ibid.

21. Boris Shor and Nolan McCarty, "Two Decades of Polarization in American State Legislatures," *Journal of Political Institutions and Political Economy* 3, no. 4 (December 2022): 360.

22. Thomas B. Edsall, "No Hate Left Behind," *New York Times*, March 13, 2019, https://www.nytimes.com/2019/03/13/opinion/hate-politics.html.

23. Steven Levitsky and Daniel Ziblatt, *How Democracies Die* (New York: Crown, 2018), 135.

24. Ibid., 153.

25. "Cloture Motions," United States Senate, accessed May 2023, https://www.senate.gov/legislative/cloture/clotureCounts.htm.

26. David A. Graham, "We've Entered the Era of 'Total Politics,'" *Atlantic*, April 15, 2023, https://www.theatlantic.com/ideas/archive/2023/04/tennessee-house-expel-democrats-greg-abbott-pardon/673734/.

27. Levitsky and Ziblatt, *How Democracies Die*, 109.

28. Ben Kamisar, "Two-thirds of Republicans Still Don't Believe Biden Was Elected Legitimately," NBC News, October 25, 2022, https://www.nbcnews.com/meet-the-press/meetthepressblog/two-thirds-republicans-still-dont-believe-biden-was-elected-legitimate-rcna53880.

29. Karen Yourish, Larry Buchanan, and Denise Lu, "The 147 Republicans Who Voted to Overturn Election Results," *New York Times*, January 7, 2021, https://

www.nytimes.com/interactive/2021/01/07/us/elections/electoral-college
-biden-objectors.html.

30. Jesse T. Clark and Charles Stewart III, "The Confidence Earthquake: Seismic
Shifts in Trust in the 2020 Election," MIT Election Lab, July 15, 2021, https://
papers.ssrn.com/sol3/papers.cfm?abstract_id=3825118.

31. Kathy Frankovic, "Belief in Conspiracies Largely Depends on Political Identity," YouGov, December 27, 2016, https://today.yougov.com/topics/politics/ar
ticles-reports/2016/12/27/belief-conspiracies-largely-depends-political-iden.

32. Warren Fiske, "Fact-Check: Did Democrats Suggest 2016 Presidential Election Was Stolen?," PolitiFact, October 10, 2022, https://www.statesman.com
/story/news/politics/politifact/2022/10/10/2016-election-fact-check-demo
crats-hillary-clinton-bernie-sanders/69548196007/.

33. *Fair Fight Action, Inc., et al. v. Brad Raffensperger, et al.*, United States District
Court for the Northern District of Georgia, Atlanta Division, accessed May
2023, https://storage.courtlistener.com/recap/gov.uscourts.gand.257857/gov.u
scourts.gand.257857.916.0_1.pdf.

34. Clark and Stewart, "The Confidence Earthquake."

35. John Opdycke, interview with author, June 1, 2023.

36. "Party Affiliation," Gallup, accessed March 2023, https://news.gallup.com
/poll/15370/party-affiliation.aspx.

37. "States Where Registered Independents Outnumber Both Major Political Parties," Independent Voter News, last updated November 21, 2022, https://ivn
.us/2018/08/08/9-states-registered-independents-outnumber-major-political
-parties.

PART II: A LOSE-LOSE-LOSE SYSTEM

1. "Who We Are," Blue Dog Coalition, accessed May 2023, https://bluedogcau
cus-golden.house.gov/.

2. Kal Munis and Robert Saldin, "The Democrats' Rural Problem," *Washington
Monthly*, July 28, 2022, https://washingtonmonthly.com/2022/07/28/the-dem
ocrats-rural-problem/.

3. Nathan Gonzales, "Blue Dog Democrats Facing Decimation," *Roll Call*, August 3,
2022, https://rollcall.com/2022/08/03/blue-dog-democrats-facing-decimation/.

4. Kurt Schrader, interview with author, March 30, 2023.

5. Mychael Schnell, "House Democrat Who Initially Voted against Coronavirus
Relief Bill Says He'll Vote for Senate Version," *The Hill*, March 8, 2021, https://
thehill.com/homenews/house/542214-house-democrat-who-voted-against
-coronavirus-relief-bill-says-hell-vote-for/.

6. Keith Salazar (@k_salazar2020), "can't wait for your primary opponent
in 2022," Twitter, March 9, 2021, https://twitter.com/k_salazar2020/sta
tus/1369480357221965826.

7. Kurt Schrader, interview with author, March 30, 2023.

8. Burgess Everett and Marianne Levine, "The Power of 10: Inside the 'Unlikely
Partnership' That Sealed an Infrastructure Win," *Politico*, August 10, 2021,

https://www.politico.com/news/2021/08/10/senate-infrastructure-bipartisan
-partnership-502722.

9. Heather Caygle and Sarah Ferris, "9 Dems Threaten Mutiny over Pelosi's Budget
    Plan," *Politico*, August 13, 2021, https://www.politico.com/news/2021/08/13/9
    -dems-threaten-mutiny-over-pelosis-budget-plan-504408.

10. Emily Cochrane and Jim Tankersley, "Democrats Scrounge for Votes to Pass
    $3.5 Trillion Budget Plan," *New York Times*, August 23, 2021, https://www.ny
    times.com/2021/08/23/us/politics/democrats-budget-infrastructure.html.

11. Kurt Schrader, interview with author, March 30, 2023.

12. Ibid.

13. Ibid.

14. Ibid.

15. Betsy Hammond, "Republicans Sue to Block Democrats' 'Obvious, Extreme,
    Partisan Gerrymander' of Oregon Congressional Districts," *Oregonian*, Octo-
    ber 11, 2021, https://www.oregonlive.com/politics/2021/10/republicans-sue
    -to-block-democrats-obvious-extreme-partisan-gerrymander-of-oregon-con
    gressional-districts.html.

16. "What Redistricting Looks Like in Every State," *FiveThirtyEight*, July 19, 2022,
    https://projects.fivethirtyeight.com/redistricting-2022-maps/oregon/.

17. "Oregon's 5th Congressional District," Ballotpedia, accessed May 2023, https://
    ballotpedia.org/Oregon%27s_5th_Congressional_District.

18. Kurt Schrader, interview with author, March 30, 2023.

19. Eugene Scott and David Weigel, "Rep. Kurt Schrader Loses Primary in Oregon's
    5th District," *Washington Post*, May 27, 2022, https://www.washingtonpost
    .com/politics/2022/05/27/kurt-schrader-loses-primary-oregons-5th-district/.

20. Kurt Schrader, interview with author, March 30, 2023.

21. Ibid.

22. Scott and Weigel, "Rep. Kurt Schrader Loses Primary in Oregon's 5th District."

23. Kurt Schrader, interview with author, March 30, 2023.

24. Jim Saksa, "Where Have All the Centrists Gone? Rep. Stephanie Murphy Has
    an Idea," *Roll Call*, October 12, 2022, https://rollcall.com/2022/10/12/where
    -have-all-the-centrists-gone-rep-stephanie-murphy/.

THREE: BAD FOR VOTERS

1. Mark Niesse, "Faith in Georgia Elections Rises as Fraud Frenzy Fades, AJC Poll
    Shows," *Atlanta Journal-Constitution*, January 30, 2023, https://www.ajc.com
    /politics/ajc-poll-voter-confidence-increases-split-opinions-on-election-law
    /RMH42EFFH5AKPCHVKDC7VZWXCY/?state=refreshTokenFallback.

2. "Data Hub—November 8, 2022, General Election," Georgia Secretary of State,
    https://sos.ga.gov/data-hub-november-8-2022-general-election.

3. Niesse, "Faith in Georgia Elections Rises as Fraud Frenzy Fades."

4. Author analysis based on "Partisan Affiliations of Registered Voters," Ballotpe-
    dia, accessed May 2023, https://ballotpedia.org/Partisan_affiliations_of_regis
    tered_voters.

5. David Wasserman, "Introducing the 2022 Cook Partisan Voting Index," *Cook Political Report*, July 13, 2022, https://www.cookpolitical.com/cook-pvi/2022-partisan-voting-index/introducing-2022-cook-partisan-voting-index.

6. Emily Risch, "Monopoly Politics 2020: The Root of Dysfunction in the U.S. House of Representatives," FairVote, December 2020, https://fairvote.org/report/monopoly_politics_2020_the_root_of_dysfunction_in_the_u_s_the_the_u_s_house_of_representatives/.

7. Ibid.

8. "Monopoly Politics 2024," FairVote, accessed May 2023, https://fairvote.org/report/monopoly-politics-2024/.

9. "Why People Identify With—or Lean Toward—a Political Party," Pew Research Center, August 9, 2022, https://www.pewresearch.org/politics/2022/08/09/why-people-identify-with-or-lean-toward-a-political-party/.

10. "Moderates Nearly Extinct in the U.S. House," FairVote, August 7, 2013, https://fairvote.org/moderates-nearly-extinct-in-the-u-s-house/.

11. David Wasserman, "House Recap: The Five Biggest Takeaways from 2022's Photo Finish," *Cook Political Report*, December 1, 2022, https://www.cookpolitical.com/analysis/house/house-overview/house-recap-five-biggest-takeaways-2022s-photo-finish.

12. Nicholas T. Davis and Lilliana Mason, "Sorting and the Split-Ticket: Evidence from Presidential and Subpresidential Elections," *Political Behavior* 38, no. 2 (August 2015): 337–54.

13. "The Partisan Breakdown of Florida's New Map," *FiveThirtyEight*, July 19, 2022, https://projects.fivethirtyeight.com/redistricting-2022-maps/florida/.

14. "What Redistricting Looks Like in Every State," FiveThirtyEight, July 19, 2022, https://projects.fivethirtyeight.com/redistricting-2022-maps/.

15. Nathaniel Rakich, "The New National Congressional Map Is Biased Toward Republicans," *FiveThirtyEight*, June 15, 2022, https://fivethirtyeight.com/features/the-new-national-congressional-map-is-biased-toward-republicans/.

16. Wasserman, "Introducing the 2022 Cook Partisan Voting Index."

17. Bill Bishop, "For Most Americans, the Local Presidential Vote Was a Landslide," Daily Yonder, December 17, 2020, https://dailyyonder.com/for-most-americans-the-local-presidential-vote-was-a-landslide/2020/12/17/.

18. Wendy K. Tam Cho, James G. Gimpel, and Iris Hui, "Voter Migration and the Geographic Sorting of the American Electorate," University of Kentucky, 2012, https://www.uky.edu/AS/PoliSci/Peffley/pdf/Sniderman/Cho%20Gimpel%20Hui_UK_Dec10.pdf.

19. Gregory J. Martin and Steven W. Webster, "Does Residential Sorting Explain Geographic Polarization?" *Political Science Research and Methods*, March 23, 2018, https://web.stanford.edu/~gjmartin/papers/partisan_sorting_density_R1.pdf.

20. Dave Wasserman (@Redistrict), "Here's the breakdown of Whole Foods/Cracker Barrel counties won by past new presidents," December 8, 2020, https://twitter.com/redistrict/status/1336349272950890497?lang=en.

21.	Tim Wallace and Krishna Karra, "The True Colors of America's Political Spectrum Are Gray and Green," *New York Times*, September 2, 2020, https://www.nytimes.com/interactive/2020/09/02/upshot/america-political-spectrum.html.

22.	David Wasserman, "Realignment, More Than Redistricting, Has Decimated Swing House Seats," *Cook Political Report*, April 5, 2023, https://www.cookpolitical.com/cook-pvi/realignment-more-redistricting-has-decimated-swing-house-seats?check_logged_in=1.

23.	"State Legislative Elections, 2022," Ballotpedia, https://ballotpedia.org/State_legislative_elections,_2022.

24.	Cassandra Handan-Nader, Andrew C. W. Myers, and Andrew B. Hall, "Polarization in State Legislative Elections," Stanford University, February 5, 2022, https://stanforddpl.org/papers/handan-nader_myers_hall_polarization_2022/handan-nader_myers_hall_polarization_2022.pdf.

25.	All turnout rates are percentages of the voting-age population and are sourced from each state's secretary of state. The overall general election turnout is courtesy of the U.S. Elections Project (https://www.electproject.org/2022g). States with nonpartisan primaries were excluded from this analysis as were states without any competition in their top of the ticket primaries.

26.	"Election Results Archive," Secretary of the Commonwealth of Massachusetts, https://electionstats.state.ma.us/elections/search/year_from:2022/year_to:2022/stage:General; "2022 November General Election Turnout Rates," US Elections Project, May 2, 2023, https://www.electproject.org/2022g.

27.	Alan S. Gerber, Gregory A. Huber, Daniel R. Biggers, and David J. Hendry, "Why Don't People Vote in U.S. Primary Elections? Assessing Theoretical Explanations for Reduced Participation," *Electoral Studies* 45 (February 2017): 119–29.

28.	Taylor Johnston and Christine Zhang, "2022 Midterm Primary Election Calendar," *New York Times*, January 25, 2023, https://www.nytimes.com/interactive/2022/us/elections/midterm-elections-calendar.html.

29.	Joshua M. Scacco, Lauren Hearit, Lauren Potts, Jeff Sonderman, and Natalie Jomini Stroud, "Primary Election Coverage: What Types of News Engage Audiences," Center for Media Engagement, October 11, 2016, https://mediaengagement.org/research/election-coverage/.

30.	"Political Engagement and Activism," Pew Research Center, June 12, 2014, https://www.pewresearch.org/politics/2014/06/12/section-5-political-engagement-and-activism/.

31.	"Political Engagement among Typology Groups," Pew Research Center, November 9, 2021, https://www.pewresearch.org/politics/2021/11/09/political-engagement-among-typology-groups/.

32.	Elaine Kamarck and Alexander R. Podkul, "The 2018 Primaries Project: The Ideology of Primary Voters," Brookings Institution, October 23, 2018, https://www.brookings.edu/research/the-2018-primaries-project-the-ideology-of-primary-voters/.

33. "Party Affiliation," Gallup, accessed May 2023, https://news.gallup.com /poll/15370/party-affiliation.aspx.

34. V. O. Key Jr., *Southern Politics in State and Nation* (New York: Alfred A. Knopf, 1949), 407.

35. "Smith v. Allwright," Justia US Law, accessed May 2023, https://supreme.justia .com/cases/federal/us/321/649/#661.

36. "Partisan Affiliations of Registered Voters," accessed May 2023.

37. All references to states' primary participation rules are courtesy of the National Conference of State Legislatures and Open Primaries.

38. "Partisan Affiliations of Registered Voters," accessed May 2023.

39. "Our Veterans Deserve Better. They Deserve Open Primaries," Open Primaries, accessed May 2023, https://d3n8a8pro7vhmx.cloudfront.net/openprim aries/pages/4228/attachments/original/1564591956/OP_Veterans_Fact_Sheet _V3.pdf?1564591956.

40. "Trends in Party Affiliation among Demographic Groups," Pew Research Center, March 20, 2018, https://www.pewresearch.org/politics/2018/03/20/1 -trends-in-party-affiliation-among-demographic-groups/.

41. "Taxpayer Funding: The Cost of Closed Primaries," Open Primaries, accessed May 2023, https://www.openprimaries.org/wp-content/uploads/2022/02/Tax payer-Funding-The-Cost-of-Closed-Primaries.pdf.

42. John Opdycke, interview with author, June 1, 2023.

43. Daniel Yudkin, "Americans Exaggerate the Extremism of the Other Side," CNN, November 14, 2019, https://www.cnn.com/2019/11/14/opinions/percep tion-gap-republican-democrat-yudkin/index.html.

44. Erin Durkin, Joe Anuta, and Janaki Chadha, "Dan Goldman Wins Free-for-All New York House Seat," *Politico*, August 24, 2022, https://www.po litico.com/news/2022/08/24/free-for-all-new-york-house-primary-too-close -to-call-00053459.

45. "Enrollment by Congressional District," New York State Board of Elections, accessed May 2023, https://www.elections.ny.gov/EnrollmentCD.html.

46. According to the *Cook Political Report*'s ratings of House races.

47. Rachel Hutchinson, "Fewest Votes Wins: Plurality Victories in 2022 Primaries," FairVote, October 2022, https://fairvote.app.box.com/s/xmnjolsmcqd3rkgwy ustbihatjn2lber.

48. Marc Fortier, "Gary Johnson Throws in the Towel in NH," Amherst Patch, November 29, 2011, https://web.archive.org/web/20120615045936/http://am herst.patch.com/articles/gary-johnson-throws-in-the-towel-in-nh.

49. Evan McMorris-Santoro, "Is Mitt Romney Afraid of Gary Johnson?" Talking Points Memo, June 12, 2012, https://talkingpointsmemo.com/election2012/is -mitt-romney-afraid-of-gary-johnson.

50. Barry C. Burden, Bradley Jones, and Michael S. Kang, "Sore Loser Laws and Congressional Polarization," *Legislative Studies Quarterly* 39, no. 3 (August 2014): 299–325.

51. Chapman Rackaway and Joseph Romance, *Primary Elections and American*

Politics: The Unintended Consequences of Progressive Era Reform (Albany: State University of New York Press, 2022), 167.

52. Joe Setyon, "Poll: 72% of Americans Support School Choice," Goldwater Institute, March 2, 2022, https://www.goldwaterinstitute.org/poll-72-of-americans-support-school-choice/; J. Baxter Oliphant, "Top Tax Frustrations for Americans: The Feeling That Some Corporations, Wealthy People Don't Pay Fair Share," Pew Research Center, April 7, 2023, https://www.pewresearch.org/short-reads/2023/04/07/top-tax-frustrations-for-americans-the-feeling-that-some-corporations-wealthy-people-dont-pay-fair-share/.

53. Danielle M. Thomsen, "Ideological Moderates Won't Run: How Party Fit Matters for Partisan Polarization in Congress," *Journal of Politics* 76, no. 3 (July 2014): 786–97.

54. Ibid.

55. John Adams, "Letter to John Penn," Adams Papers, Founders Online, March 27, 1776, https://founders.archives.gov/documents/Adams/06-04-02-0026-0003.

FOUR: BAD FOR THE COUNTRY

1. Robert Samuelson, "Robert Samuelson: Politics Now Exaggerates Differences," *Orange County Register*, October 25, 2010, https://www.ocregister.com/2010/10/25/robert-samuelson-politics-now-exaggerates-differences/.

2. Mark Barabak, "The Earthquake That Toppled Eric Cantor: How Did It Happen?," *Los Angeles Times*, June 11, 2014, https://www.latimes.com/nation/politics/politicsnow/la-pn-earthquake-toppled-cantor-20140611-story.html.

3. Jeb Bush, "A Republican Case for Immigration Reform," *Wall Street Journal*, June 30, 2013, https://www.wsj.com/articles/SB10001424127887324328204578571641599272504.

4. Ezra Klein, "Wanted: 20 House Republicans to Save Congress," *Washington Post*, January 17, 2013, https://www.washingtonpost.com/news/wonk/wp/2013/01/17/wanted-20-house-republicans-to-save-congress/.

5. Bryan Baker, "Estimates of the Unauthorized Immigrant Population Residing in the United States: January 2014," Department of Homeland Security, June 2017, https://www.dhs.gov/sites/default/files/publications/Unauthorized%20Immigrant%20Population%20Estimates%20in%20the%20US%20January%202014_1.pdf.

6. Braden Goyette, "Eric Cantor: DREAMers Shouldn't Be 'Kids Without a Country,'" *HuffPost*, June 30, 2013, https://www.huffpost.com/entry/eric-cantor-dream-act_n_3523786.

7. Jeanne Batalova, Sarah Hooker, and Randy Capps, "DACA at the Two-Year Mark: A National and State Profile of Youth Eligible and Applying for Deferred Action," Migration Policy Institute, August 2014, https://www.migrationpolicy.org/research/daca-two-year-mark-national-and-state-profile-youth-eligible-and-applying-deferred-action.

8. Goyette, "Eric Cantor: DREAMers Shouldn't Be 'Kids Without a Country.'"

9. Eric Cantor, interview with author, May 5, 2023.
10. Ibid.
11. Ibid.
12. Seung Min Kim, "Cantor Loss Kills Immigration Reform," *Politico*, June 10, 2014, https://www.politico.com/story/2014/06/2014-virginia-primary-eric-can tor-loss-immigration-reform-107697.
13. Bolt Media Group, "We Deserve Better PAC," YouTube video, June 3, 2013, https://www.youtube.com/watch?v=jaE2SZgo5wg.
14. John Pudner, interview with author, March 29, 2023.
15. Dara Lind, "Read Eric Cantor's Anti-'Amnesty' Campaign Mailers," *Vox*, June 10, 2014, https://www.vox.com/2014/6/10/5798834/read-eric-cantors-an ti-amnesty-campaign-mailers.
16. "Data from the Virginia Department of Elections," Virginia Department of Elections, accessed May 2023, https://historical.elections.virginia.gov/elec tions/search/year_from:2014/year_to:2014/office_id:5/district_id:27260 /stage:Primaries.
17. Eric Cantor, interview with author, May 5, 2023.
18. Nate Cohn, "Did Democratic Voters Defeat Eric Cantor? Probably Not," *New York Times*, June 11, 2014, https://www.nytimes.com/2014/06/12/upshot/did -democratic-voters-defeat-eric-cantor-probably-not.html.
19. Eric Cantor, interview with author, May 5, 2023.
20. Aaron Blake, "Make No Mistake: Immigration Reform Hurt Eric Cantor," *Washington Post*, June 11, 2014, https://www.washingtonpost.com/news/the -fix/wp/2014/06/11/yes-immigration-reform-hurt-eric-cantor/.
21. Amber Phillips, "'They're Rapists.' President Trump's Campaign Launch Speech Two Years Later, Annotated," *Washington Post*, June 16, 2017, https://www .washingtonpost.com/news/the-fix/wp/2017/06/16/theyre-rapists-presidents -trump-campaign-launch-speech-two-years-later-annotated.
22. Bradley Jones, "Majority of Americans Continue to Say Immigrants Strengthen the U.S.," Pew Research Center, January 31, 2019, https://www.pewresearch .org/short-reads/2019/01/31/majority-of-americans-continue-to-say-immi grants-strengthen-the-u-s/.
23. Alexander Bolton, "Abolishing ICE Becomes Dem Litmus Test," *The Hill*, June 30, 2018, https://thehill.com/homenews/senate/394920-abolishing-ice -becomes-dem-litmus-test/.
24. Kevin Robillard, "Abolishing ICE Isn't Very Popular (Yet)," *HuffPost*, July 3, 2018, https://www.huffpost.com/entry/abolishing-ice-not-popular-yet_n_5b3 a3916e4b08c3a8f6c803d?pn=.
25. Eli Yokley, "Ahead of 2020, Democratic Voters Are Moving Left on Im- migration," Morning Consult, August 28, 2019, https://morningconsult .com/2019/08/28/ahead-2020-democratic-voters-moving-left-immigration.
26. Robillard, "Abolishing ICE Isn't Very Popular (Yet)."
27. "NEW POLL: Overwhelming Majority of U.S. Voters across Political Spec- trum Support Legislation for Dreamers Paired with Border Security," FWD.us,

October 27, 2022, https://www.fwd.us/news/new-poll-overwhelming-major
ity-of-u-s-voters-across-political-spectrum-support-legislation-for-dreamers
-paired-with-border-security.

28. Alex Samuels, "How Democrats Became Stuck on Immigration," *FiveThirty-Eight*, March 30, 2021, https://fivethirtyeight.com/features/how-democrats
-became-stuck-on-immigration/.

29. "US Undocumented Immigrant Population Estimates," ProCon/Encyclopaedia
Britannica, last updated June 22, 2022, https://immigration.procon.org/us-un
documented-immigrant-population-estimates/#2022.

30. John Gramlich, "Monthly Encounters with Migrants at U.S.-Mexico Border
Remain Near Record Highs," Pew Research Center, January 13, 2023, https://
www.pewresearch.org/short-reads/2023/01/13/monthly-encounters-with-mi
grants-at-u-s-mexico-border-remain-near-record-highs/.

31. "A Sober Assessment of the Growing U.S. Asylum Backlog," Transactional Records
Access Clearinghouse, December 22, 2022, https://trac.syr.edu/reports/705/.

32. "CCPI Rankings," CCPI, accessed May 2023, https://ccpi.org/ranking/.

33. "Deloitte Report: Inaction on Climate Change Could Cost the US Economy
$14.5 Trillion by 2070," Deloitte, January 25, 2022, https://www2.deloitte.com
/us/en/pages/about-deloitte/articles/press-releases/deloitte-report-inaction
-on-climate-change-could-cost-the-us-economy-trillions-by-2070.html.

34. Kimberly Amadeo, "U.S. Education Rankings Are Falling Behind the Rest of
the World," *The Balance*, March 26, 2023, https://www.thebalancemoney.com
/the-u-s-is-losing-its-competitive-advantage-3306225.

35. Claire Parker, "U.S. Health-Care System Ranks Last among 11 High-Income
Countries, Researchers Say," *Washington Post*, August 5, 2021, https://www
.washingtonpost.com/world/2021/08/05/global-health-rankings/.

36. "Obesity, Race/Ethnicity, and COVID-19," Centers for Disease Control and
Prevention, accessed August 2023, https://www.cdc.gov/obesity/data/adult
.html.

37. "Risks and Threats from Deficits and Debt," Committee for a Responsible
Federal Budget, July 14, 2022, https://www.crfb.org/papers/risks-and-threats
-deficits-and-debt.

38. "Debt to GDP Ratio by Country 2023," World Population Review, accessed
May 2023, https://worldpopulationreview.com/country-rankings/debt-to-gdp
-ratio-by-country.

39. "Risks and Threats from Deficits and Debt," Committee for a Responsible Federal Budget, July 14, 2022, https://www.pdsdc.org/docs/default-source/clip
/informational-bulletin-2023-2024.pdf?sfvrsn=ee369bd0_0.

40. Tami Luhby, "Social Security Will Not Be Able to Pay Full Benefits in
2034 if Congress Doesn't Act," CNN, March 31, 2023, https://www.cnn
.com/2023/03/31/politics/social-security-benefits-decrease/index.html.

41. "Retirees Face a $17,400 Cut if Social Security Isn't Saved," Committee for a Re-
sponsible Federal Budget, August 8, 2023, https://www.crfb.org/blogs/retirees
-face-17400-cut-if-social-security-isnt-saved.

42. "Notable & Quotable: Reagan on Compromise," *Wall Street Journal*, October 20, 2015, https://www.wsj.com/articles/notable-quotable-reagan-on-compromise -1445379280.

43. Robert Burgdorf Jr., "Why I Wrote the Americans with Disabilities Act," *Washington Post*, July 24, 2015, https://www.washingtonpost.com/posteverything /wp/2015/07/24/why-the-americans-with-disabilities-act-mattered/.

44. Eric Garcia, "Bob Dole's Disability Rights Legacy Marked the End of a Bipartisan Era," *New Republic*, December 5, 2021, https://newrepublic.com/ar ticle/162491/bob-dole-obit-disability-legacy.

45. "Should the Senate Approve the 'Americans with Disabilities Act of 1989'?," *Congressional Digest*, December 1989, 294.

46. "Federal Elections 92: Election Results for the U.S. President, the U.S. Senate, and the U.S. House of Representatives," Federal Elections Commission, accessed May 2023, https://www.fec.gov/resources/cms-content/documents /federalelections92.pdf.

47. "Milbank: Washington Forgets the Art of Friendship," *Denver Post*, July 28, 2015, https://www.denverpost.com/2015/07/28/milbank-washington-forgets -the-art-of-friendship/.

48. Sarah E. Anderson, Daniel M. Butler, and Laurel Harbridge-Yong, *Rejecting Compromise: Legislators' Fear of Primary Voters* (Cambridge, UK: Cambridge University Press, 2020), 66.

49. Ibid., 1–2.

50. David Wasserman, "Primary Scorecard: House GOP Veers towards Trump, Democrats Tack Less Left," *Cook Political Report*, September 9, 2022, https://www.cookpolitical.com/analysis/house/house -charts/primary-scorecard-house-gop-veers-towards-trump-democrats -tack-less?redirect=63f4fd4112b22.

51. Elaine Kamarck, "Lessons from the 2022 Primaries—What Do They Tell Us about America's Political Parties and the Midterm Elections?," Brookings Institution, September 8, 2022, https://www.brookings.edu/blog/fixgov/2022/09/08 /lessons-from-the-2022-primaries-what-do-they-tell-us-about-americas-polit ical-parties-and-the-midterm-elections/.

52. Elaine Kamarck and James Wallner, "Anticipating Trouble: Congressional Primaries and Incumbent Behavior," *R Street Policy Study*, no. 156, October 2018, https://www.brookings.edu/wp-content/uploads/2018/10/GS_10292018_Pri maries-and-Incumbent-Behavior.pdf.

53. Ibid.

54. Eric Cantor, interview with author, May 5, 2023.

55. Richard Barton, "Congress Is Polarized. Fear of Being 'Primaried' Is One Reason," *Washington Post*, June 10, 2022, https://www.washingtonpost.com/poli tics/2022/06/10/primaries-gridlock-polarization-congress-schrader-extremists/.

56. Benjamin I. Page and Martin Gilens, *Democracy in America?: What Has Gone Wrong and What We Can Do about It* (Chicago: University of Chicago Press, 2020), 68.

57. Miguel Schor, "Why the Solution to the Debt Ceiling Crisis (and to Our Dysfunctional Federal Government) Can Be Found in Alaska," *Des Moines Register*, April 2, 2023, https://www.desmoinesregister.com/story/opinion/columnists/iowa-view/2023/04/02/alaska-ranked-choice-voting-solving-dysfunctional-government/70064843007/.

58. Dalibor Rohac, Liz Kennedy, and Vikram Singh, "Drivers of Authoritarian Populism in the United States," Center for American Progress, May 10, 2018, https://www.americanprogress.org/article/drivers-authoritarian-populism-united-states/.

59. Elena Holodny, "The US has been Downgraded to a 'Flawed Democracy,'" Business Insider, January 25, 2017, https://www.businessinsider.com/economist-intelligence-unit-downgrades-united-states-to-flawed-democracy-2017-1.

60. Julia Jacobo, "This Is What Trump Told Supporters Before Many Stormed Capitol Hill," ABC News, January 7, 2021, https://abcnews.go.com/Politics/trump-told-supporters-stormed-capitol-hill/story?id=75110558.

61. Adam Carlson, "Liz Cheney Says Jan. 6 Work Is Worth Losing Her House Seat; Committee May Subpoena Ginni Thomas," ABC News, July 24, 2022, https://abcnews.go.com/Politics/liz-cheney-jan-work-worth-losing-house-seat/story?id=87327833.

62. Lisa Hagen, "Poll: A Third of Americans Question Legitimacy of Biden Victory Nearly a Year Since Jan. 6," U.S. News & World Report, December 28, 2021, https://www.usnews.com/news/politics/articles/2021-12-28/poll-a-third-of-americans-question-legitimacy-of-biden-victory-nearly-a-year-since-jan-6.

63. Kevin Arceneaux and Rory Truex, "Donald Trump and the Lie," *Perspectives on Politics* (March 2022): 1–17.

64. "60 Percent of Americans Will Have an Election Denier on the Ballot This Fall," *FiveThirtyEight*, updated November 8, 2022, https://projects.fivethirtyeight.com/republicans-trump-election-fraud/.

65. Kamarck, "Lessons from the 2022 Primaries."

66. Michael Graham, "Morse, Mowers Skip Debates Hosted by 'Election Integrity' Group," *NH Journal*, August 14, 2022, https://nhjournal.com/morse-mowers-skip-debates-hosted-by-election-integrity-group/.

67. "Open Letter from Retired Generals and Admirals," Flag Officers 4 America, May 10, 2021, https://img1.wsimg.com/blobby/go/fb7c7bd8-097d-4e2f-8f12-3442d151b57d/downloads/2021%20Open%20Letter%20from%20Retired%20Generals%20and%20Adm.pdf?ver=1620643005025.

68. Maggie Astor, "Right After Primary Win, Bolduc Reverses Support for Election Lies," *New York Times*, September 15, 2022, https://www.nytimes.com/2022/09/15/us/politics/don-bolduc-nh.html.

69. "Bolduc Shares 'Bottom-Up' Campaign Approach, Slams Dems' Failures: 'Enough Is Enough,'" Fox News, September 15, 2022, https://www.foxnews.com/video/6312358456112#sp=show-clips.

70. Amber Phillips, "What an Election Denier Could Do If Elected Secretary of

State," *Washington Post*, September 19, 2022, https://www.washingtonpost
.com/politics/2022/09/19/election-deniers-secretary-state/.

71. "Arizona Secretary of State Election, 2022," Ballotpedia, accessed May 2023,
    https://ballotpedia.org/Arizona_Secretary_of_State_election,_2022.

72. Phillips, "What an Election Denier Could Do If Elected Secretary of State."

73. "Jim Marchant," Ballotpedia, accessed May 2023, https://ballotpedia.org/Jim_
    Marchant.

74. Adrian Blanco, Daniel Wolfe, and Amy Gardner, "Tracking Which 2020 Elec-
    tion Deniers Are Winning, Losing in the Midterms," *Washington Post*, last
    updated December 18, 2022, https://www.washingtonpost.com/politics/inter
    active/2022/election-deniers-midterms/.

75. Daniel Nichanian, "Meet the First Election Denier Poised to Win for Secretary
    of State This Year," *Bolts*, August 19, 2022, https://boltsmag.org/wyoming-first
    -election-denier-secretary-of-state/.

76. "Views of Election Administration and Confidence in Vote Counts," Pew
    Research Center, October 31, 2022, https://www.pewresearch.org/poli
    tics/2022/10/31/views-of-election-administration-and-confidence-in-vote
    -counts/.

77. "Voting Laws Roundup: December 2021," Brennan Center for Justice, last up-
    dated January 12, 2022, https://www.brennancenter.org/our-work/research-re
    ports/voting-laws-roundup-december-2021.

78. Stef W. Kight, "19 States Enacted Voting Restrictions This Year," *Axios*, De-
    cember 21, 2021, https://www.axios.com/2021/12/21/states-restrictive-voting
    -bills-2021-election.

79. Annie Linskey, "Democrats Spend Tens of Millions Amplifying Far-Right
    Candidates in Nine States," *Washington Post*, September 12, 2022, https://www
    .washingtonpost.com/politics/2022/09/12/democrats-interfere-republican
    -primaries/.

80. Jonathan Weisman, "Democrats Aid Far-Right Candidate against Republican
    Who Backed Impeachment," *New York Times*, July 26, 2022, https://www.ny
    times.com/2022/07/26/us/politics/democrats-john-gibbs-peter-meijer.html.

81. James O'Rourke and Lisa Hayes, "Meet John Gibbs: The Trump Republican
    Who Took Down Peter Meijer," *Gander*, August 18, 2022, https://gandernews
    room.com/2022/08/15/meet-john-gibbs-the-trump-republican-who-took
    -down-peter-meijer.

82. "Political Leaders Denounce Democrats Who Elevate Election Deniers in Re-
    publican Primaries," Issue One, August 1, 2022, https://issueone.org/articles
    /political-leaders-denounce-democrats-who-elevate-election-deniers-in-re
    publican-primaries/.

FIVE: BAD FOR THE PARTIES

1. Aliza Astrow and Lanae Erickson, "Overcoming the Democratic Party Brand,"
   Third Way, November 7, 2023, https://www.thirdway.org/memo/overcoming
   -the-democratic-party-brand.

2. Ibid.
3. Rich Kremer, "Wisconsinites Have a Negative View of Sen. Ron Johnson. It May Not Hurt His Reelection Chances," Wisconsin Public Radio, October 10, 2022, https://www.wpr.org/sen-ron-johnson-wisconsin-reelection-republi cans-democrats-mandela-barnes-polling.
4. Eli Yokley, "Ron Johnson Is Unpopular in Wisconsin. Can He Win Anyway?" Morning Consult, January 25, 2022, https://pro.morningconsult.com/trend -setters/ron-johnson-unpopular-in-wisconsin-can-he-win-anyway.
5. All expenditure data presented here is from OpenSecrets, https://www.opense crets.org/.
6. Andrew Kaczynski and Em Steck, "Mandela Barnes Has Signaled Support for Removing Police Funding and Abolishing ICE—Despite Ad Claiming Other- wise," CNN, October 7, 2022, https://www.cnn.com/2022/10/07/politics/kfile -mandela-barnes-signaled-support-abolish-ice.
7. "Biden Approval Rating," FiveThirtyEight, accessed May 2023, https://projects .fivethirtyeight.com/biden-approval-rating/.
8. "Historical Inflation Rates: 1914–2023," US Inflation Calculator, accessed May 2023, https://www.usinflationcalculator.com/inflation/historical-inflation-rates/.
9. Charlie Cook, "The Midterms May Come Down to the Last Gust of Political Wind," Cook Political Report, October 20, 2022, https://www.cookpolitical.com /analysis/national/national-politics/midterms-may-come-down-last-gust-po litical-wind.
10. Marley Parish,"Oz Clarifies Abortion Views, Fetterman Capitalizes on Con- flicting Views in Senate Race," Pennsylvania Capital-Star, September 11, 2022, https://www.penncapital-star.com/election-2022/oz-clarifies-abortion-views -fetterman-capitalizes-on-conflicting-views-in-senate-race/.
11. Sahil Kapur and Frank Thorp V, "McConnell Says Republicans May Not Win Senate Control, Citing 'Candidate Quality,'" NBC News, August 18, 2022, https://www.nbcnews.com/politics/2022-election/mcconnell-says-republi cans-may-not-win-senate-control-citing-candidate-rcna43777.
12. David Wasserman, "House Recap: The Five Biggest Takeaways from 2022's Photo Finish," Cook Political Report, December 1, 2022, https://www.cook political.com/analysis/house/house-overview/house-recap-five-biggest-take aways-2022s-photo-finish?redirect=64161d4775b1b.
13. Nate Cohn, "Trump's Drag on Republicans Quantified: A Five-Point Penalty," New York Times, November 16, 2022, https://www.nytimes.com/2022/11/16 /upshot/trump-effect-midterm-election.html.
14. Philip Wallach, "We Can Now Quantify Trump's Sabotage of the GOP's House Dreams," Washington Post, November 15, 2022, https://www.washingtonpost .com/opinions/2022/11/15/data-trump-weighed-down-republican-candidates/.
15. Greg Orman, "The House Speaker Standoff and Final Five Voting," RealClear- Politics, January 6, 2023, https://www.realclearpolitics.com/articles/2023/01/06 /negotiating_with_terrorists_isnt_a_long-term_solution_148694.html.
16. Unite America (@uniteamerica), "McCarthy's Primary Problem," Twitter,

January 5, 2023, https://twitter.com/uniteamerica/status/16111100319861514
24?s=43&t=MVM8tr3X-DEx0c_scDc2qw.

17. Philip Klein, "Kevin McCarthy Elected Speaker in Name Only," *National Review*, January 7, 2023, https://www.nationalreview.com/corner/kevin-mccar
thy-elected-speaker-in-name-only/.

18. Melanie Zanona and Heather Caygle, "Pelosi, AOC, Gaetz: The Dam Is Breaking on Playing in Primary Battles," *Politico*, August 28, 2020, https://www
.politico.com/news/2020/08/28/pelosi-ocasio-cortez-gaetz-congress-support
-primary-battles-403794.

19. Jeff Bartos, interview with author, April 17, 2023.

20. Charles Schumer, "End Partisan Primaries, Save America," *New York Times*,
July 21, 2014, https://www.nytimes.com/2014/07/22/opinion/charles-schumer
-adopt-the-open-primary.html.

21. William Saletan, "That McCarthy PAC Concession? It Could Elect Far-Right
Candidates in 2024," Bulwark, January 9, 2023, https://www.thebulwark.com
/that-mccarthy-pac-concession-it-could-elect-far-right-candidates-in-2024/.

22. Alexandria Ocasio-Cortez (@AOC), "No one gets to complain about primary challenges again," Twitter, August 20, 2020, https://twitter.com/AOC/sta
tus/1296498853517176832.

23. Gabby Birenbaum, "In a Victory for Progressives, the DCCC Ends Its Consultant Blacklist," *Vox*, March 10, 2021, https://www.vox.com/2021/3/10/22323348
/dccc-consultant-blacklist-maloney-aoc.

24. Chris Deaton, "The Primary Problem Derails McCarthy's Bid," Unite America, January 4, 2023, https://www.uniteamerica.org/news-article/the-primary
-problem-derails-mccarthys-bid.

25. Ronald Brownstein, "The Four Quadrants of American Politics," *Atlantic*,
March 17, 2023, https://www.theatlantic.com/politics/archive/2023/03/house
-of-representatives-equity-research-institute-usc-analysis/673422/.

26. Chapman Rackaway and Joseph Romance, *Primary Elections and American
Politics: The Unintended Consequences of Progressive Era Reform* (Albany: State
University of New York Press, 2022), 11.

27. Ibid., 129.

28. Clara Elizabeth Fanning, *Selected Articles on Direct Primaries* (Minneapolis:
H. W. Wilson, 1911), 110.

29. Jonathan Rauch and Ray La Raja, "Too Much Democracy Is Bad for Democracy," *Atlantic*, December 2019, https://www.theatlantic.com/magazine/ar
chive/2019/12/too-much-democracy-is-bad-for-democracy/600766/.

30. Jeff Bartos, interview with author, April 17, 2023.

31. Newell Normand, "Newell: Nungesser Gives Full-Throated Defense of Louisiana's Open Primary System," *Audacy*, April 20, 2021, https://www.audacy.com
/wwl/news/nungesser-gives-full-throated-defense-of-open-primary-system.

32. Steven Levitsky and Daniel Ziblatt, *How Democracies Die* (New York: Crown,
2018), 38–39.

33. Rauch and La Raja, "Too Much Democracy Is Bad for Democracy."

34. Seth Hill, "Sidestepping Primary Reform: Political Action in Response to Institutional Change," *Political Science Research and Methods* 10, no. 2 (October 2020): 1–17.

35. R. Michael Alvarez and J. Andrew Sinclair, *Nonpartisan Primary Election Reform: Mitigating Mischief* (New York: Cambridge University Press, 2015), 42–44.

36. Jennifer Proto, "Major Party Nominating Procedures in States with Conventions," OLR Research Report, January 17, 2019.

37. Ernest Luning, "Dave Williams Says Colorado GOP Won't Apologize for Beliefs, Wants to Close Primaries," Colorado Politics, March 25, 2023, https://www.coloradopolitics.com/elections/colorado-republicans-new-chair-closed-primaries-dave-williams/article_bf25cab4-c8fc-11ed-9dde-8718dd624381.html.

38. Sefakor Ashiagbor, *Political Parties and Democracy in Theoretical and Practical Perspectives* (Washington, DC: National Democratic Institute for International Affairs, 2008), 17.

39. Rauch and La Raja, "Too Much Democracy Is Bad for Democracy."

PART III: THE BETTER ALTERNATIVE

1. Grace L. Miller, "The Origins of the San Diego Lincoln-Roosevelt League, 1905–1909," *Southern California Quarterly* 60, no. 4 (1978): 421–43.

2. Jack Santucci, "Ranked-Choice Voting Didn't Solve Our Problems in the Last Century. And It Won't Today," Medium, July 29, 2022, https://medium.com/3streams/ranked-choice-voting-didnt-solve-our-problems-in-the-last-century-and-it-won-t-today-5bda00988a0c.

3. "Where Is Ranked Choice Voting Used?" FairVote, accessed July 2023, https://fairvote.org/our-reforms/ranked-choice-voting-information/#where-is-ranked-choice-voting-used.

4. George W. Norris, "The One-House Legislature," *Annals of the American Academy of Political and Social Science* 181 (September 1935): 50–58.

5. Will Chambers, "Granges Plan Initiation of Two Measures," *Seattle Star,* March 7, 1934, https://www.newspapers.com/clip/111675954/wa-state-grange-announces-initiative/.

6. "Action Is Assured: State Grange Files Blanket Primary Initiative," *Bellingham Herald,* November 3, 1934, https://www.newspapers.com/clip/111728589/grange-submits-over-80k-signatures-to-se/.

7. "Brief of Amicus Curiae: Alaskan Voters for an Open Primary (AVOP) in Support of Respondents," Supreme Court of the United States, March 31, 2000, https://www.findlawimages.com/efile/supreme/briefs/99-401/99-401fo6/brief.pdf.

8. "California Proposition 198, Open Blanket Primary Election Initiative (March 1996)," Ballotpedia, accessed May 2023, https://ballotpedia.org/California_Proposition_198,_Open_Blanket_Primary_Election_Initiative_(March_1996).

9. *California Democratic Party, et al., Petitioners v. Bill Jones, Secretary of State of California, et al.*, VotesCount, accessed May 2023, https://www.votescount.us /Portals/16/mar2k/suprect.htm.

10. "History of Washington State Primary Systems," Washington Secretary of State, accessed July 2023, https://www.sos.wa.gov/elections/data-research/history -laws-and-litigation/history-washington-state-primary-systems.

11. "Washington Initiative 872, Top-Two Primaries Measure (2004)," Ballotpedia, accessed May 2023, https://ballotpedia.org/Washington_Top_Two_Prima ries,_Initiative_872_(2004).

12. *Washington State Grange v. Washington State Republican Party et al.*, Supreme Court of the United States, March 18, 2008, https://www.scotusblog.com/wp -content/uploads/2008/03/06-713.pdf.

SIX: THE PRIMARY SOLUTION

1. "Poverty Status in the Last 12 Months," U.S. Census Bureau, accessed May 2023, https://data.census.gov/table?q=S1701:+POVERTY+STATUS+IN+THE+PAST +12+MONTHS&g=010XX00US$0400000,&tid=ACSST5Y2020.S1701.

2. "US States by Race 2023," World Population Review, accessed May 2023, https://worldpopulationreview.com/states/states-by-race.

3. David Wasserman, Sophie Andrews, Leo Saenger, Lev Cohen, Ally Flinn, and Griff Tatarsky, "2020 National Popular Vote Tracker," *Cook Political Report*, accessed May 2023, https://www.cookpolitical.com/2020-national-popular-vote -tracker.

4. "Contributions to Gubernatorial Candidates in Mississippi 2015," Follow the Money, accessed May 2023, https://www.followthemoney.org/show -me?s=MS&y=2015&c-r-ot=G&gro=c-t-id.

5. "Short, Dem Candidate for Governor: Miss. Leaders Have Failed," WAPT, updated June 2, 2015, https://www.wapt.com/article/short-dem-candidate-for -governor-miss-leaders-have-failed/2093902.

6. Ben Mayer, "Robert Gray's Unlikely Primary Win in Mississippi Draws Suspicion, Shock," MSNBC, September 10, 2015, https://www.msnbc.com /msnbc/robert-gray-unlikely-primary-win-mississippi-draws-suspicion -shock-msna679671.

7. Campbell Robertson, "Chosen by Mississippi Democrats, Shy Trucker Is at a Crossroad," *New York Times*, September 7, 2015, https://www.nytimes .com/2015/09/08/us/shy-trucker-emerges-as-democrats-pick-for-mississippi -governor.html.

8. "Mississippi Gubernatorial Election 2015," Ballotpedia, accessed May 2023, https://ballotpedia.org/Mississippi_gubernatorial_election,_2015.

9. Tyler Bridges, "'You're Crazy If You Believe That': John Bel Edwards Takes Remarkable Journey to Improbable Landslide in Governor's Race," *Advocate*, December 15, 2015, https://www.theadvocate.com/baton_rouge/news/politics /elections/article_e4dd2ddd-518a-5a8e-85f6-a13717f8c0c5.html.

10. Kat Tenbarge, "John Bel Edwards Was Narrowly Re-Elected as Governor of

Louisiana. He's Not a Typical Democrat," *Business Insider*, November 17, 2019, https://www.businessinsider.com/john-bel-edwards-life-bio-re-election-of -conservative-democrat-2019-11.

11. "U.S. Senator Caught in 'D.C. Madam' Scandal," CBS News, July 9, 2007, https:// www.cbsnews.com/news/senator-caught-in-dc-madam-scandal/.

12. Brock Sues, "Dardenne Endorses Edwards for Governor," WBRZ, November 5, 2015, https://www.wbrz.com/news/dardenne-endorses-edwards-for-governor/.

13. Bridges, "'You're Crazy If You Believe That.'"

14. "Louisiana Gubernatorial Election 2015."

15. "Federal Poverty Level (FPL)," HealthCare.gov, accessed May 2023, https:// www.healthcare.gov/glossary/federal-poverty-level-fpl/.

16. Bobby Jindal, "Gov. Bobby Jindal: Why I Opposed Medicaid Expansion," NOLA, July 23, 2013, https://www.nola.com/opinions/article_c0155e08-f87b -5c8f-b4e3-092a5b095991.html.

17. "LSU Survey: Medicaid Expansion Has 72% Approval," Louisiana Department of Health, April 11, 2017, https://ldh.la.gov/news/4216.

18. John Bel Edwards, interview with author, June 1, 2023.

19. Daniel Malloy, "David Vitter Open to Medicaid Expansion in Louisiana," *Atlanta Journal-Constitution*, June 16, 2014, https://www.ajc.com/blog/politics /david-vitter-open-medicaid-expansion-louisiana/MykNIwTdxDeEUx86hWl RZN/.

20. Marsha Shuler, "Louisiana Medicaid Expansion Gains Republican Support, Heads to Senate Floor for Final Passage," *Advocate*, June 2, 2015, https://www .theadvocate.com/baton_rouge/news/politics/legislature/article_4d5a8b6d -5a40-5838-bae0-07948ecec7c9.html.

21. Richard Fausset and Abby Goodnough, "Louisiana's New Governor Signs an Order to Expand Medicaid," *New York Times*, January 12, 2016, https://www .nytimes.com/2016/01/13/us/louisianas-new-governor-signs-an-order-to-ex pand-medicaid.html.

22. "Gov. Edwards Celebrates the 5-Year Anniversary of Medicaid Expansion That Continues to Save Lives, Jobs, Rural Hospitals and Reduce the Number of Uninsured Louisianans," State of Louisiana, Office of the Governor, July 1, 2021, https://gov.louisiana.gov/index.cfm/newsroom/detail/3253.

23. Ibid.

24. Melinda Deslatte, "Louisiana Governor Election Won't Uproot Medicaid Expansion," Associated Press, September 18, 2019, https://apnews.com/article/3a 1d333dcf2b4e78a969428b29a0a9ad.

25. "Healthcare on the Ballot," Ballotpedia, accessed May 2023, https://ballotpedia .org/Healthcare_on_the_ballot.

26. Geoff Pender, "Who's Opposed to Mississippi Medicaid Expansion and Why?," Mississippi Today, November 15, 2022, https://mississippitoday .org/2022/11/15/medicaid-expansion-opposition-why/.

27. Louise Norris, "Medicaid Eligibility and Enrollment in Mississippi," Healthinsurance.org, March 9, 2023, https://www.healthinsurance.org/medicaid/mississippi/.

28. Geoff Pender, "Poll: 80% of Mississippians Favor Medicaid Expansion," Mississippi Today, January 18, 2023, https://mississippitoday.org/2023/01/18/medicaid-expansion-mississippi-poll/.

29. John Bel Edwards, interview with author, June 1, 2023.

30. Grace Reinke, "A Stronger EITC Can Mitigate Sales Tax Increase," Louisiana Budget Project, February 2, 2016, https://www.labudget.org/2016/02/a-stronger-eitc-can-mitigate-sales-tax-increase/.

31. Kaylee Poche, "Clay Schexnayder Selected as New Louisiana House Speaker; See Other Leadership Picks," Gambit, January 13, 2020, https://www.nola.com/gambit/news/the_latest/clay-schexnayder-selected-as-new-louisiana-house-speaker-see-other-leadership-picks/article_99c7d8f6-3652-11ea-915a-fb12a2275a6d.html.

32. Edwards, interview with author, June 1, 2023.

33. Billy Nungesser, interview with author, May 1, 2023.

34. Frederick J. Boehmke and Paul Skinner, "State Policy Innovativeness Revisited," State Politics & Policy Quarterly 12, no. 3 (September 2012): 303–29.

35. "Bipartisan Index," The Lugar Center, https://www.thelugarcenter.org/ourwork-Bipartisan-Index.html.

36. "Louisiana's Long-Term Election Experiment: How Eliminating Partisan Primaries Improved Governance and Reduced Polarization," Unite America, November 2022, https://www.uniteamericainstitute.org/research/louisianas-long-term-election-experiment-how-eliminating-partisan-primaries-improved-governance-and-reduced-polarization.

37. Seth Hill, "Sidestepping Primary Reform: Political Action in Response to Institutional Change," Political Science Research and Methods 10, no. 2 (October 2020): 1–17.

38. Christian Grose, "Reducing Legislative Polarization: Top-Two and Open Primaries Are Associated with More Moderate Legislators," Journal of Political Institutions and Political Economy 1, no. 2 (June 2020): 267–87.

39. Seattle Times Editorial Board, "The Times Recommends: Marilyn Strickland for the 10th Congressional District," Seattle Times, July 8, 2022, https://www.seattletimes.com/opinion/editorials/the-times-recommends-marilyn-strickland-for-the-10th-congressional-district/.

40. "Endorsements," Beth Doglio, accessed May 2023, https://www.bethdoglio.com/endorsements/.

41. "Didier Polls in Single Digits, but Palin Endorsement Created Buzz," Tri-City Herald, June 27 2010, https://www.newspapers.com/image/822467738/?clipping_id=111685010&fcfToken=eyJhbGciOiJIUzI1NiIsInR5cCI6IkpXVCJ9.eyJmcmVlLXZpZXctaWQiOjgyMjQ2NzczOCwiaWF0IjoxNjc3NTE1ODk1LCJleHAiOjE2Nzc2MDIyOTV9._rUPzX3Y49He3yzYuNkEJM9_j1yzWBUy-a2o-i6Ba_U.

42. Mike Faulk, "Former State Ag Director Newhouse Officially Joins 4th District Race," Yakima Herald-Republic, February 21, 2014, https://archive.ph/20140221202416/http://www.yakimaherald.com/community/lowervalley/

sunnysidecontent/1944182-8/newhouse-declares-for-hastings-seat-in-con
gress.

43. Arnold Schwarzenegger and Ro Khanna, "Don't Listen to the Establishment
     Critics. California's Open Primary Works," *Washington Post*, June 18, 2018,
     https://www.washingtonpost.com/news/posteverything/wp/2018/06/18/dont
     -listen-to-the-establishment-critics-californias-open-primary-works/.

44. Richard Barton, "California's Top-Two Primary: The Effects on Electoral Poli-
     tics and Governance," Unite America Institute, June 2023, https://docsend
     .com/view/hnmec525w7bzy48p.

45. Charles Munger Jr., "California's Top-Two Primary: A Successful Reform," USC
     Schwarzenegger Institute, February 22, 2019, http://schwarzenegger.usc.edu
     /institute-in-action/article/californias-top-two-primary-a-successful-reform.

46. Lee Drutman, "Why Hasn't the Top-Two Primary Been More Transformative?"
     New America, July 1, 2021, https://www.newamerica.org/political-reform/re
     ports/what-we-know-about-congressional-primaries-and-congressional-pri
     mary-reform/why-hasnt-the-top-two-primary-been-more-transformative.

47. Jesse Crosson, "Extreme Districts, Moderate Winners: Same-Party Challenges,
     and Deterrence in Top-Two Primaries," *Political Science Research and Methods*
     9, no. 3 (March 2020): 1–17.

48. "FairVote's Fix for Top Two in California," FairVote, June 18, 2013, https://fair
     vote.org/fairvote-s-fix-for-top-two-in-california/.

49. Katherine Gehl, "The Case for the Five in Final Five Voting," *Constitutional
     Political Economy* (January 2023): doi.org/10.1007/s10602-022-09386-6.

50. Katherine Gehl, interview with author, June 14, 2023.

51. Jeremy Rose, "Primary Runoff Elections and Decline in Voter Turnout, 1994–
     2002," FairVote, accessed May 2023, https://fairvote.org/report/primary-run
     offs-report-2022/.

52. "Louisiana's Long-Term Election Experiment: How Eliminating Partisan Pri-
     maries Improved Governance and Reduced Polarization," Unite America,
     November 2022, https://www.uniteamericainstitute.org/research/louisianas
     -long-term-election-experiment-how-eliminating-partisan-primaries-im
     proved-governance-and-reduced-polarization.

53. Chris Lisinski, "Accord Clears Way for E-Sigs on Ballot Questions," *Lowell Sun*,
     April 30, 2020, https://www.lowellsun.com/2020/04/30/accord-clears-way-for
     -e-sigs-on-ballot-questions/.

54. "Research and Data on RCV in Practice," FairVote, accessed May 2023, https://
     fairvote.org/resources/data-on-rcv/#comefrombehind-winners.

55. John Opdycke, interview with author, June 1, 2023.

SEVEN: ALASKA'S PROOF OF CONCEPT
1.   "Indian Affairs: Alaska Region," U.S. Department of the Interior, accessed May
     2023, https://www.bia.gov/regional-office/alaska-region#:~:text=Alaska%20
     Region%20(Sub%20Navigation)&text=More%20than%20180%2C000%20
     Tribal%20members.

2. Bill Walker, interview with author, 2017.

3. Lee Revis, "Walker Running for Governor 2014," *Valdez Star*, May 1, 2013, https://web.archive.org/web/20140905012757/https://valdezstar.net/sto ry/2013/05/01/main-news/walker-running-for-governor-2014/304.html.

4. "About Governor Walker," State of Alaska, accessed May 2023, https://web.ar chive.org/web/20150930004431 /http://gov.alaska.gov/Walker/governors-offi ce/meet-bill-walker.html.

5. *Working Title* documentary, directed by AJ Schnack, Polestar Productions, 2024.

6. Bill Walker, "Gov. Bill Walker: The Hard Truth about Alaska's Oil Revenue," *Anchorage Daily News*, updated June 29, 2016, https://www.adn.com/commentary /article/gov-bill-walker-hard-truth-about-alaskas-oil-revenue/2015/01/08/.

7. Scott Kendall, interview with author, March 28, 2023.

8. Alex DeMarban and Yereth Rosen, "'Day of Reckoning': Gov. Walker Vetoes Hundreds of Millions in Spending, Caps Permanent Fund Dividend at $1,000," *Anchorage Daily News*, June 29, 2016, https://www.adn.com/poli tics/2016/06/29/walker-budget-vetoes-include-capping-permanent-fund-div dends-at-1000/.

9. "1994 General Election Official Results: Statewide Summary," Alaska Division of Elections, November 8, 1994, https://www.elections.alaska.gov/Core/ Archive/94GENR/result94.php#govltg.

10. "Mark Begich," Ballotpedia, accessed May 2023, https://ballotpedia.org/Mark_ Begich.

11. "Statement of Support for Alaska Ballot Measure 1," FairVote, July 2002, https:// archive.fairvote.org/?page=1467.

12. "Alaska Automatic Runoff Voting Initiative, Measure 1 (August 2002)," Ballotpedia, accessed May 2023, https://ballotpedia.org/Alaska_Automatic_Run off_Voting_Initiative,_Measure_1_(August_2002).

13. Scott Kendall, interview with author, March 28, 2023.

14. Ibid.

15. "Initiative Petition List," Alaska Division of Elections, accessed July 2023, https://www.elections.alaska.gov/Core/initiativepetitionlist.php#19AKBE.

16. Andrew Kitchenman, "Judge Approves Signature Gathering for Initiative That Would Change State Elections," Alaska Public Media and KTOO, October 28, 2019, https://www.ktoo.org/2019/10/28/judge-approves-signature-gathering -for-initiative-that-would-change-state-elections/.

17. "Meyer v. Alaskans for Better Elections," Justia US Law, accessed May 2023, https://law.justia.com/cases/alaska/supreme-court/2020/s-17629.html.

18. Scott Kendall, interview with author, March 28, 2023.

19. *Working Title* documentary, directed by AJ Schnack, Polestar Productions, 2024.

20. Scott Kendall, interview with author, March 28, 2023.

21. Nat Herz, "Gov. Dunleavy Says He'll Vote No on Oil Tax Increase, Election Overhaul Initiatives," KTOO, October 15, 2020, https://www.ktoo.org/2020/10/15

/gov-dunleavy-says-hell-vote-no-on-oil-tax-increase-election-overhaul-initia
tives/.

22. Russell Berman, "The Political-Reform Movement Scores Its Biggest Win
Yet," *Atlantic*, January 26, 2021, https://www.theatlantic.com/politics/ar
chive/2021/01/congress-reform-ranked-choice-voting/617821/.

23. Mark Begich and Sean Parnell, "Alaska's Election Initiative Is Rank," *Wall Street
Journal*, July 23, 2020, https://www.wsj.com/articles/alaskas-election-initiative
-is-rank-11595545790.

24. Jacob Begich, "Why Alaska Needs Ranked-Choice Voting," *Anchorage Daily
News*, July 31, 2021, https://www.adn.com/opinions/2020/07/31/why-alaska
-needs-ranked-choice-voting/.

25. *Working Title* documentary, directed by AJ Schnack, Polestar Productions,
2024.

26. Catherine Giessel, interview with author, May 31, 2023.

27. *Working Title* documentary, directed by AJ Schnack, Polestar Productions,
2024.

28. Catherine Giessel, interview with author, May 31, 2023.

29. Andrew Kitchenman, "Senate President Giessel Faces Primary Challenge for
Anchorage Seat," Alaska Public Media, August 11, 2020, https://alaskapublic
.org/2020/08/11/senate-president-giessel-faces-primary-challenge-for-ancho
rage-seat/.

30. Catherine Giessel, interview with author, May 31, 2023.

31. Ibid.

32. Ibid.

33. Ibid.

34. Ibid.

35. Claire Stremple, "Alaska Senate Passes Major One-Time Education Funding
Increase," *Alaska Beacon*, May 18, 2023, https://alaskabeacon.com/2023/05/18
/alaska-senate-passes-major-one-time-education-funding-increase/.

36. Catherine Giessel, interview with author, May 31, 2023.

37. Tea Party Express, "TVAd: Liberal Lisa Murkowski vs. Conservative Joe
Miller—U.S. Senate, Alaska," YouTube video, August 17, 2010, https://www
.youtube.com/watch?v=pfBrbxvTDNg.

38. "Tea Party Express/Our Country Deserves Independent Expenditures,"
OpenSecrets, accessed May 2023, https://www.opensecrets.org/political-ac
tion-committees-pacs/tea-party-express-our-country-deserves/C00454074
/independent-expenditures/2010.

39. Patti Epler, "Alaska Senate Race: The Untold Story of Lisa Murkowski's Write-in
Decision," *Anchorage Daily News*, November 11, 2010, https://www.adn.com
/politics/article/alaska-senate-race-untold-story-lisa-murkowski-s-write-deci
sion/2010/11/12/.

40. Lisa Murkowski, interview with author, June 16, 2023.

41. Ibid.

42. Ibid.

43. "Roll Call Vote 111th Congress—2nd Session," United States Senate, accessed June 2, 2023, https://www.senate.gov/legislative/LIS/roll_call_votes/vote1112 / vote_111_2_00278.htm.

44. Aaron Blake, "Murkowski Becomes Third GOP Senator to Back Gay Marriage," *Washington Post*, June 19, 2013, https://www.washingtonpost.com/news/post -politics/wp/2013/06/19/murkowski-becomes-third-gop-senator-to-back -gay-marriage/.

45. Leigh Ann Caldwell, "Obamacare Repeal Fails: Three GOP Senators Rebel in 49–51 Vote," NBC News, July 28, 2017, https://www.nbcnews.com/politics /congress/senate-gop-effort- repeal-obamacare-fails-n787311.

46. James Brooks, "Alaska Sen. Lisa Murkowski Calls on President Trump to Resign, Questions Her Future as a Republican," *Anchorage Daily News*, January 8, 2021, https://www.adn.com/politics/2021/01/08/alaska-sen-lisa-murkowski-calls -on-president-trump-to-resign-questions-her-future-as-a-republican/.

47. Caroline Vakil, "Trump Goes after 'RINO' Murkowski During Alaska Rally: 'She's Worse than a Democrat,'" *The Hill*, July 9, 2022, https://thehill.com /homenews/campaign/3551248-trump-goes-after-rino-murkowski-during -alaska-rally-shes-worse-than-a-democrat/.

48. Jeanette Lee, "Cheney's and Murkowski's Fates Tied to Their States' Primary Systems," Fulcrum, August 19, 2022, https://thefulcrum.us/Elections/Voting /cheney-murkowski-primaries.

49. Amy Walter, Jessica Taylor, and David Wasserman, "A Tale of Two Primary (Systems)," *Cook Political Report*, August 17, 2022, https://www.cookpolitical .com/analysis/senate/2022-primaries/tale-two-primary-systems?redirect=62fe 5fb76df16.

50. David Lauter, "Essential Politics: How Three Pro-Impeachment Republicans Escaped Trump's Wrath in Primaries," *Los Angeles Times*, August 19, 2022, https://www.latimes.com/politics/newsletter/2022-08-19/three-pro-impeach ment-republicans-escaped-trumps-wrath-reform-that-works-made-it-possi ble-essential-politics.

51. Henry Olsen, "Lisa Murkowski Is Showing the Limits of Political Extremism," *Washington Post*, August 18, 2022, https://www.washingtonpost.com/opin ions/2022/08/18/murkowski-alaska-senate-results-ranked-choice/.

52. Calder McHugh, "The Impeachment Revenge Tour's Unexpected Fall-out," Politico, August 17, 2022, https://www.politico.com/newsletters /politico-nightly/2022/08/17/the-impeachment-revenge-tours-unexpected -fallout-00052554?nname=politico-nightly&nid=00000170-c000-da87 -af78-e185fa700000&nrid=0000014c-2414-d9dd-a5ec-34bc65180004&nlid =2670445&cid=hptb_primary_0.

53. Azi Paybarah, "Who Is Mary Peltola, the First Alaska Native in Congress?," *Washington Post*, September 1, 2022, https://www.washingtonpost.com/poli tics/2022/08/31/mary-peltola-alaska-special-election-palin/.

54. Kayla Gallagher and Madison Hall, "Sarah Palin Complimented Mary Peltola as 'a Real Alaskan Chick' in Texts after the Democrat Beat Palin in a Special House

Election," *Business Insider*, September 1, 2022, https://www.businessinsider.com /palin-texted-mary-peltola-calling-her-a-real-alaskan-chick-after-win-2022-9.

55. Paul Best, "Former Alaska Gov. Sarah Palin Knocks Ranked-Choice Voting after Election Loss," Fox News, September 1, 2022, https://www.foxnews.com /politics/former-alaska-gov-sarah-palin-knocks-ranked-choice-voting-elec tion-loss.

56. Tom Cotton (@TomCottonAR), "60% of Alaska voters voted for a Republican, but thanks to a convoluted process and ballot exhaustion—which disenfranchises voters—a Democrat 'won,'" Twitter, August 31, 2022, https://twitter .com/TomCottonAR/status/1565139542000246784?s=20.

57. "RCV Detailed Report: General Election, State of Alaska, November 8, 2022," Alaska Division of Elections, November 30, 2022, https://www.elections.alaska .gov/results/22GENR/US%20REP.pdf.

58. Joe Lancaster, "Ranked Choice Voting Worked in Alaska. Sarah Palin Came to CPAC to Complain about It," *Reason*, March 7, 2023, https://reason .com/2023/03/07/ranked-choice- voting-worked-in-alaska-sarah-palin-came -to-cpac-to-complain-about-it/.

59. "Washington's 3rd Congressional District Election, 2022," Ballotpedia, accessed May 2023, https://ballotpedia.org/Washington%27s_3rd_Congressional_Dis trict_election,_2022.

60. Bill Walker, interview with author, 2017.

61. Author analysis of Alaska's election results.

62. "Alaska's Elections Reforms: Voter Perceptions & Experiences," McKinley Research Group, March 2023, https://mckinleyresearch.com/wp-content/up loads/2023/04/MRG-Alaska-Voter-Perceptions-Report-Mar2023.pdf.

63. Jeannette Lee and Jay Lee, "Alaska Primary Voters Had More Choice in 2022," Sightline Institute, November 4, 2022, https://www.sightline.org/2022/11/04 /alaska-primary-voters-had-more-choice-in-2022/.

64. Ryan Williamson, "Evaluating the Effects of the Top-Four System in Alaska," R Street Institute, January 2023, https://www.rstreet.org/wp-content/up loads/2023/01/REALFINAL_policy-short-no-122-no-embargo.pdf.

65. Ibid.

66. Lee and Lee, "Alaska Primary Voters Had More Choice in 2022."

67. Wesley Early, "In a Historic First, Alaskans Set to Elect 3 LGBTQ Lawmakers to State Legislature," Alaska Public Media, November 18, 2022, https:// alaskapublic.org/2022/11/18/in-a-historic-first-alaskans-set-to-elect-3-lgbtq -lawmakers-to-state-legislature/.

68. Lee and Lee, "Alaska Primary Voters Had More Choice in 2022."

69. "Alaska's Elections Reforms: Voter Perceptions & Experiences."

70. Bryan Metzger, "Sarah Palin Came All the Way to CPAC to Campaign against the Election System That Cost Her Alaska's House Seat," *Business Insider*, March 3, 2023, https://www.businessinsider.com/sarah-palin-cpac-election -system-house-seat-ranked-choice-voting-2023-3.

71. Roger Sollenberger, "The Fake Church Behind Sarah Palin's Crusade Against

Voting," *Daily Beast*, August 3, 2023, https://www.thedailybeast.com/the-fake
-church-behind-sarah-palins-crusade-against-voting?ref=scroll.

72. Ibid.

73. Lisa Murkowski, interview with author, June 16, 2023.

74. Scott Kendall, interview with author, March 28, 2023.

EIGHT: A BETTER WAY TO PICK A PRESIDENT

1. Erin Doherty, "Biden v. Trump: The Rematch That Nobody Really Wants,"
Axios, April 25, 2023, https://www.axios.com/2023/04/25/2024-trump-biden
-presidential-rematch.

2. Lydia Saad, "Trump and Clinton Finish with Historically Poor Images," *Gallup*,
March 24, 2022, https://news.gallup.com/poll/197231/trump-clinton-finish
-historically-poor-images.aspx.

3. Heather Long, "Voters Say This Is the Ultimate 'Lesser of Two Evils' Election," *CNNMoney*, October 13, 2016, https://money.cnn.com/2016/09/25/news
/economy/donald-trump-hillary-clinton-lesser-of-two-evils/.

4. Kelcie T. Grega, "Fact Check: Who Won? Trump, Clinton or 'Did Not Vote'?,"
Arizona Republic, November 30, 2016, https://www.azcentral.com/story/news
/politics/fact-check/2016/11/30/fact-check-map-did-not-vote-donald-trump
-hillary-clinton/94576656/.

5. "Republican Convention 2016," www.thegreenpapers.com, accessed May 2023,
http://www.thegreenpapers.com/P16/R.

6. "Democratic Convention 2016," www.thegreenpapers.com, accessed May 2023,
https://www.thegreenpapers.com/P16/D.

7. Ed Pilkington, "Americans Elect Forced to Abandon Campaign to Break Two-
Party System," *The Guardian*, May 15, 2012, https://www.theguardian.com
/world/2012/may/15/americans-elect-abandons-campaign.

8. Gideon Resnick and Sam Stein, "Howard Schultz Gets Shouted down at Book
Event: 'Don't Help Elect Trump!'," *The Daily Beast*, January 29, 2019,https://
www.thedailybeast.com/howard-schultz-gets-shouted-down-at-book-event
-dont-help-elect-trump.

9. Nick Troiano and Charles Wheelan, "Opinion | Run, Howard, Run!," *Wash-
ington Post*, January 27, 2019, https://www.washingtonpost.com/opinions
/2019/01/27/run-howard-run/.

10. "Ranked Choice Voting: The Solution to the Presidential Primary Predicament," *Unite America Institute*, June 2020, https://docsend.com/view
/jnu3d442irjgaagb.

11. "Public Funding of Presidential Elections," *Federal Election Commission*, 2012,
https://www.fec.gov/introduction-campaign-finance/understanding-ways
-support-federal-candidates/presidential-elections/public-funding-presiden
tial-elections/.

12. "Level the Playing Field et al. v. Federal Election Commission," United States
District Court for the District of Columbia, accessed May 2023, https://www
.fec.gov/resources/legal-resources/litigation/lpf_lpf_complaint2.pdf.

13. "Ranked Choice Voting: The Solution to the Presidential Primary Predicament," Unite America Institute, June 2020, https://docsend.com/view/jnu3d442irjgaagb.
14. Ibid.
15. "Data & Tools," International Institute for Democracy and Electoral Assistance, accessed May 2023, https://www.idea.int/data-tools.
16. Kevin Johnson, "To Fix the Electoral College, Change the Way Its Votes Are Awarded," *Governing*, December 11, 2020, https://www.governing.com/now/To-Fix-the-Electoral-College-Change-the-Way-Its-Votes-Are-Awarded.html.
17. "Past Attempts at Reform," FairVote, accessed May 2023, https://fairvote.org/archives/the_electoral_college-past_attempts_at_reform/?gclid=Cj0KCQjw3JanBhCPARIsAJpXTx4NToRK1rDkm4_Sir1tsp-T6I7QvoqptGjuDdSGr7d9Yhqw8BOeFWoaArCzEALw_wcB.
18. Jeff Stein, "The Real Obstacle to Voter Turnout in Democratic Primaries: Caucuses," *Vox*, May 2, 2016, https://www.vox.com/2016/5/2/11535648/bernie-sanders-closed-primaries-caucuses.
19. John Delaney, interview with author, April 19, 2023.
20. Open Primaries, "Rules in Your State," www.openprimaries.org, accessed May 2023, https://www.openprimaries.org/rules-in-your-state/.
21. Rob Richie, "The Case for a One-Person, One-Vote National Primary to Nominate Our Presidential Candidates in 2020," *In These Times*, June 2, 2016, https://inthesetimes.com/article/ the-case-for-a-one-person-one-vote-national-primary-to-elect-our-president.

PART IV: THE PATH TOWARD NATIONWIDE REFORM

1. Michael D. Shear, "Biden to Sign Bill to Protect Same-Sex Marriage Rights," *New York Times*, December 13, 2022, https://www.nytimes.com/2022/12/13/us/politics/biden-same-sex-marriage-bill.html.
2. James Dao, "Same-Sex Marriage Issue Key to Some G.O.P. Races," *New York Times*, November 4, 2004, https://www.nytimes.com/2004/11/04/politics/campaign/samesex-marriage-issue-key-to-some-gop-races.html.
3. Marc Solomon, interview with author, March 29, 2023. All quotes from Solomon in this chapter are from this interview.
4. Mackenzie Weinger, "Evolve: Obama Gay Marriage Quotes," *Politico*, May 9, 2012, https://www.politico.com/story/2012/05/evolve-obama-gay-marriage-quotes-076109.
5. Amy Sherman, "Hillary Clinton's Changing Position on Same-Sex Marriage," PolitiFact, June 17, 2015, https://www.politifact.com/factchecks/2015/jun/17/hillary-clinton/hillary-clinton-change-position-same-sex-marriage/.
6. MJ Lee, Betsy Klein, and Kevin Liptak, "Biden to Sign into Law Same-Sex Marriage Bill, 10 Years after His Famous Sunday Show Answer on the Issue," CNN, December 13, 2022, https://www.cnn.com/2022/12/13/politics/white-house-same-sex-marriage-signing-ceremony/index.html.

7. Kevin Cirilli, "Portman for Gay Marriage after Son Comes Out," *Politico*, March 15, 2013, https://www.politico.com/story/2013/03/rob-portman-gay -marriage-stance-088903.

8. Justin McCarthy, "Record-High 60% of Americans Support Same-Sex Marriage," Gallup, May 19, 2015, https://news.gallup.com/poll/183272/record -high-americans-support-sex-marriage.aspx.

9. Marc Solomon, *Winning Marriage: The Inside Story of How Same-Sex Couples Took on the Politicians and Pundits—and Won* (Lebanon, NH: ForeEdge, 2014), 96.

10. Chris Geidner, "The 2005 Decision to Go Forward with the Fight for Marriage Equality," BuzzFeed News, June 21, 2015, https://www.buzzfeednews.com/ar ticle/chrisgeidner/the-2005-decision-to-go-forward-with-the-fight-for-mar riage.

11. Outtraveler Staff, "V.P. Cheney on Gay Relationships: 'Freedom Means Freedom for Everyone,'" *Advocate*, August 25, 2004, https://www.advocate.com /news/2004/08/25/vp-cheney-gay-relationships-quotfreedom-means-freedom -everyonequot-13491.

12. Elaine S. Povich, "Without Obergefell, Most States Would Have Same-Sex Marriage Bans," Stateline, July 7, 2022, https://stateline.org/2022/07/07/without -obergefell-most-states-would-have-same-sex-marriage-bans/.

NINE: WINNING: ONE STATE AT A TIME

1. Abel Maldonado, interview with author, May 30, 2023.

2. Ibid.

3. Ibid.

4. Ibid.

5. Steve Peace, interview with author, March 31, 2023.

6. Ibid.

7. Charles Munger Jr., interview with author, April 19, 2023.

8. Jennifer Steinhauer, "In Budget Deal, California Shuts $41 Billion Gap," *New York Times*, February 19, 2009, https://www.nytimes.com/2009/02/20 /us/20california.html.

9. Abel Maldonado, interview with author, May 30, 2023.

10. "The Real History: California's Top-Two Nonpartisan Primary Electoral Reform," IVN Network, April 23, 2018, https://ivn.us/posts/the-real-history-cal ifornias-top-two-nonpartisan-primary-electoral-reform.

11. Abel Maldonado, interview with author, May 30, 2023.

12. Charles Munger Jr., interview with author, April 19, 2023.

13. Steve Peace, interview with author, March 31, 2023.

14. Carlo Macomber, "Poll: Voters Overwhelmingly Support Eliminating Partisan Primaries, Requiring Majority Winners," Unite America, August 7, 2023, https://www.uniteamerica.org/news-article/poll-voters-overwhelmingly-sup port-eliminating-partisan-primaries-requiring-majority-winners.

15. "Bipartisan Momentum in the 117th: Key Senate Influencers," BPC Action, May

2023, https://bpcaction.org/wp-content/uploads/Senate-Influencers-117th-Co ngress.pdf.

16. "Bipartisan Momentum in the 117th: Key Efforts," BPC Action, May 2023, https://bpcaction.org/wp-content/uploads/Bipartisan-Initiatives-117th-Con gress.pdf.

17. Jason Grumet, BPC email newsletter, Bipartisan Policy Center, 2022.

18. Sula P. Richardson, "Term Limits for Members of Congress: State Activity," Congressional Research Service, June 4, 1998, https://www.everycrsreport .com/reports/96-152GOV.html.

19. Danielle Allen, "Our Democracy is Menaced by Two Dragons. Here's How to Slay Them," *Washington Post*, July 20, 2023, https://www.washingtonpost .com/opinions/2023/07/20/gerrymandering-electoral-college-solution-de mocracy/.

20. Joshua Ferrer and Michael Thorning, "2022 Primary Turnout: Trends and Les- sons for Boosting Participation," Bipartisan Policy Center, March 2023, https:// bipartisanpolicy.org/download/?file=/wp-content/uploads/2023/03/Primary -Turnout-Report_R03.pdf.

21. Lee Drutman, "What We Know About Redistricting and Redistricting Re- form," New America, September 2022, https://d1y8sb8igg2f8e.cloudfront.net /documents/What_We_Know_About_Redistricting_and_Redistricting_Re form___Vlt6sZ8.pdf.

22. Matthew Nelson, "Independent Redistricting Commissions Are Associated with More Competitive Elections," *PS: Political Science & Politics* 56, no. 2 (April 2023): 207–12.

23. Carl von Clausewitz, "On War: Book III—of Strategy in General," Clause- witz Homepage, 1873, https://www.clausewitz.com/readings/OnWar1873 /BK3ch01.html.

24. Kent Thiry, interview with author, 2023. All other quotes from Thiry in this chapter are from this interview, unless otherwise noted.

25. John Opdycke, interview with author, June 1, 2023.

26. Jesse Paul, "Unaffiliated Voters This Year Cast More Ballots in Colorado Re- publican Primaries Than Ever Before," *Colorado Sun*, July 5, 2022, https://colo radosun.com/2022/07/05/unaffiliated-voters-colorado-2022-primaries/.

27. "State of Reform: An Analysis of the Impact and Progress of Four Political Re- forms," Unite America Institute, May 2023, https://www.uniteamericainstitute .org/research/state-of-reform.

28. Kaitlin LaCasse, interview with author, April 20, 2023. All other quotes from LaCasse in this chapter are from this interview, unless otherwise noted.

29. Chloe Maxmin, interview with author, April 19, 2023. All other quotes from Maxmin in this chapter are from this interview, unless otherwise noted.

30. "Actions for LD231," State of Maine Legislature, accessed May 2023, https:// legislature.maine.gov/LawMakerWeb/dockets.asp?ID=280078305.

31. Anita Kumar and Rosalind S. Helderman, "McDonnell Vetoes State Redis- tricting Bill," *Washington Post*, April 15, 2011, https://www.washingtonpost

.com/local/politics/mcdonnell-vetoes-state-redistricting-bill/2011/04/14
/AFOO2HlD_story.html.

32. "Campaign Finance Reports, Schedule D: Expenditures," Virginia State Board
of Elections, April 1 to June 30, 2019, https://cfreports.elections.virginia.gov
/Report/ScheduleD/170588?page=2.

33. "Seattle, Washington, Proposition 1A and 1B, Approval Voting Initiative and
Ranked-Choice Voting Measure (November 2022)," Ballotpedia, accessed May
2023, https://ballotpedia.org/Seattle,_Washington,_Proposition_1A_and_1B,_
Approval_Voting_Initiative_and_Ranked-Choice_Voting_Measure_(Novem
ber_2022).

34. Leslie R. Crutchfield, *How Change Happens: Why Some Social Movements Succeed While Others Don't* (Hoboken, NJ: Wiley, 2018), 13.

35. Aimee Picchi and Kate Gibson, "NRA, Long Viewed as Invincible, Faces Shrink-
ing Membership and Revenue," CBS News, May 27, 2022, https://www.cbs
news.com/news/nra-national-rifle-association-membership-revenue-2022/.

36. Heather Knight, "Moms' Group's Tactics Show There Is Cause for Optimism about Gun Control," *SFGATE*, October 15, 2017, https://www.sfgate
.com/news/article/Moms-group-s-tactics-show-there-is-cause-for-12278589
.php?t=8603837d09.

37. "About Us," RepresentUS, accessed May 2023, https://represent.us/about/.

38. Brian Schwartz, "Federal and State Spending on 2022 Elections Set to Top
$16.7 Billion, Making Them the Most Expensive Midterms Ever," CNBC,
November 3, 2022, https://www.cnbc.com/2022/11/03/2022-midterm-election
-spending-set-to-break-record.html.

39. Rob Stein, "Scaling a Sustainable Cross Partisan Constituency for Change," Democracy Fund, 2018, https://docsend.com/view/cpyysycwqmk54w2n.

40. Laura Arnold, interview with author, September 12, 2022.

41. Charles Munger Jr., interview with author, April 19, 2023.

42. Ibid.

43. Marc Merrill and Kathryn Murdoch, "How Philanthropy Could Fix America's Broken Politics," *Fortune*, August 6, 2020, https://fortune.com/2020/08/06
/american-politics-2020-elections-campaign-reform-politlcal-philanthropy/.

44. John Delaney, interview with author, April 19, 2023.

45. Ben Pershing, "Delaney, Md. Democrats Work to Show Unified Front after
Newcomer's Primary Win," *Washington Post*, April 4, 2012, https://www.wash
ingtonpost.com/local/md-politics/delaney-md-democrats-work-to-show-uni
fied-front-after-newcomers-primary-win/2012/04/04/gIQA6u0GvS_story.html.

46. John Delaney, interview with author, April 19, 2023.

47. John Delaney, "The Solution to Fixing Dysfunction in Congress," *Washington Post*, September 2, 2014, https://www.washingtonpost.com/opinions/the
-solution-to-fixing-dysfunction-in-congress/2014/09/02/0f0d0a9a-31e6-11e4
-9e92-0899b306bbea_story.html.

48. John Delaney, interview with author, April 19, 2023.

49. Edward B. Foley, "Requiring Majority Winners for Congressional Elections:

Harnessing Federalism to Combat Extremism," *Lewis and Clark Review* 26, no. 2 (November 2022), 399.

50. Joshua Ferrer and Michael Thorning, "2022 Primary Turnout," Bipartisan Policy Center, March 6, 2023, https://bipartisanpolicy.org/report/2022-primary-turnout/.

51. "Governing in a Polarized America: A Bipartisan Blueprint to Strengthen our Democracy," Bipartisan Policy Center, June 24, 2014, https://bipartisanpolicy.org/download/?file=/wp-content/uploads/2019/03/BPC-CPR-Report.pdf.

52. "Election Type: General / Office: U.S. House of Representatives / Year: 1824 to 1825," A New Nation Votes, https://elections.lib.tufts.edu/?f%5Belection_type_sim%5D%5B%5D=General&f%5Boffice_id_ssim%5D%5B%5D=ON125&range%5Bpub_date_facet_isim%5D%5Bbegin%5D=1824&range%5Bpub_date_facet_isim%5D%5Bend%5D=1825&search_field=dummy_range.

53. Evan Andrews, "Why Is Election Day a Tuesday in November?" History Channel, November 2, 2020, https://www.history.com/news/why-is-election-day-a-tuesday-in-november.

54. John Opdycke, interview with author, June 1, 2023.

55. *United States v. Classic*, 313 U.S. 299 (1941)," Justia,https://supreme.justia.com/cases/federal/us/313/299/.

TEN: OVERCOMING OBJECTIONS TO PRIMARY REFORM

1. "The Electoral College, Congress and Representation," Pew Research Center, April 26, 2018, https://www.pewresearch.org/politics/2018/04/26/5-the-electoral-college-congress-and-representation/#should-the-allocation-of-senate-seats-or-the-size-of-the-house-be-changed.

2. Ann Brown, "Ranked-Choice Ballot Initiative Would Destroy Alaska's Voting System," Anchorage Daily News, December 17, 2019, https://www.adn.com/opinions/2019/12/18/ranked-choice-ballot-initiative-would-destroy-alaskas-voting-system/.

3. Internal poll by Unite America.

4. Kal Munis and David C. W. Parker, "A Modest Proposal to Improve Montana's Politics: Ranked Choice Voting and Top Four Primaries Considered," *Salon*, June 6, 2020, https://static1.squarespace.com/static/580ab33829687f686ad6cbb1/t/6164cead9f93f02cba78e6d7/1633996461870/Munis+Parker+Top+Four+%2B+RCV+in+Montana.pdf.

5. "Senate Bill No. 566," Montana Legislature, 2023, https://leg.mt.gov/bills/2023/billpdf/SB0566.pdf.

6. "Jon Tester," Ballotpedia, accessed May 2023, https://ballotpedia.org/Jon_Tester.

7. Rebecca Falconer, "Alexandria Ocasio-Cortez Criticizes Moderate 'Meh' Policies," *Axios*, March 10, 2019, https://www.axios.com/2019/03/10/ocasio-cortez-criticizes-meh-policies-552179259.

8. Ro Khanna, interview with author, August 24, 2022.

9. Mark Noack, "Ro Khanna Makes Economic Case for Green New Deal," *Mountain View Voice*, May 20, 2019, https://www.mv-voice.com/news/2019/05/20/ro-khanna-makes-economic-case-for-green-new-deal.

10. Jeff Stein, "With Trumpcare Dead and Obama Gone, Progressives Are Putting Medicare for All Back on the Table," *Vox*, March 29, 2017, https://www.vox.com/policy-and-politics/2017/3/29/15056672/single-payer-democrats-medicare.

11. Ayman Mohyeldin, "Rep. Ro Khanna on Passing Voting Rights Legislation: 'This Is an Obligation, a Duty,'" MSNBC, September 18, 2021, https://www.msnbc.com/ayman-mohyeldin/watch/rep-ro-khanna-on-passing-voting-rights-legislation-this-is-an-obligation-a-duty-121271365982/.

12. Emily Singer, "Bernie Sanders Introduces 'College for All Act' to Make Public Colleges Tuition-Free," *Mic*, April 3, 2017, https://www.mic.com/articles/173013/bernie-sanders-introduces-college-for-all-act-to-make-public-colleges-tuition-free#.jnzt4UpDR.

13. Michael Kruse, "Ro Khanna's Apology Tour. And Why Trump Voters Love It," *Politico*, August 26, 2022, https://www.politico.com/news/magazine/2022/08/26/ro-khanna-midwest-policy-democrat-00052660.

14. Chris Cioffi, "Not a 'Monster': Why Rep. Ro Khanna Still Goes on Fox News," *Roll Call*, August 10, 2022, https://rollcall.com/2022/08/10/why-rep-ro-khanna-still-goes-on-fox-news/.

15. Mike Gallagher and Ro Khanna, "Two Congressmen Offer a Bipartisan Plan to 'Drain the Swamp,'" *USA Today*, June 21, 2017, https://www.usatoday.com/story/opinion/2017/06/01/two-congressmen-offer-bipartisan-plan-drain-swamp/102189506/.

16. "Sen. Bill Cassidy," Heritage Action for America, accessed May 2023, https://heritageaction.com/scorecard/members/C001075/117.

17. "Louisiana Scorecard," FreedomWorks, accessed May 2023, https://www.freedomworks.org/scorecard/state/LA/.

18. "Congressional Scorecard: Bill Cassidy," Club for Growth, May 2023, https://www.clubforgrowth.org/scorecards/app/?party=all&chamber=S&yr=2021&state=all&rep=cassidy.

19. Cameron Cawthorne, "Cassidy Defends 2017 Tax Cuts Targeted by Biden, Pointing to Wage Growth among Low Earners," Fox News, May 2, 2021, https://www.foxnews.com/politics/cassidy-defends-2017-tax-cuts-targeted-by-biden-wage-growth.

20. U.S. Senator Bill Cassidy, M.D. (@SenBillCassidy), "Today's decision recognizes that an unborn child has a right to life," Twitter, June 24, 2022, https://twitter.com/SenBillCassidy/status/1540345835619340288.

21. "Louisiana's Senator Bill Cassidy Says He Uses His AR-15 to Kill Feral Pigs," *Economic Times*, May 27, 2022, https://economictimes.indiatimes.com/news/international/us/louisianas-senator-bill-cassidy-says-he-uses-his-ar-15-to-kill-feral-pigs/articleshow/91841234.cms.

22. Sahil Kapur, "Senate Group Eyes Social Security Changes as Biden Hits

Republicans over Benefits," NBC News, March 3, 2023, https://www.nbcnews. com/politics/congress/senate-group-social-security-changes-biden-hits-re-publicans-rcna73307.

23. Mike Allen, "GOP Sen. Cassidy Warns of 'True Colors' Test," *Axios*, October 17, 2021, https://www.axios.com/2021/10/17/bill-cassidy-conservative-louisiana-hbo.

24. Andrew Kitchenman, "Sponsors of Complex 'Alaska's Better Elections Initiative' Say Its Benefits Are Clear," Alaska Public Media, November 25, 2019, https://alaskapublic.org/2019/11/25/sponsors-of-complex-alaskas-better-elec tions-initiative-say-its-benefits-are-clear/.

25. Sam Karlin, "GOP Disagreement Emerges over Whether to Change Louisiana's Unique Open Primary Elections," *Houma Today*, March 30, 2021, https://www.houmatoday.com/story/news/state/2021/03/30/gop-disagree ment-emerges-over-whether-change-louisianas-unique-open-primary-elec tions/7059675002/.

26. Carla Marinucci, "Limbaugh Seeks to Sow Chaos in Democrats' Race," *SF-GATE*, April 27, 2008, https://www.sfgate.com/politics/article/Limbaugh -seeks-to-sow-chaos-in-Democrats-race-3286535.php.

27. E. Frank Stephenson, "Strategic Voting in Open Primaries: Evidence from Rush Limbaugh's 'Operation Chaos,'" *Public Choice* 148, no. 3⁄4 (September, 2011): 445, 456.

28. R. Michael Alvarez and Jonathan Nagler, "Analysis of Crossover and Strategic Voting," California Institute of Technology and University of California, September 1997, https://web.archive.org/web/20100625234325/http://polmeth .wustl.edu/media/Paper/alvar99b.pdf.

29. Annie Linskey, "Democrats Spend Tens of Millions Amplifying Far-Right Candidates in Nine States," *Washington Post*, September 12, 2022, https://www .washingtonpost.com/politics/2022/09/12/democrats-interfere-republican -primaries/.

30. Email blast from Pudner's organization, Take Back Our Republic.

31. Erin Carman and Jay Wendland, "Ranking Works: An Examination of Ranked Choice Voting in New York City," Unite America Institute, February 2022, https://docsend.com/view/wurzmdn5rrcze66w.

32. Kyrene Gibb and Quin Monson, "Voter Experience in the 2021 Utah RCV Pilot Program," Y2 Analytics, 2021, https://le.utah.gov/interim/2021/pdf/00004023 .pdf.

33. "Alaska's Election Reforms: Voter Perceptions and Experiences," McKinley Research Group, March 2023, https://mckinleyresearch.com/wp-content/up loads/2023/04/MRG-Alaska-Voter-Perceptions-Report-Mar2023.pdf.

34. Sarah John and Andrew Douglas, "Candidate Civility and Voter Engagement in Seven Cities with Ranked Choice Voting," *National Civic Review* 106, no. 1 (Spring 2017): 25–29.

35. Tom Cotton (@TomCottonAR), "Ranked-choice voting is a scam to rig elections," Twitter, August 31, 2022, https://twitter.com/TomCottonAR/sta tus/1565139540834222080.

36. Rob Richie, interview with author, April 14, 2022.

37. *Baber v. Dunlap*, Casetext, accessed May 2023, https://casetext.com/case/baber-v-dunlap.

38. Sean Murphy, "Bond, Golden and Poliquin run for District 2, Again," Spectrum News, October 19, 2022, https://spectrumlocalnews.com/me/maine/news/2022/10/19/bond--golden-and-poliquin-run-for-district-2--again.

39. Alan Greenblatt, "When Parties Can't Control Primaries," *Governing*, July 22, 2022, https://www.governing.com/now/when-parties-cant-control-primaries.

40. "Measuring the Effects of Ranked Choice Voting in Republican Primaries," Center for Campaign Innovation, August 2, 2022, https://campaigninnovation.org/research/measuring-the-effects-of-ranked-choice-voting-in-republican-primaries.

41. Rob Richie, "Ranked Choice Voting May Affect Partisan Outcomes, but It Always Helps Voters," FairVote, November 9, 2018, https://fairvote.org/ranked_choice_voting_may_affect_partisan_outcomes_but_it_always_helps_voters/.

42. Jennifer C. Braceras, "Ranked-Choice Voting Threatens to Distort Election Outcomes," *Boston Globe*, December 12, 2019, https://www.bostonglobe.com/2019/12/12/opinion/no-it-threatens-distort-election-outcomes/.

43. Matthew Simonson, "Mathematical Democracy: Mission Impossible? Maybe not . . ." *AMS*, November 2016, https://blogs.ams.org/mathgradblog/2016/11/21/mathematical-democracy-mission-impossible-not/.

44. "Florida League's Change of Position on Amendment 3 (FL)," League of Women Voters of Florida, September 4, 2020, https://lwvfl.org/florida-leagues-change-of-position-on-amendment-3-fl/.

45. "Progressive Left," Pew Research Center, November 9, 2021, https://www.pewresearch.org/politics/2021/11/09/progressive-left/.

46. Matthew Isbell, "'Top-Two' Will Bleach Minority-Districts in Florida," MCI Maps, July 16, 2020, https://mcimaps.com/top-two-will-bleach-minority-districts-in-florida/.

47. Brenda Carr, interview with author, April 18, 2023.

48. "A Troubling Flip-Flop by the League of Women Voters of Florida," *Orlando Sentinel*, November 16, 2020, https://www.orlandosentinel.com/2020/11/16/a-troubling-flip-flop-by-the-league-of-women-voters-of-florida-editorial/.

49. "Open Primaries Empower Communities of Color," Open Primaries, accessed May 2023, https://www.openprimaries.org/wp-content/uploads/2022/01/POC_Party_Politics_Sheet_V2.pdf.

50. Ibid.

51. Andrea Benjamin and Barry C. Burden, "Consequences of Final-Five Voting for Communities of Color," Elections Research Center at the University of Wisconsin-Madison, October 22, 2021, 4, https://elections.wisc.edu/consequences-of-final-five-voting-for-communities-of-color/.

52. Ibid.

53. Ibid., 8.

54. Ibid., 23.

55. Christian Grose, "Reducing Legislative Polarization: Top-Two and Open Primaries Are Associated with More Moderate Legislators," *Journal of Political Institutions and Political Economy* 1, no. 2 (June 2020): 267–87.

56. Jesse Crosson, "Extreme Districts, Moderate Winners: Same-Party Challenges, and Deterrence in Top-Two Primaries," *Political Science Research and Methods* 9, no. 3 (March 2021): 1–17; J. Andrew Sinclair, Ian O'Grady, Brock McIntosh, and Carrie Nordlund, "Crashing the Party: Advocacy Coalitions and the Nonpartisan Primary," *Journal of Public Policy* 38, no. 3 (November 2017): 1–32.

57. Jeffrey B. Lewis, Keith Poole, Howard Rosenthal, Adam Boche, Aaron Rudkin, and Luke Sonnet, "Voteview: Congressional Roll-Call Votes Database," Voteview, 2023, https://voteview.com/.

58. Richard Barton, interview with author, February 24, 2023.

59. See, for instance: John Sides, Chris Tausanovitch, Lynn Vavreck, and Christopher Warshaw, "On the Representativeness of Primary Electorates," *British Journal of Political Science* 50, no. 2 (March 2018): 1–9; and Alan I. Abramowitz, "Don't Blame Primary Voters for Polarization," *Forum* 5, no. 4 (January 2008): https://doi.org/10.2202/1540-8884.1210.

60. Elaine C. Kamarck and James Wallner, "Anticipating Trouble: Congressional Primaries and Incumbent Behavior," *R Street Policy Study*, no. 156, October 2018, https://www.brookings.edu/wp-content/uploads/2018/10/GS_10292018_Primaries-and-Incumbent-Behavior.pdf.

61. Ibid.

62. Steve Peace, interview with author, March 31, 2023.

CONCLUSION

1. Erika Ryan, Patrick Jarenwattananon, and Elissa Nadworny, "Congress is Older Than Ever. It Hasn't Always Been This Way.," NPR, November 10, 2022, https://www.npr.org/2022/11/10/1135856127/congress-is-older-than-ever-it-hasnt-always-been-this-way.

2. Sara Morrison and Christian Paz, "3 Winners and 3 Losers from Congress's TikTok Hearing," *Vox*, March 23, 2023, https://www.vox.com/technology/23653884/tiktok-hearing-shou-chew-winners-losers.

3. Evann Gastaldo, "Congressman Ridiculed over TikTok WiFi Question," *Newser*, March 24, 2023, https://www.newser.com/story/333119/congressman-ridiculed-over-tiktok-wifi-question.html.

4. Charlie Wheelan, interview with author, June 8, 2020.

5. Jeffrey M. Jones, "Support for Third U.S. Political Party at High Point," Gallup, February 15, 2021, https://news.gallup.com/poll/329639/support-third-political-party-high-point.aspx.

6. Steve Peace, interview with author, March 31, 2023.

7. Luke Mullins, "The Terrifying Story of the Congressional Baseball Shooting," *Washingtonian*, May 28, 2018, https://www.washingtonian.com/2018/05/28/terrifying-story-of-the-congressional-baseball-shooting-steve-scalise/.

8. "Office of the Commonwealth's Attorney—City of Alexandria," Office of the

Commonwealth's Attorney, City of Alexandria, October 6, 2017, https://media
.alexandriava.gov/docs-archives/commattorney/info/17-001---simpson-field
-shooting---final-10.06.17.pdf.

9. Charles R. Davis, "Pelosi Attack Suspect Says He was Motivated by Politics,
Telling Police that Democrats had been 'Persecuting' Trump," *Business Insider*,
January 27, 2023, https://www.businessinsider.com/pelosi-attack-suspect-tells
-police-motivated-by-right-wing-views-2023-1.

10. Mark Mellman, "Mellman: How Many Endorse Political Violence?," *The Hill*,
June 22, 2022, https://thehill.com/opinion/3531987-mellman-how-many-en
dorse-political-violence/.

11. Steven Levitsky and Daniel Ziblatt, "How Wobbly Is Our Democracy?," *New
York Times*, January 27, 2018, https://www.nytimes.com/2018/01/27/opinion
/sunday/democracy-polarization.html.

12. David Thornburgh, interview with author, March 31, 2023.

13. Scott Kendall, interview with author, March 28, 2023.

INDEX

Note: Page numbers in italics refer to figures.

Cruz, Ted, 8–9, 262
Cuomo, Andrew, 212

Dardenne, Jay, 146
Daschle, Tom, 241
D.C. Madam, 146, 147
debates, in presidential election, obstacles
　to independent candidates, 196
deciding ballots, percentage of voters
　casting, 153–54
Defense of Marriage Act of 1996, repeal
　of, 208
Delaney, John, 201, 239–40
democracy, U.S.
　bedrock principles of, 110
　citizens' dissatisfaction with, 273
　impact of election denial on,
　　113–14
　majority rule as bedrock principle of,
　　227–28
　and tools for change, 274
　Trump as threat to, 110–16
Democratic Congressional Campaign
　Committee, 124
Democratic Party
　candidates' necessary positions for
　　success, 89
　commitment to democracy, 115
　extremist candidates, as liability,
　　117–18
　flawed primary system of, 196
　interference in 2022 Republican
　　primaries, 114–15, 253
　loss of rural support, 60
　and political machine system, 30
　primarying of moderates, 44–47
　views on immigration as backlash
　　against Trump, 99–100
Democratic-Republican Party, 25–26
Didier, Clint, 156–57
direct primaries. See primaries, direct
disinformation, as commonly cited
　problem, 2
dislike of other party, increase in, 72
districts, House
　redistricting of, 4, 73

redistricting in 2022, 73–74
　See also competitive House districts,
　　decline of; gerrymandering
Doglio, Beth, 156
Dole, Bob, 104–5
Donnelly, Joe, 47
DREAM Act of 2001, 96, 100
Drutman, Lee, 41
Dunleavy, Mike, 173, 184–85
Durbin, Dick, 96
DW-Nominate ideology score, 262

echo chambers, partisan
　creation by partisan primaries, 84–85
　misperceptions bred by, 85
Economist Intelligence Unit, 110–11
Edgmon, Bryce, 172
education reform inaction, political
　polarization and, 101–2
Edwards, Donna, 46
Edwards, Edwin, 139–40
Edwards, John Bel, 146–47, 149–50
Election Day, national, establishment of,
　241
election denial
　by Clinton in 2016, 54
　and erosion of public trust in elections,
　　114
　impact on 2022 elections, 113–14
　impact on our democracy, 113–14
　increase in, 54–55
　and state election reforms, 114
　by Trump in 2020, 81
　by Trump, reasons for Republican
　　support for, 111–12
election interference
　by Democrats, in 2022 Republican
　　primaries, 114–15, 253
　party raiding, 231, 252–53
election of 1976, 193
election of 2004, 209
election of 2008
　and primary party raiding, 252–53
　same-sex marriage as issue in, 210
　Unity08 plan for bipartisan presidential
　　ticket, 193

Major League Baseball, and claimed voter
suppression in Georgia, 67
Maldonado, Abel
election to state assembly, 217–18
fight for open primaries in California,
218–20
political career, 217
Mallott, Byron, 168–69
Manchin, Joe, 61
Mann, Thomas, 49
Marchant, Jim, 113–14
Marino, Tom
author's run against, 9–11
as partisan representative, 9, 11–12
Markey, Ed, 124
Maryland
gerrymandering in, 239–40
Unite America candidate support in,
169
and vocal minority's control of
primaries, 46
Mason, George, 199
Massachusetts
campaign for RCV, 237
election of 2022 primary turnout, 77
general elections, lack of competition
in, 68–69
online signature collection during
COVID, 163
and same-sex marriage, 209, 211–12
Mathias, Art, 188
Maxmin, Chloe, 231–32
Mayhew, David, 7
McBath, Lucy, 65
McCain, John, 96, 171, 179
McCarthy, Kevin
difficult election as House Speaker,
121–22
power ceded to extreme Republicans,
122–23, 124
as speaker in name only, 122–23
McCarty, Nolan, 50
McConnell, Mitch, 8, 120
McCormick, David, 18–19
McLeod-Skinner, Jamie, 64–65
McMullin, Evan, 192

media
fragmentation of, and rise of
extremism, 41–42
minimal attention to primary elections,
77–78
niche, influence on partisan activists,
21
online, and freeing of candidates from
party influence, 123
and primary reform campaign, 244–45
on top-four nonpartisan primaries,
181
median voter theorem, *91*, 91–92
Medicaid expansion
Louisiana's acceptance of, 147–49
Republicans' opposition to, 147–48
as will of majority, 148–49
Meijer, Peter, 115
Merrill, Marc, 13, 238
military voters, and RCV, 255–56
Millennial Action Project, *280*
Miller, Joe, 46, 177
Mississippi
gubernatorial election of 2015, 145
open partisan primaries in, 144
Missouri, Unite America candidate
support in, 169
Moms Demand Action, 236
Montana, success of nonpartisan
primaries in, 247–48
Moore, Ivan, 180–81
Moore, Stephen, 43
Morse, Chuck, 113
Mourdock, Richard, 47
MoveOn.org, 44, 45, 46
Munger, Charles Jr., 218–20, 237–38
Murdoch, Kathryn, 13, 238
Murkowski, Lisa
on Alaska's top-four election system,
188–89
and election of 2010, write-in general
election victory, 46, 177–79
and election of 2022, reelection in top-
four system, 180–81
first appointment by governor father,
177–78